The Centenary History of St. Matthew's Church and Parish, Northampton

The Centenary History of St. Matthew's Church and Parish, Northampton

Mona C. Harrison

The Pentland Press Limited
Edinburgh · Cambridge · Durham

© M. Harrison 1993

First published in 1993 by
The Pentland Press Ltd.
1 Hutton Close
South Church
Bishop Auckland
Durham

All rights reserved.
Unauthorised duplication
contravenes existing laws.

ISBN 1 85821 061 5

Typeset by Elite Typesetting Techniques, Southampton.
Printed and bound by Antony Rowe Ltd., Chippenham.

Foreword

John Betjeman once said that the greatest artistic treasure of England lay in its parish churches and as I go round the village churches of Northamptonshire with their history running back over hundreds of years I am deeply conscious of the truth of this.Every century since the Middle Ages has given us here arches and windows, statues and painting, primitive woodwork and wonderful roofs.

The people of the past were not afraid to bring their own particular creative insights and skills to the building and decoration of their churches. It is the especial achievement of St Matthew's that a church just a century old has had the same courage in bringing the artistic vision of our own times to the service of worship and faith.

It is in the tradition of this diocese as one thinks of the windows of Evie Hone, Jean Barrilet, John Piper and Patrick Reyntiens in All Hallows Wellingborough, of the paintings of Henry Bird and Christopher Fiddes in Earls Barton, of Comper's St Mary's Wellingborough, of Maureen Colpman's bronze in Duston, of Kenneth Leighton's Eucharistic setting for the Cathedral's 750th or John Joubert's Anthem for the diocese's 450th celebrations. It is a great tradition in the diocese and of that tradition St Matthew's is the crown.

Now all this is more than a matter of just decorating church buildings. It is the church giving the artist a chance to express religious feeling and insight which is then held within the worship of a congregation and the prayer of any who care to pass by.

In the Decade of Evangelism we are thinking in too shallow a way. We see a return to Christianity as being expressed in bringing people into church and refuting the perpetual newspaper cry of 'empty pews'. That is a consummation devoutly to be wished for, but it does not meet a concern even more fundamental. I believe, especially as a result of my experience in radio and television, that we have lost our place, as a Christian Church, in the deepest thinking of the nation.

In past time, people who rejected the Christian Faith knew what they were rejecting and the insights of that Faith were part of the furniture of their minds. Matthew Arnold's poem 'Dover Beach' is an anguished cry concerning the loss of a shared faith and knowledge. Philip Larkin's 'Church Going' is much more bleak for it speaks of a time when faith and doubt and knowledge have all, equally, disappeared. That arid vision is, I believe, a possibility for England, now.

To resist it we need not simply to get the men and women of our country back inside our churches but, more seriously, to re-capture their hearts and minds. Your century of careful and beautiful worship, of intelligent preaching, of commissioning some of the finest of our painters and composers and sculptors and poets has been an especial contribution in the battle for the soul of our nation.

Their work has given much to the church but it has not just been all one way.

I visited the Henry Moore Exhibition at the Royal Academy. Your statue had a special place and there in the gallery it emanated a power which one could actually feel. The power came not simply from the magnificent vision and genius of the sculptor. It came, also, because for years that statue had stood in St Matthews 'where prayer has been valid'. The statue had given much to the Church and the Church had given back much to the statue.

This has been your special gift to us for a hundred years. I thank you for it and wish you well into your next century.

Your sincere friend and Bishop,
William Petriburg

Contents

	Page
Foreword	v
Acknowledgements	ix
List of Photographs	xi
List of Figures	xiii
Photograph Credits	xv
Preface	xvii
1 Early Days	1
2 The New Church	8
3 Extracts from the Souvenir Booklet	14
4 From 1893	25
5 1900 – Before and After	30
6 The Church Overseas	35
7 Back to St. Matthew's	37
8 The End of an Era	42
9 The Day Schools	46
10 The 1914–1918 War	48
11 Post-War and the New Parochial Church Council	54
12 Mission	59
13 Anglo-Catholicism	63
14 The Hussey Family and Others	67
15 Thirty-sixth Northampton (St. Matthew's) Boy Scouts	72
16 Dedication Festivals	77
17 Coming Retirement	82
18 War	86

19	1943 – Jubilee Year	91
20	Criticism	97
21	The End of the War	99
22	People	105
23	Music at St. Matthew's	110
24	A New Vicar – 1955	117
25	1957 to 1960	123
26	1961 – A Momentous Year	130
27	An Interregnum and a New Vicar	134
28	1964 to 1966	138
29	Overseas Contacts	143
30	Another Interregnum and a New Vicar	146
31	The Seventy-Fifth Anniversary Year – 1968	150
32	Changes Ahead?	155
33	The Eightieth Anniversary and After	160
34	Music from 1965 – Michael Nicholas	163
35	Music with Stephen Cleobury	168
36	And Afterwards	172
37	St. Matthews Voluntary Aided Junior Mixed School	175
38	A New Year and a New Vicar – John Ivor Morton	182
39	1977 to 1983	187
40	The Last Decade of the Church's Century	192
41	Music with Andrew Shenton, in the last decade of the Church's century	198
42	The Centenary Years – 1991–1993 (from Foundation Stone to New Church)	206

Family Trees:	
– The Phipps Family	215
– The Hussey Family	216
– The Atherton Family	217
The Staff of St. Matthew's Church, Northampton	218
The Choir of St. Matthew's Church, Northampton, Commissioned Works	221
Bibliography	223
Index of Persons	225

Acknowledgements

The list of those people who have helped to provide material for this book is a very long one and any attempt to put down names would inevitably leave some out. The help ranged from casual conversations to long interviews and many letters. I am most grateful to everyone concerned and I also apologise to those who could have contributed but were somehow missed. I would, however, like to offer my sincere thanks to Patrick Rawlinson for the great care he has devoted to the preparation and production of all the illustrations.

I apologise for all the names and events which I have not included. Time and length had to limit the book but I hope it gives a true survey of 100 eventful and prayerful years at St. Matthew's Church.

Mona Harrison
1993

List of Photographs

	Page
John Rowden Hussey, first vicar of St. Matthew's, 1893–1937.	2
Pickering Phipps senior, in whose memory the church was built.	9
View as built showing Nave, West Window and Baptistry. Note the absence of the wrought iron screens (added 1894), also the temporary choir stalls.	15
The High Altar and Reredos with the now removed sanctuary lamps.	19
The SE. aspect of the church, as it appeared c. 1900 before the vicarage was added.	23
The NW. aspect as it is today.	24
Charles King, organist and Director of Music 1895–1934.	28
The 'Great War' memorial listing the 126 parishioners who died for their country.	55
The 36th. Northampton (St. Matthew's) Scout Group in 1948 with their Scoutmaster, Arthur Wilson, seated centre, second row.	74
The 31st. Northampton (St. Matthew's) Guide Company parading into church on St. George's Day, 1969.	75
Fred Stallard (curate) at his farewell party in 1940.	89
The Henry Moore 'Madonna and Child' (1944) framed by the magnificent wrought iron screen surrounding the Lady Chapel.	95
Jack and the Beanstalk pantomine, Christmas 1948. Jack and Jill were played by Marjorie Guilbert and Joy Teasdale respectively.	101
Graham Sutherland's 'Crucifixion' painting, hung in the South Transept in 1946.	103
Walter Hussey having his autograph book signed by comedian Jimmy Edwards, who opened the church fete in 1947.	107

List of Photographs

	Page
A rehearsal of the Northampton Bach Choir conducted by Alec Wyton (nearest the camera), who was also organist and choirmaster.	113
Walter Hussey (vicar), on right, welcoming the operatic soprano Kirsten Flagstad in 1948.	114
Stephen Cleobury at the organ console.	169
Canon John I. Morton, vicar of St. Matthew's since 1975.	183
A memorial ceramic panel for the former St. Matthew's Church School and headmaster, E. G. Ashby.	185
Number 5 of 14 stations of the Cross (1987), the work of David Thomas.	190
The Lady Chapel, showing Triptych and Stained Glass Windows. Standing in front of the altar is Michael Fountaine (curate).	193
An aerial view of the church and grounds taken in August 1990. The Parish Centre, built in 1968, is on the left.	197
Daniel Ludford-Thomas 'Choirboy of the Year' B.E.T. award in 1986.	201
Malcolm Pollard's 'Risen Christ' was dedicated by the Bishop of Blackburn, the Right Reverend Alan Chesters, on St. Matthew's Day, 1992.	210
Parish outing on 25.7.92 to Derbyshire Well Dressing. Church members grouped round one of the displays at Stony Middleton. Amongst the parishioners is Ray Allen (churchwarden), second from right.	211
The church boasts a Carillon of twelve bells played via this keyboard. Bellringer in this instance is Matthew Hobden.	211
The Clergy and Choir after the 10.15 service on 28.2.93. Seated centre of second row, from left to right, are – Alan March (ordinand), Canon John Morton (vicar) and Rev. Stephen Cope (curate), flanked by retired priests Leslie Bearman and Methuen Clarke.	212
The Right Reverend and Rt. Hon. Lord Bishop of London. Dr. David Hope, in procession with the youth services, Mothering Sunday 1993. The occasion was used for all baptised in St. Matthew's to renew their vows.	213
The SW. aspect of the church and vicarage as they appear today.	214

List of Figures

	Page
Service Sheet covers for:	
(i) The order for laying the foundation Stone;	
(ii) The order of the Consecration of the Permanent Church.	11
The Pulpit.	17
St. Matthew as depicted on the front of the Lady Chapel Altar.	21
Baptistry and Font.	22
Certificate of Baptism in the time of J. Rowden Hussey.	80
Commissioned Music I 'Justus quidem tu es Domine' composed by Peter Dickinson for John Bertalot and St. Matthew's choir:	
(i) Cover;	127
(ii) Original Manuscript.	128
Commissioned Music II 'The Covenant of the Rainbow' composed by Gordon Crosse for Michael Nicholas and St. Matthew's Choir.	152
Commissioned Music III 'The Spacious Firmament' composed by Herbert Sumsion for Andrew Shenton and St. Matthew's Choir (original manuscript).	200

Photograph Credits

Photographer/ Custodian	Print/Plate Number
St. Matthew's Church	1, 6, 7, 21, 23
R. J. F. Rawlinson	2
P. I. Rawlinson	3, 8, 9, 13, 16–20, 22, 25, 27, 29, 30
P. M. Rawlinson collection	4
S. Cleobury collection	5
F. Stallard collection	10
M. Snedker collection	11
Northants. County Record Office	12, 15
Canon M. Clarke collection	14
G. Smith collection	24
B. Ludford-Thomas collection	26
J. Stirling	28

Preface

by the Reverend Canon John Morton, M.A., Vicar

I paid my first visit to Northampton in 1957. Arriving by train from the West Country after a long journey, improved by the sort of good lunch that British Railways still supplied, I caught a bus which transported me through the gathering darkness of a early spring evening right through the centre of a town, still busy with last-minute Saturday shoppers.

Eventually I was set down near the bulk of St. Matthew's Church and made my way to the adjoining Parsonage, never imagining for a moment that one day it would be my home for almost two decades.

The purpose of my visit was to ascertain whether the Vicar, at that time Charles Mackenzie, would think me a suitable person to serve my title, my ministerial apprenticeship, at St. Matthew's.

In those days such matters were settled informally and personally. The church had not begun to imitate the techniques of corporate commerce and if it looked for any model on which it might up-date its procedures, the Armed Services, or the Civil Service, were seen as offering suitable guidance.

The Principal of my Theological College, who knew my nature well, had handed me a bunch of eight letters from priests whom he also knew and valued, and told me to select one to visit as a prospective training Vicar. From his letter and from his description of St. Matthew's, Charles Mackenzie of St. Matthew's, Northampton, seemed to have much to offer. So I made my selection.

My memories of that first visit to St. Matthew's are, after thirty-five years, somewhat patchy. I warmed instantly to Mackenzie, though I felt troubled by his almost quasi-military insistence on loyalty in his assistants. Yet the next day when I saw him in action in church I recognised his gifts as an evangelist, for his preaching style was robust and the content of his sermon, though muffled by St. Matthew's deplorable acoustics, hit home. He had introduced a simple mid-morning Parish Communion, which, like many other priests of his generation who had inherited a non-communicating Sung Mass as the principal parish Eucharist, he hoped would gradually supersede the later sung service. Though he had not thought it perhaps prudent to touch on the problems of the parish, this and other changes he had made at St. Matthew's had involved him in much stressful dispute, hence, as I later learned, his disturbing emphasis on loyalty.

On the Sunday afternoon of my visit I began to recognise the unmistakable signs of influenza and my capacity for picking up impressions was correspondingly diminished. All I wanted was to get home to bed. Perhaps this unfortunate occurrence influenced my later decision not to come to St. Matthew's. In fact, it was as well, for I might well have had to cope as a raw curate with the aftermath of the sudden death of Fr. Mackenzie in the autumn of 1961. However, with the negative decision the likelihood of my ever having any further contact with St. Matthew's seemed utterly remote.

Yet, less than twenty years later, with two curacies and two incumbencies behind me, I was surprised one day to have a 'phone call asking whether I would allow my name to go forward to the patrons of St. Matthew's, the Diocesan Board of Patronage, as a possible future Vicar. The fact that St. Matthew's had cropped up once again in my life helped me to say yes! I had come to feel that my work in Cheshire was done, so I made my second-ever visit to Northampton, this time by car and to a town very different in appearance from that bustling county town I had last seen in the fifties. The Board took only a short time to make up its mind to offer me St. Matthew's and I had no hesitation in accepting. I have never regretted that decision.

The St. Matthew's of which I became Vicar in the mid-seventies struck me as being quite unchanged from the church and congregation which I had encountered with Fr. Mackenzie. Both for better and for worse the changes which had overtaken the whole Church of England in the last two decades seemed to have made little impression on the church. The morning services were still well attended at a time when many churches were beginning to experience contraction. The pattern of worship still proclaimed the adherence of the congregation to a eucharistically centred spirituality. The conduct of services placed the parish in the centre of the mainstreams of Anglican Catholic opinion, firmly sacramental but unequivocally Anglican. The Solemn Eucharist sung by an excellent choir had not, as Charles Mackenzie had hoped, withered. A pattern of services had evolved which seemed to meet the experienced needs of the people. The said service had crept later in time, the Solemn Eucharist had become a people's communion. The overall impression was of stability, rooted in traditional devotion.

There were, however, few indications that St. Matthew's was alert to, let alone had responded to, the changes in thinking about worship which were current in the rest of the Church. All Sunday celebrations were Eastward facing at the distant High Altar. The Series II services had recently been adopted but there was no enthusiasm for the modern language liturgy. St. Matthew's was conservative and proud of it!

Perhaps that resistance to change was inevitable in a church where, quite exceptionally in the twentieth century, son had succeeded father as incumbent, so that one family of priests had led the church for nearly sixty years. Similarly, the use of a cathedral repertory of music at services does not encourage change, since the best traditional church music was written for the Prayer Book and Missal. Maybe also there is in Northampton people, to a marked degree, that suspicion of novelty which characterises most people's approach to religion. The church building was also designed to form a suitable setting for the worship Anglo-Catholics valued. If Matthew Holding did not favour a dim, he certainly aimed at a religious light and atmosphere. His lofty, lengthy church was meant to lead the eye to a distant altar, where dignified ceremony would proclaim the unchanging otherness of God. The ideal was worship by impression, by appeal to the aesthetic senses, rather than by community participation. Within the terms of what was sought, the design was highly successful. Then as now, I have always felt that our church building had a rather severe 'Cistercian' atmosphere. St. Matthew's is a very different place during worship, when robes and vestments fill the chancel and clouds of incense film the vision, than on a dark December afternoon, when its great spaces are full of dark shadows. Nonetheless, it is at any time a distinguished building, a noble parish church, now lifted well above the ordinary, because it houses, thanks to Dean Hussey, two works of modern religious art of the first rank. Our church will always be a wonderful testimony to the generosity and sense of responsibility which led successful Victorian businessmen to feel that they must give back to the God who had blessed them with prosperity. That impulse was the direct result of profound Christian faith. It is notable that those who enjoy affluence today are more likely to use excess profits to buy a second home abroad and yet another luxury car. The faith which led Pickering Phipps' relatives to donate St. Matthew's and most that is in it, has withered, along with the world of low wages and long hours for workers, which made the accumulations of comfortable fortunes so widely possible. St. Matthew's, as locals never tire of letting a newcomer know, was built from the profits of beer, yet it would never have taken shape, without the costly Christian belief of the donors.

Across the century we are celebrating, the torch of faith has been handed on. This great building inspired affection because for so many it was the setting for the worship and instruction which gave them a faith for life. They have not for the most part been people of great means, but what they had they gave unstintingly, both time and money, so that the altar might be well served; the choir stalls filled; the increasingly expensive building maintained; in order that the original vision of those who founded church and parish might be sustained. Almost without interruption across this hundred years of witness, the daily Eucharist has been upheld; the solemn Sunday celebrations continued; the young and old of the parish instructed in sacramental Anglicanism.

In only one serious matter have we capitulated to irresistible pressure. The Church School in Byron Street, an essential weapon in Canon Hussey's strategy for the parish from the first, had to close in 1977. Matters were well advanced before I came as Vicar. Neither parish nor diocese could afford the suggested replacement buildings, so a link with the origins of church work in the Kingsley district was severed. The school was a mission outpost and a sympathetic Head ensured that the clergy were made aware of all the pastoral problems the children reported. We continue to suffer from its closure both from the point of view of impact on the district at large and through the loss of contact with youngsters and their families which has resulted from its demise. I shall always cherish the memory of a mass Baptism we planned before this breach occurred, when Archdeacon Marsh and I christened nearly fifty of the children at one great service. When some of them come to see me now to be married, they too recall the great day!

St. Matthew's was, from the first, conceived as essentially a parish church, serving a well-marked, densely populated, district. Though at first the parish was divided geographically and socially by the Kettering Road, there seems to have been little sense in worshippers of 'us' and 'them', even when behind the older 'poet' streets a council estate took shape, between the wars. Even in the more fluid circumstances created by the motor car, it remains firmly a parish church. One third of the names of those on the electoral roll reside within the ecclesiastical parish, and a third of those who do not, once did, and often live just outside. The clergy are still much occupied with the Baptisms, Marriages and Burials of parishioners, though social and local factors seem to have led to a decrease in the first two categories. Of course, the church's particular spiritual, aesthetic and musical tradition does mean that it is used by a body of outsiders, but they are content to embrace rather than dominate a parish-based community.

Ours is, by the meagre standards of late twentieth-century England, a strong church and the 270 or so names on the roll are a fair guide to the number of those seriously engaged with our church. It is as well, for the beneficence of the past has bequeathed us a church building expensive both to maintain and to use. Happily, the generosity of Walter Hussey has gone some way to alleviating the burden of provision for fabric upkeep, but the cost of day-to-day running, which is considerable, has to fall on the shoulders of worshippers. As the first century of St. Matthew's closes, it is good to report that they are providing for this more generously than ever before.

It would not be right to close this foreword without some conjectures about the future. Clearly it is not easy to see how St. Matthew's can cope with the demands of the twenty-first century, without strengthening its local base. The call of the Decade of Evangelism to draw in those on the fringes of Church life, especially the young who feel a lack of direction in their lives, has a particular resonance for our congregation. If for no better reason, maintenance compels mission.

But successful mission would pose questions we are still tending to shirk, particularly about the style and content of our worship. Most modern people have not the cultural resources to derive benefit from the principal acts of worship. They would probably look for an informality, a directness, a degree of participation, which we presently cannot offer. I wonder how much longer we can refuse to grasp the nettle of a re-ordering of the church, so that a central altar around which all can gather, becomes the focus of our worship, rather than one at the end of a distant sanctuary. We already experiment regularly with such an arrangement but on a temporary basis. Yet if, as it should be, such a re-ordering is to be more than a re-arrangement of furnishings, it must be underpinned across the congregation by an acceptance of the more biblically-based view of the Eucharist as a community action in which all actively participate. The acceptance of such a view will also have repercussions in the field of music and ceremonial. These and kindred questions about forms of worship, and rites, are ones I feel must be faced early by our congregation as we move into our second century.

They are made all the more difficult in that none of us, in our quest to be more relevant to our neighbourhood, wishes to lose those special excellencies for which our church is rightly valued. Our choir has been a nursery of gifted church musicians; the tradition of patronage of the arts, begun by Walter Hussey in his outstanding ministry, we have steadfastly continued. But any Vicar of St. Matthew's will always find himself balanced on a knife edge in seeking to conserve these valuable traditions, whilst endeavouring to shape a church truly fitted for its ordinary parishioners. St. Matthew's has never been an eclectic shrine for an esoteric clientèle, nor must it ever be allowed to become such, if it is to serve the Lord, to whose glory it was built and the ordinary people of God for whom it was erected.

For my part I can look back on the eighteen years in which I have served the church with intense happiness. I carry in my heart the memory of some outstanding and moving acts of worship. I am grateful for the fact that never for one day have I felt unused or unneeded in this parish of 7,000 souls. But, above all, I thank God for the loyalty of my people to their church, and for the kindness, understanding and warmth they have shown to me personally, as to all previous parish priests.

At St. Matthew's I have met and been encouraged by a few saints. They were shaped by the life and worship of our beloved church, and they, in the last resort, are St. Matthew's greatest treasures, for our church was built and given to nourish them.

As long as it continues to produce them in the incredibly different and difficult circumstances of our times, it will fulfil the hopes and prayers of those who, one hundred years ago, provided our church to the glory of God and the service of his people.

J. I. Morton
Vicar

1

Early Days

One winter's day in 1888, a young man was to be seen in the developing suburb of Kingsley Park. John Rowden Hussey was seeking lodgings in the area. Rowden was twenty-four, having been born on 11th January 1864 at Milston, Wiltshire, the youngest son of John Compton Hussey, a gentleman farmer, Master of Foxhounds and a Churchwarden, and of Susannah, née Pearce. On both sides Rowden's grandparents were also farmers and the families had lived around the Salisbury area of Wiltshire for a long time.

John Rowden Hussey was treading a different path. His father had been much influenced by Dr. Wordsworth, the Bishop of Salisbury, who did not think much of Oxford Colleges, so Rowden had been taught by the Bishop, a most academic man, who believed that anyone could learn Greek to read the New Testament in the original! After school in Marlborough, and some private tuition, Rowden had gone to Salisbury Theological College and, on Sunday 6th March 1887, had been ordained as a Deacon in the parish church of St. James', Trowbridge, by the Lord Bishop of Sarum, and earlier in 1888 had been ordained priest. As a Deacon he had been appointed to the parish of Belgrave, north of Leicester, under the Vicar, the Rev'd. Charles Gray, and now, when he had expected to stay in Belgrave for a number of years, Bishop Magee of Peterborough had appointed him as Curate-in-Charge of a Mission Church in this new suburb within the parish of Kingsthorpe. William Conner Magee had been Bishop of Peterborough since 1869 and was particularly concerned with the Church Extension Society, which had been formed in Northampton in 1875. The population of the town of Northampton had expanded to nearly 50,000 and was still growing. Four new churches had recently been built, St. Lawrence's in 1877/8; St. Michael's in 1882; St.

John Rowden Hussey, first vicar of St. Matthew's, 1893–1937.

Mary's, Far Cotton, in 1885 and St. Paul's was being built. Kingsley was the next area to be considered. The Bishop was to provide his stipend and license him to do the 'spadework' for an eventual new parish. Rowden had already travelled the two miles along the tramway to the village of Kingsthorpe to visit the Vicar, the Rev'd. Edward Tuson.

Kingsthorpe was a big parish, bounded by Moulton and Abington on the east; Boughton to the north; the river Nene on the west and the town of Northampton on the south. With developing industry, Northampton was growing rapidly and new houses were extending into Kingsthorpe parish, making it difficult to administer from the old village. Until 1850, Kingsthorpe had been annexed to St. Peter's, Northampton. In 1877, the St. Paul's parish was formed from part of Kingsthorpe and part of St. Sepulchre's, later in 1888, it was decided to consider a new parish for the developing area of Kingsley.

So, here he was, potential Curate-in-Charge of the Kingsley Park Mission. A small population and no church! The houses consisted of the first blocks built from Oliver Street to Chaucer Street and joined by Junction Road.

Northampton in the late 1880s was not the easiest town in which to be an Anglican priest; it had a national reputation for atheism, following the election of the Liberal M.P. Charles Bradlaugh, who had been elected in 1880 but had been unable to take his seat until 1886 as he refused to take the oath. There was also a strong Non-Conformist element in the town, in fact many of the Chapels were large, rich and powerful. In contrast to the sober, in all senses, Methodists and Baptists and Congregationalists, some of the 'cobblers' who were still, in many cases, working in their own homes and were paid when they took in the finished work on Fridays, had a reputation for drunkenness on Saturdays!

There was distinction at the time, between the 'workers' who were mostly Liberal and Non-Conformist, and the 'bosses' who were mostly Conservative and Church, often representing the County families, though many of the shoe manufacturers and others were staunchly Baptist.

In Kingsley Park, the new 'poet' streets, Byron Street, Shelley Street, etc., were of smallish houses built in terraces, and the new occupants were mostly small shopkeepers, shoemakers, etc. On the other side of the Kettering Road, the area to be Phippsville, the houses were to be larger, particularly towards the main road, and became occupied by people of a higher social class.

This was the area where Rowden Hussey was to settle, outside the old town but to some extent a reflection of it. The Methodist Chapel, on the

Kingsley side, had already been built, and the strictly teetotal were already casting disapproving eyes at the Phippsville side, belonging to the Phipps family of brewers!

John Rowden Hussey walked alone round his future 'parish', realising that this would be the last time he could do this as an 'unknown', a queer feeling to be essentially invisible! But time pressed, he had to get back to Belgrave and he still needed lodgings for his official arrival.

Friday 11th January 1889 was Rowden Hussey's twenty-fifth birthday and he had found lodgings at 147 Park Crescent, at the Kettering Road end of Colwyn Road and the edge of the Race Course. How to begin?

Recently the doors had opened for the Kingsley Park Infant Day School on the east side of Byron Street. A circular letter sent to every home invited parishioners to the Byron Street schoolroom for the first Eucharist to be held on Sunday 20th January, the second Sunday in Epiphany. Rowden had no church furnishings, so he borrowed some wooden candlesticks from a friendly neighbour and Communion vessels from the Rev'd. Arthur Snowden, Vicar of St. Michael's, 'next door'. The schoolroom was icy, so he lit the fire, prepared an altar on a small table, arranged a few chairs and rang the school bell! He must have wondered if anyone would come, despite the circulars, his contacts and his prayers. To his relief, sixteen communicants came, the forerunners of many more. God had heard his prayers – or were they merely curious to see the new Curate? Future Sundays would answer that!

In 1889 it was quite a challenge to start the Mission with a Eucharist service, but John Rowden Hussey had been much influenced by the Oxford Movement, although its origin was long before his birth. The revival of older practices, altar candles, the mixed chalice, the eastward position, vestments, etc., were all still matters of passionate controversy and Rowden was anxious to run the Mission on Anglo-Catholic lines, a true venture of faith, needing courage and conviction which he certainly possessed. To have a Eucharist every Sunday was unusual enough and Rowden's aim was to have a *daily* Eucharist, so that the Sacrament became the ordinary food of the Faithful. For the time being he was restricted by the building. He could only use the schoolroom out of school hours, and the school was impeded by the chairs piled for the services. It was agreed that an 'Iron Church' should be erected behind the school, and this was achieved in mid-April, three months into his Ministry.

In his first three months, Rowden had been very busy. He had Churchwardens, Mr. George Weed and Mr. Fred Chouler; Sidesmen, Mr. Robins and Mr. Lowe; a Choirmaster, Mr. Kean; Miss Smith as 'organist' to play the harmonium; Mr. J. Kean as Sunday School Superintendent and a Mr. Percival, who lived in Shelley Street, as Caretaker. At 8.00 a.m. every Sunday there was Holy Communion, followed at 10.00 a.m. by the Sunday School classes for the children; 11.00 a.m. was Mattins with the Litany and a Sermon; and Evensong was at 6.30 p.m. On first Sundays, there was Holy Communion at the 11.00 a.m. service and on the last Sunday of the month, there was a Children's Service at 2.30 p.m.

April 1889 saw the publication of the first Parish Magazine, for the price of one (old) penny. In it Rowden announced that the new church would be dedicated on Palm Sunday; he thanked his parishioners for their many kindnesses and the support he had received; 'Services,' he said, 'were well attended, the Sunday School had 113 scholars and the parish school had over 100 on its roll.'

On Palm Sunday, 14th April, over fifty were present at the 8.00 a.m. Communion when Rowden himself celebrated, and there was a large congregation at 11.00 a.m. Mattins, when Canon Hull, the Rural Dean, took the service. The choir, of four men and six boys, were wearing cassocks and surplices, another 'first'! At Evensong, with the Rt. Rev'd. the Lord Bishop of Leicester, the church was packed. There was a processional hymn, the Bishop preached from Acts 8.35, 'the readiness of God to teach when man was ready to hear' – the church was dedicated and the Mission Church became St. Matthew's!

The first Easter was an important occasion for the new congregation. Rowden was anxious to make his parishioners aware of the importance of the Church's Year and he was also aware of the impact of introducing different priests and different ideas on special occasions. He reminded his flock of the importance of the Prayer Book instruction to Communicate at least three times a year 'of which Easter shall be one'. At Easter the church was well decorated with flowers, the singing was said to be good and there were seventy-two communicants!

On Easter Tuesday came the first Parochial Tea. One of Rowden's strong beliefs was the importance of socialising, having a good time together; getting to know people; getting them to know each other, and this was particularly vital in a newly growing neighbourhood, where people were moving in at frequent intervals. The Parochial Tea, in the schoolroom, attracted over 200 people and twenty-five ladies provided trays of food. There was a short service in the church and the meal was followed by a concert. Rowden took the opportunity to outline what had been achieved; Mr. George Weed, the churchwarden, spoke and the

Rev'd. William Law, the curate from Belgrave, had come to wish success to the Mission. Various ladies, gentlemen and one child sang, gave readings or played the piano, even William Law contributed by singing 'Ole King Cole' and all felt that the gathering had been a great success. It was the first of many such occasions.

Organisation makes things happen, so Rowden Hussey firmly believed. He himself worked unceasingly, but he had the common sense to involve the laity at an early stage, at a time when 'Lay Ministry' was uncommon. Visiting was very important and, at first, Rowden himself went to every house as often as he could, always wearing his cassock, but, realising that, as the number of houses increased rapidly, he was facing an impossible task, he conceived the idea of District Visitors. In these early days he persuaded six ladies to be responsible for seven streets (later he needed nearly forty) – Junction Road, Chaucer and Moore Streets, Shelley Street, Byron Street, Milton Street and Oliver Street were the nucleus at that time.

Daily Evensong was said at 6.00 p.m., Mattins and the Litany at 10.00 a.m., at first only twice a week, but later daily. Herbert Cuthbert was his first baptism and, sadly, his first funeral service was for Frederick Chouler, his churchwarden who was greatly esteemed in the parish. From the first, choral music was to play an important part in the worship at St. Matthew's and a cricket club was started to involve the choir and to encourage the men and boys who were interested. There was a Choral Evensong on the Eve of Ascension Day, when the Rev'd. Augustus Miller of Wootton preached, and there were twenty communicants at the 6.30 a.m. Eucharist on Ascension Day itself.

Money was a constant problem, the church building had still to be paid for, and Rowden invited subscriptions for that and also for a Sunday School Treat. A Parochial Picnic was arranged for Tuesday 9th July at 1s. 6d. a head. The Summer Picnic, which was to become an annual event, was an outing to Castle Ashby. The brakes left Kingsley at 1.30 p.m. by which time 120 had assembled. The party went over Castle Ashby House and gardens, visited the church and had tea in the grounds of the Falcon Inn. Unfortunately it rained in the evening, but stopped for the return journey, leaving at 8.30 p.m. and arriving in Kingsley at 10.15 p.m. It was rated a most successful occasion.

On 20th August, Rowden Hussey and the Churchwardens took the Choir to a meal at the Falcon at Castle Ashby and finished the day with a cricket match. Another 'first' was a Flower Service, mainly for the children, from which the flowers went to the Infirmary, and on 21st September was held the first celebration of St. Matthew's Day, an occasion which was to loom large in later years. Harvest Festival in October with Choral Evensong; a Confirmation Service in November at St. Michael's Church (classes preceding had been held for boys and girls on different evenings of the week); a Sale of Work and Concerts to raise money. The basic pattern of the Church's Year, both liturgically and socially, was becoming established.

Christmas was a great occasion. Rowden emphasised the importance of Advent, the need to prepare; to be regular and attentive in Church attendance; the need for self-examination and regular communions. During Advent, he had special services every Tuesday evening, which he took himself, and persuaded the Rev'd. Albert Oldroyd of Raunds to preach each Thursday evening.

On Christmas Day there were seventy-three communicants. To greet the New Year of 1890, 250 people attended a tea in the Schoolroom, followed by Evensong with Carols in the Church and then a concert in the Schoolroom. The Mothers' Meeting had a special tea and service and the choirboys were entertained to tea at Kingsthorpe Hall before Christmas and by Mr. and Mrs. Weed of Kingsley Road early in the New Year, followed a couple of days later by a similar tea for the men of the choir. Rowden's mixture of services and socials was popular!

Eighteen-ninety was a year when the previous year's work was consolidated and services made more meaningful, together with further innovations. In May came the first meeting of the Communicants' Guild, which was to meet once a month for Instruction and Devotion; at most meetings there was to be a special speaker to initiate discussion and, on a practical level, it was decided that the members would be responsible for the cleaning of the Altar and Sanctuary.

The Parochial Church Picnic in July went to Overstone and was again a success, as was the Choir Outing to Lamport. The Northampton Church Guild Union Annual Festival was held at St. Matthew's, as was the November Confirmation.

In December, the year ended with the great news from Mr. Pickering Phipps that a new and substantial church would be built for the new parish.

2

The New Church

The Phipps Family had been prominent in Northampton for over half a century. Coming from farming stock, James Phipps of Bugbrooke had married Elizabeth Pickering in 1771 and their eldest son, christened Pickering, had founded a brewery in Towcester and then, in Northampton, had founded the brewery at South Bridge. It was his grandson, another Pickering Phipps, who had been head of the firm of Phipps & Co.; had been M.P. for Northampton and later for South Northants; Alderman of Northampton Borough and twice Mayor. In 1860 he had gone to live in Collingtree, in the newly built Grange, where he became interested in farming and agricultural matters. He was much esteemed, a good host and liberal to charities, a good Churchman and a generous subscriber to the cost of new churches in the expanding town. Some time before, he had acquired a large piece of land to the east of the Kettering Road on which to build a housing estate to be called Phippsville. This on the opposite side from the Kingsley Park Estate which was being developed by the Northampton Freehold Building Society. Alderman Phipps had indicated that he was prepared to provide a piece of land on which a permanent church could be built.

Unfortunately, on 14th September 1890, he died at the relatively early age of sixty-three. He and his wife had had nine children of whom six grew up and, although their father had made no gift of land or financial provision towards the new church in his will, they, with their mother, decided to build a new St. Matthew's Church in his memory. The late Mr. Phipps' daughters were to give the land, nearly an acre, fronting the Kettering Road, with a new road alongside, and his son would pay for the building at a cost of around £20,000. His widow would donate the East window and the organ. It was Alderman Phipps' son, another Pickering

Pickering Phipps senior, in whose memory the church was built.

Phipps, who made the great announcement in December 1890, a great boost for the New Year. He was not much older than Rowden Hussey and they became great friends.

The Northampton architect, Matthew Holding, was commissioned to produce a Gothic design for the new church. It was to seat about 1,000 people and all seats would be free, a tribute to the Free and Open Church cause, as well as a memorial to the man who had contributed so much to his native town. One of the last official acts within the diocese of Bishop Magee was to assist in the plans for the new church. The Bishop had been translated to the Archbishopric of York in the spring of 1891 but sadly died of influenza a few weeks later.

The Patronal Festival of 1891 was to be the time for the new Bishop of Peterborough, the Rt. Rev'd. Mandell Creighton, to lay the Foundation Stone of the new St. Matthew's. Flags and bunting were arranged along and across the roads; a triple arch of evergreens and crimson bunting was constructed, bearing the Royal Arms and the Prince of Wales' Feathers; there was a smaller arch at the actual entrance to the site and there were decorated poles along the road. Kingsley was *en fête*!

The Mayor and Corporation processed from the Town Hall, together with the Chief of Police and a police escort. The Bishop, with the choir and many clergy, met the Civic procession at the Borough boundary, together with the Phipps family, Mr. Pickering Phipps leading with the new processional cross, his first gift to the church. A service was held in the 'iron church' and then, despite heavy rain, all proceeded to the site singing 'Onward Christian Soldiers'. The 15 cwt. stone inscribed 'To the glory of God and in memory of Pickering Phipps J.P. . . . .' was duly laid by the Bishop, using a silver-gilt trowel and a mallet bound with silver-gilt.

After the Benediction, 250 people crowded into the school for luncheon, and to see a painting of the late Mr. Phipps, as well as plans and drawings of the new church. There were toasts and speeches, and the celebrations continued with further special services over the weekend.

On 26th August 1893, the *London Gazette* published an Order in Council dated from Osborne House on the Isle of Wight, forming the new parish of St. Matthew in Northampton. The Ecclesiastical Commission declared the parish would consist of 'all that part of the parish of Kingsthorpe in the county of Northamptonshire and the diocese of Peterborough, which is bounded on the NE. by the parish of Abington . . . upon the South by the new parish of St. Michael and All Angels, Northampton . . . upon the SW. partly by the new parish of St. Paul, Northampton and on the NW. by an imaginary line commencing upon the boundary which

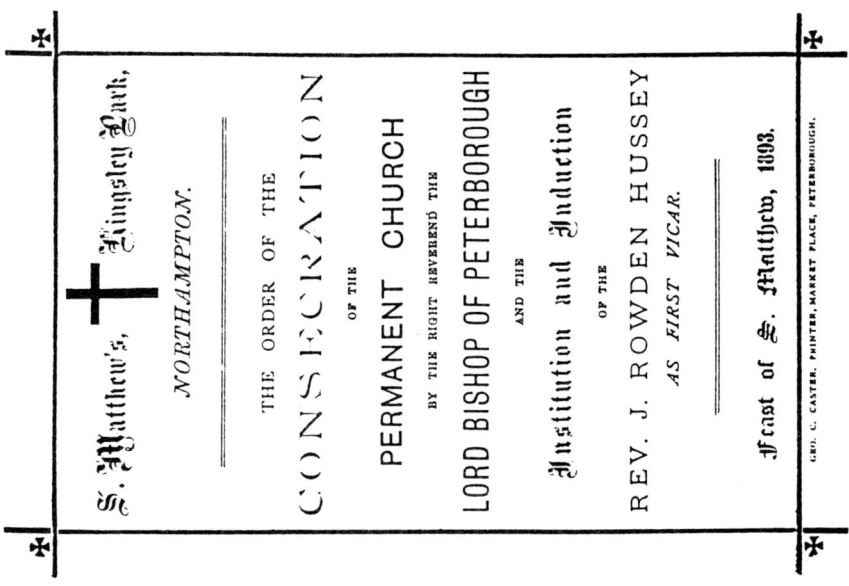

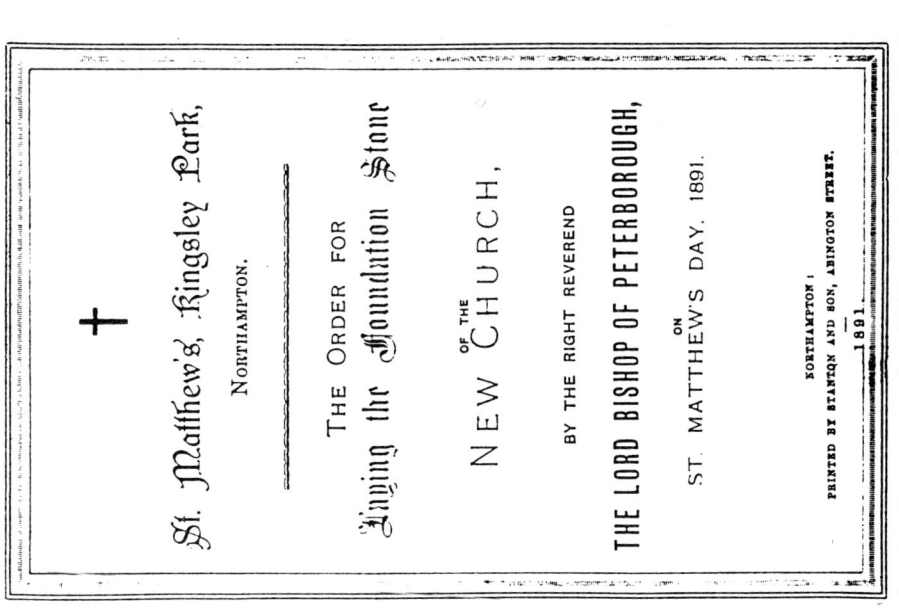

Service Sheet covers for: (i) The order for laying the Foundation Stone;
(ii) The Order of the Consecration of the Permanent Church.

divides the said new parish of St. Paul from the parish of Kingsthorpe at the centre of the bridge or culvert which carries Gipsy Lane, otherwise known as Peach's Lane, over the brook called or known as Sourlands Brook and extending thence NE.-ward along the middle of the said brook for seventy-one and a quarter chains to the point where it crosses the public footpath leading from Kingsthorpe Farm into the Northampton and Kettering High Road, upon the boundary which divides the parish of Kingsthorpe from Abington.'

The church was to be consecrated on St. Matthew's Day, 21st September 1893, at 11.00 a.m. by the Rt. Rev'd. the Bishop of Peterborough, followed immediately by Holy Communion. There would be special preachers for all the services. Holy Communion would be celebrated daily throughout the octave, culminating on Sunday 1st October.

'The noble structure built by the present Mayor of Northampton, Mr. Henry Martin, from the fine designs of Mr. Matthew Holding, reared its head by degrees, public interest in its completion proportionately deepened until a degree of attention had been aroused which is without parallel in the religious history of our ancient Borough.' This was the introduction to an article in the *Northampton Herald* describing the new church 'as an eloquent tribute to noble and unbounded liberality, as well as a memorial to one whose genial face and kindly heart endeared him, without distinction, to all.'

Crowds gathered long before 11.00 a.m.; decorations flapped in the breeze and at last the sun came out, in contrast to the wet and stormy weather which had marked the Stone-laying!

Admission to the church had to be by ticket as a great deal of room was needed for the civic and clerical dignitaries. The clergy robed in the old church and the procession was again led by Mr. Phipps as Crucifer. He was followed by the choir and the Guild Banner of St. Matthew. Over 100 clergy from the Peterborough diocese and beyond were followed by the Churchwardens, Mr. John Haviland and Mr. H. L. Philp; leading the Bishop of Leicester, the Diocesan Secretary, the Bishop's Secretary, the Chancellor, with the Bishop of Peterborough and his chaplains coming last. The processional hymn was 'Forward Be Our Watchword'. The Civic procession came from the Guildhall, consisting of representatives of the Police under the Chief Constable; members of the Fire Brigade; the Town Crier; the Beadle; the Town Clerk; the Mayor with the Recorder and members of the Corporation. The two processions met at the West door. The Churchwardens presented the petition, exactly at 11.00 a.m., praying the Bishop to consecrate the church, as the procession circled the church, the twenty-fourth Psalm was sung by the huge congregation. The beautiful service of Consecration followed ending with the 'Te Deum'. Mr. Pickering Phipps, now patron of the living, presented the Rev'd. John Rowden Hussey 'to be admitted to the cure of souls of the parish of St. Matthew'. The first Vicar was then instituted by the Bishop of Peterborough and afterwards inducted by the Bishop of Leicester, Archdeacon Thicknesse. Holy Communion was celebrated by Bishop Creighton assisted by the new Vicar. The Organist during the service was Dr. G. C. Martin from St. Paul's Cathedral and the address was by the Bishop of Leicester. The whole service lasted for two and a half hours!

At the Stone-laying, marquees had had to be used to make room for everyone at the luncheon, but on this occasion even that would have been inadequate; the party proceeded to the Town Hall in Northampton, where Mr. and Mrs. Pickering Phipps entertained 400 people to luncheon. Speeches and toasts followed; to the Donors, the Architect, the Builder, the Preacher and the Success of St. Matthew's. Back in Kingsley at 6.00 p.m. a Parochial Tea for another 400 was a great success and was attended by the Phipps family, the new Vicar and others. Evensong was at 8.00 p.m., when Bishop Mandell Creighton preached, and the church was full to overflowing.

Indeed a great day!

3

Extracts from the Souvenir Booklet (Published 1893)

St. Matthew's Church – Phipps Memorial

The Exterior

A visitor may with advantage take a first general view of the building as it is approached from the road from Northampton, and will probably be struck with the size and general outline of the whole. The long sky-line of the Nave and Chancel is boldly broken by a lofty flèche, rising some 40 ft. above the ridge of the roof. The flèche is of timber, wholly covered with lead, and with tall pinnacles at the angles, pierced gables between each. Attention may next be directed to the range of tall Clerestory windows, with intervening flying buttresses carried down to the aisle walls. The grouping of the richer South Transept, with the subordinate and less elaborate Organ Chamber adjoining, and the lower and simple range of Vestry buildings beneath, may be noticed in passing. Proceeding eastward, the exterior of the Chancel Apse comes into view. This consists of five bays of traceried windows each of three lights, divided between with tall buttresses of considerable projection, and capped with a parapet of sunk and moulded panel work, with pinnacles at each angle; and the whole apse is flanked on each side with tall circular turrets, rising above the main ridge, while the roof of the apse is finished with a lead hip knob and an iron cross. The North side of the church shows considerable variation from the South, for here we find the side chapel makes a distinc-

Extracts from the Souvenir Booklet 15

View as built showing Nave, West Window and baptistry. Note the absence of the wrought iron screens (added 1894), also the temporary choir stalls.

tive feature toward the new cross-road, and the addition of a small North porch (intended more especially for access to the Chapel) should not be overlooked. Continuing a walk along the North side, we reach the Tower and the main North Doorway, which is enriched with arcades and niches. The sculpture in these niches represents Our Lord calling St. Matthew from the Receipt of Custom. Crossing now the Main Road, and even to some distance into Byron Street, a good view may be obtained of the West Front, and notice may be taken of the grouping of the west windows, with the arrangement of three lights in the centre, and with two-light windows on each side, also the adjacent South-west buttresses and circular turret, which gives some balance to the work at the opposite angle. The exterior walling of the Church is of local stone quarried at Kingsthorpe.

The Nave

The nave consists of six bays, and each intervening pier has an arrangement of engaged and disengaged shafts to the height of the pier caps, when the former become engaged in the walls, and run up in connection with the main wall shafts, which latter support a series of moulded and pierced cross arches, which span the Nave at each pier division, and carry the eye onward to the Chancel Arch, which is at the same level. The smaller shafts to the Nave receive the arches over the Clerestory windows, and give a depth and continuity to the Clerestory arcade.

Transepts

The North Transept has a wide arch opening into the Side Chapel, and the floor space of this Transept is so arranged as to be seated in continuation of the Chapel area, and to be used at times in conjunction with it. The South Transept is also made largely contributory to the success of the Organ Chamber, and for passage of sound from the Organ into the body of the church.

Pulpit

The Pulpit is mainly composed of moulded and polished alabaster, the base consisting of a series of larger shafts of alabaster, with smaller intervening shafts of Levanto marble. The upper portion is divided into a series of panels with traceried heads, and divided by shafts of polished Breche Sanquin marble. A small sunk arcading runs round the lower portions of the panels, and the upper portion of each is filled with subjects in sculpture representing great and remarkable occasions of preaching. The carved ornamentation may be noticed as well as the manner in which the marble steps to it are formed by a continuation of the steps to the Chancel.

Lectern

This stands upon a broad raised slab of marble, and is a reproduction of the celebrated Southwell Eagle. This is the work of Messrs. T. Potter &

Extracts from the Souvenir Booklet 17

The Pulpit.

Sons, of South Molton Street, London, and is the gift of Mr. and Mrs. James Barry.

Litany Desk

This is of wainscot oak, with sunk and panelled ends and traceried front, and is in keeping with the adjacent fittings. The Desk, with the vellum-bound Litany Book, is the gift of Mr. Thomas Phipps of Towcester.

The Books

The large Bible for the Eagle Lectern in the Nave is a Cambridge Imperial Quarto, red-lined, the gift of Miss Dunkley of Collingtree. There are two Prayer Books for the Church Offices in great primo, quarto, red rubricated – the gifts of Mr. W. H. Lamb and Mr. J. J. Walker. Also the books in great primo, octavo, for the Altar, Litany Desk, and for use at occasional offices. All these books are bound wholly in white vellum, with the sides and backs ornamented with surface toolings, being adaptations of the artistic characteristic of white skin bindings. An inscription runs round the margin of the covers of the books, inside, recording their gifts to the church.

The Chancel

Ascending a broad flight of polished marble steps, we reach the Chancel, with an attractive groined roof composed wholly of stone, the compartments of the side Arcades and the Apse sub-divisions being carefully balanced, and the proportions of the windows and introduction of finer and more delicate detail may be noticed. The South side is broken up into two stages of lofty superimposed Arcades, which both open into the Organ Chamber to the full height of the Chancel.

Minstrel's Gallery

This interesting feature is interposed between the North arcade to the Chancel and the Clerestory above, after the manner of a Trifolium. It is reached by a winding staircase from the Chapel aisle, and is capable of holding an orchestra of some twenty musicians.

Apse Windows

This magnificent series of stained glass windows, upon which much study and pains have been bestowed, are the gift of Mrs. Pickering Phipps, of Collingtree, and are an offering full of deep teaching and holy sentiment. They are the work of Messrs. Clayton & Bell of Regent Street, London, who have throughout borne in mind that the transmission of light is a primary principle, and have turned that consideration to the most artistic account. The jewel-like effect obtained by the judicious selection of glass, the rich but not heavy colouring and the admirable drawing, have together produced a result most harmonious and telling. The arrangement consists of five windows of three lights each, making fifteen windows in all, with tracing in the head of each window. Each light is divided by canopy work into three stages. In the upper stage of the centre light of the middle window is Our Lord enthroned in majesty, on either side are St. Mary the Virgin and St. John the Baptist. The remaining twelve lights have the Apostles, each holding his respective emblem and a scroll, bearing clauses from the Creed.

Chancel Floor and Stalls

The levels are divided by a fine series of well-proportioned steps in Frosterly and Pavonazza marble. The floor spaces between are proposed

The High Altar and Reredos with the now removed sanctuary lamps.

to be paved with Sicilian, Italian and other coloured marbles in a chaste and refined manner, with rich bands and interlacing borders and fillings. The Stalls for both clergy and choir are slightly raised above the Chancel floor, with backs, desks, and bookfronts all beautifully wrought in finest wainscot oak; and with elaborately perforated and traceried fronts and carved and moulded ends and terminations.

Altar

Raised upon a marble foot-pace, eight steps up from the Nave floor, and placed some distance from the east wall of the Apse, is the Altar, composed chiefly of wood, but with an alabaster front, which is divided into three main compartments, surrounded with moulded framing; and the compartments, of which the centre is the widest, are treated in sunk and moulded panel-work and tracery, beneath which are figure subjects in sculptured relief. The sculptures are parcel-gilt, and the backgrounds and mouldings are in gold and delicate colours, they are the work of Mr. W. Aumonier of New Inn Yard, Tottenham Court Road, London. A Re-Table or Gradine of moulded and polished alabaster is built up from the floor of the Apse at some clear distance from the Altar, and from it will rise the Reredos to a height of sixteen feet. This is to consist of an arrangement of figure subjects in tiers and under canopies.

Sedilia and Credence

In the South side of the Sanctuary is the Sedilia. This is triple and fills the first bay of the Apse. The recesses for the seats and the dividing-shafts, as well as the canopies and gables, are wholly of Bath stone.
The Credence Table is movable and of wainscot oak.

The Screens

Between the Arches on each side of the Chancel, and in those also of the Organ Chamber, it is proposed to place screens of delicate wrought ironwork.

The Side Chapel

The Side Chapel is divided from the aisle by an arcade of two broad arches and has an open tinted roof and a floor of marble. The Altar is made of varieties of mahogany, and richly gilt. This is the gift of Mrs. Pickering Phipps of Blisworth and was made by Mr. Henry Martin, the builder of the

Extracts from the Souvenir Booklet

St. Matthew, as depicted on the front of the Lady Chapel Altar.

church. The elaborate Triptych was also her gift. The paintings and the raised goldwork being the work of Mr. C. E. Buckeridge of Mortimer Street, London.

The windows are of stained glass and have been specially designed. The side-chapel Stalls are of wainscot oak with desks to match. These are the gift of Mr. and Mrs. Edward Phipps of Towcester.

The Baptistry

The whole of the west end of the Nave is occupied by the Baptistry, which is divided from the Nave by an arcade of three arches. The area is vaulted in stone, and is lighted by five windows. The Font is of polished marble and alabaster, varied in colour and combination. It is raised on three steps, and has a main base and shaft, quatrefoil in plan. The steps stand on a floor of white marble and are themselves of polished marble, the lowest being Frosterly, the middle Levanto and the upper step Pavonazza. The bowl is of fine transparent alabaster and is mainly square in plan, with

Baptistry and Font.

quadrant outlines at the four corners. The font has an elaborate cover of wainscot oak, raised and lowered by means of a balance weight and chains, passing over pulleys. The gift of Miss B. L. Phipps, they were made by Mr. Aumonier of London.

West Windows

The large West Windows are of stained glass.

Electric Lighting

The Church is lighted by electricity from a general plant installed in the basement under the Vestries. The motive power is a Day's Patent valveless gas engine.

Vestries

The Clergy Vestry is fitted with a small Strong Room to contain books and plate with an iron door, and presses for Vestments and Linen.
    The Choir Vestry is arranged with careful thought for the orderly robing of the Choir, the men and boys being separately provided for.

The SE. aspect of the church, as it appeared c. 1900 before the vicarage was added.

The NW. aspect as it is today.

4

From 1893

'A grand and noble church is indeed something to be thankful for. May we always remember that we can best prove our gratitude by striving to build up the souls who worship there as living stones in God's spiritual temple.'

The completion and consecration of the new church made possible a great expansion in the work for God. Rowden Hussey had always hoped to have a daily Communion Service and *now* it was possible. Holy Communion was to take place at 8.00 a.m. every day except on Thursdays, when it was to be at 7.00 a.m. 'The daily offering of the Holy Eucharist will bring the richest blessings on ourselves, our Parish and the Church of God, if we only learn to use and value the privilege aright.' Mattins was to be held on Monday, Tuesday and Saturday at 8.30 a.m., on Thursdays at 7.30 a.m. and on Wednesdays and Fridays at 8.00 p.m. and on Thursdays and Saturdays at 6.00 p.m. Whenever possible, there would be Choral Evensong on Holy Days.

It was also exciting that marriages could now be solemnised in the church and it was asked that seven days notice should be given for the publication of banns! The first wedding took place on 30th November 1893 between William Brown and Elizabeth Long; followed on 25th December, by that of Edgar Holloway and Polly Young and on 26th December, John Tate and Caroline Osborne.

A most welcome announcement was made in December 1893 – an Assistant Curate had been appointed to join the parish towards the end of Advent. The Rev'd. Leonard Alfred Pollock, M.A., had been working in Hunstanton and previously at St. Ives in Huntingdonshire. He was an M.A. of St. John's College, Cambridge, and priested at Ely in 1887. The Additional Curates' Society had made a grant of £40 per annum, on condition that £100 a year was raised by the parish and the parish collected £10 annually for the A.C.S. funds. A Clergy Fund was set up and parishioners were asked to make regular contributions, collected by the District Visitors. In later years, the A.C.S. grants were reduced to £20 and later were stopped. Unfortunately the necessary money was not readily forthcoming from the Clergy Fund and had to be made up from the general church funds, but as expenses increased this became more difficult and further appeals were made.

A number of financial problems confronted the new Vicar and the churchwardens. There were annual collections for the Sunday School Treat, in 1893 about 170 people contributed to this in amounts from 10s. 0d. (from Rowden himself) to many amounts of 2s. 6d., 6d., 3d. or 2d. – the total cost of the Day being about £10. There was still the need to pay off the debt on the School building; £13 was collected in the first year from about seventy-five people, sums again varied from 10s. 0d. to 2d. The Clergy Fund was not only concerned with providing for the Curate's stipend, the Churchwardens explained that the Endowment of the Church, £150 a year, was hardly enough for the Vicar's stipend, it was decided to adopt the old custom of giving to him the Easter Offertories as a Free Will Offering. There was the Vicarage Fund, started when the Foundation Stone was laid. Land was available by the side of the church but money had to be raised to build a Vicarage. Rowden was now living in a rented house on Kingsley Park Terrace, part of which was to be made available for Leonard Pollock. In addition to all this and the collections at services, the congregation was asked to have boxes for the Society of the Propagation of the Gospel!

The Accounts for the period from September 1893 to Easter 1894 (about six months) showed the average weekly offering to be under £8 (excluding Easter). Running costs for this period were about £150. This was reasonably covered by the offertories but there was little over to make provision for future needs and contingencies.

With the new church, Rowden had even more opportunity to welcome visiting clergy and for the Advent services he invited the Rev'd. A. Altham, Vicar of All Saints, Wellingborough, to give a course of sermons on the Wednesday evenings and in Lent 1894, the Rev'd. Canon Hull and the Rev'd. Thomas Hands of St. Lawrence's, to preach on Tuesday afternoons and Wednesday evenings respectively. Lent, Rowden said, was a time of special discipline in which God gives great and special opportunities for learning about His never-failing Love. The message that God sends year by year as Lent comes round is 'God loves you' and 'God hates sin'. Rowden suggested that everyone should 'make a rule of life, write it down and offer it to God'. Lent should be a time (1) to cure some fault; (2) to deny something; (3) to pray more and (4) to go to church more.

The Easter Offering was £95, which was a welcome addition to the Vicar's basic stipend but was also much valued by him as an expression of confidence and affection.

During the year the various groups were meeting regularly – St. Matthew's Guild, the Mututal Improvement Society, etc., and there were money-raising and social activities – the Sale of Work and Christmas Tea; the Choir Tea; Mothers' Meetings; Amateur Dramatic productions; the Parish Dinner in April; Parish Picnic and Choir Outing in the summer; the Sunday School Treat and various entertainments. The Festival of St. Matthew came round again, the Patronal Festival as well as the first Anniversary of the Consecration, when the Bishop of Peterborough was to preach and consecrate many new fittings, the pulpit, choir stalls and the Chancel Screen.

This pattern continued in subsequent years, with a pleasing increase in the number of gifts and contributions to the parish life from many people, both clerical and lay.

Rowden Hussey used the magazine, still priced at a penny and including about twelve pages of stories, household and garden hints, details of the Church Overseas and so on (an insert called The Dawn of Day), as well as some pages of parish news, to explain many points of liturgy and to introduce new ideas. In 1894 was formed the St. Matthew's Cottage Loan Society, intended 'to help the poor in times of sickness' by having articles for loan. In the first year £5. 10s. 0d. was collected and spent on suitable articles. There was also a Ladies' Working Party, formed to prepare articles for the Winter Sale of Work. Two years later, a Clothing Club was formed.

On 1st September 1895, Mr. Charles King was appointed Organist and Choirmaster, and on St. Matthew's Day that year the new Organ was to be completed together with the reredos and the altar rails. The organ, made by J. W. Walker & Sons of London, was a marvellous and specially designed instrument, following consultation with Dr. G. C. Martin of St. Paul's Cathedral, who had given recitals on the temporary organ and was to give one on the new organ, the gift of Mrs. Pickering Phipps senior. The blowing apparatus was to be electrically driven, a method claimed to be both steady and silent! There were 4 manuals, 48 stops and 2,925 pipes! Charles King, who was born in Brighton in 1857, had been a chorister at St. George's Chapel, Windsor, and then Organist at Farnham Royal and Hinckley Parish Church. He had come to Northampton in 1891

Charles King, organist and Director of Music 1895–1934.

to be Organist at the Church of the Holy Sepulchre, as a friend of the Vicar, the Rev'd. Charles Brookes, who had been Vicar at Hinckley. He had already some connection with St.Matthew's, as he had conducted the orchestra for the first performance of the Amateur Dramatic Society in 1893. In 1898 he was Conductor of the Northampton Musical Society and much concerned with the Amateur Operatic Society, as well as teaching Music at both the Northampton Boys' Grammar School and the Girls' High School, both then in Abington Street. In fact there was little in the musical life of the town where his influence was not felt.

John Eads had been Organist since the Iron Church days, and remained for some time as Mr. King's Deputy. This appointment was one of Rowden Hussey's great successes, despite the fact that he had no ear for music himself and was distinctly Victorian in his tastes. Charles King 'strengthened the choir and laid the foundations of the rich musical tradition of the church'. He much improved the standard of Sunday services and introduced many choral performances, for which he wrote some of the music, and gave organ recitals on Sunday afternoons. He remained at St. Matthew's for thirty-nine years, until he died on 16th February 1934, aged seventy-seven. His influence on the life of the church was incalculable!

At the Festival of 1895, as well as the organ, the new reredos was revealed. This is of polished alabaster and had been designed by Matthew Holding who had been asked by the donor, Mr. Pickering Phipps, to bear in mind the work in the chapels of All Souls and New College, Oxford. There were other gifts too, including a silver processional cross. The Festival was well attended, as ever, by both clergy and laity. 'Such boundless generosity provided to so beautiful and dignified a House of God, wherein we may worship.'

For three years, Leonard Pollock was a great support to his Vicar and to the growing parish. There followed quite a fast turn-over of Assistant Clergy, until Charles Peck came in 1907 and stayed to 1913. In 1898 Andrew Carr was appointed as a second curate. Despite the changes, the very fact gave new ideas and stimulation to the parish, so that, in the last years of the nineteenth century, St. Matthew's continued to grow in size, in faith and in spirituality.

5

1900 – Before and After

Since the consecration of the church in 1893, many things had happened. Probably the most important was the introduction, in January 1898, of Sung Eucharist as the main Sunday service. A choral celebration had taken place regularly on first Sundays and on Festivals; Rowden now wanted to introduce it on every Sunday. This should, he believed, be the service to which *all* should go – not a service to which *some* may stay. This is, as the Prayer Book presents it, a service in its own right. He also felt that children should attend and hear sermons (as directed in the Baptism service). It is the one service ordained by Christ. It was in many ways a courageous decision and was, inevitably, much criticised. Rowden explained his reasons to a well-attended meeting of seventy communicants and begged that they would give the change a fair trial. He assured them that he had true consideration for those who did not approve of the change but he appealed to them not to mistake prejudice or habit for Christian principle. He assured them that he had not made the alteration without a great deal of prayer. For the first three Sundays, Rowden Hussey explained his reasons again and offered to discuss anyone's personal difficulties. It was much criticised in the Local Press, letters were sent to the Bishop, and numbers dropped. Gradually many people returned and by Easter the number of communicants was again increasing. Sung Eucharist has been the main Sunday service at St. Matthew's ever since and, although today no one finds this unusual, in 1898 it was a most unusual and important decision for the spiritual life of the parish.

Around this time was founded the St. Matthew's Branch of the Parochial Missionary Association which was to increase the awareness of the congregation. The aims were to pray for Missions and Missionaries; to attend quarterly meetings; and to give subscriptions; all Communicants were invited to join.

May 1900 saw a letter in the Magazine, signed by the Churchwardens and endorsed by Andrew Carr, the Assistant Priest, and outlining the decision to proceed with the building of a Vicarage House. The letter pointed out that this would add to the Vicar's expenses and it was suggested that an Endowment Fund be set up to raise a Capital sum of at least £1,000. This would secure a grant from the Ecclesiastical Commissioners, and from such a sum a regular interest could be obtained. The Rev'd. Andrew Carr had offered to collect the money and had himself given a generous donation of £250 to start the Fund. Letters were published from the Bishops of Peterborough, Leicester and Salisbury, and soon a steady stream of donations was in being. By St. Matthew's day on 21st September, (suggested as a target date) the £1,000 had been collected. Though this was the subject of much rejoicing, it was obvious that this had to be an on-going process, to build up sound reserves for the future.

By this time, the new clock had been installed with the carillon of twelve bells. Stained glass had been put in the North and South Nave windows; these showed representative scenes from Our Lord's Life on Earth and the donor was found to be Andrew Carr, whose initiative had led to the success of the Endowment Fund. He also gave gold communion vessels.

The architect for the new Vicarage was again Matthew Holding. In 1900 the Fund stood at £800, application was made to the Ecclesiastical Commissioners and to Queen Anne's Bounty. The site has been given by Mr. Pickering Phipps on the south side of the church, and when building was to commence, with the grants, £2,000 was available. The tender of Mr. Edward Green was accepted. A new project was on its way! Maybe it was the advent of a Vicarage House which was to inspire Rowden Hussey to marry and found a family!

In 1884, Richard Atherton, his wife Grace and their family, moved from Mount Pleasant Farm, at Speke near Liverpool, where the family had farmed for some years, to Overstone Grange, near Northampton. Richard was the youngest son, born in 1831, of William and Ann Atherton, who were then farming at Fazakerley, his elder brothers being born at Orrell, all in Lancashire. By the 1850s William was farming at Speke, at the farm later taken over by his youngest son, his other sons farming nearby. Early in 1869 Richard married Grace Jane Pipes, a native of Beverley in Yorkshire, and their eldest son, Richard Percy was born in Speke in December 1870; by 1883 the family of two boys and three girls was complete. The move to Northamptonshire came in 1884 but unfortunately Richard died in May 1887, aged only fifty-five and his widow died in 1900. The three Atherton sisters, Elsie Marion aged twenty-four, Lilian Mary aged twenty and Jessie aged seventeen moved to live in Northampton, in a house called Southwood, just down St. George's Avenue, facing the Racecourse. Their brother Ernest had moved to London and Richard junior was an Assistant Master at Haileybury School. The Misses Atherton were soon regular attenders at St. Matthew's Church and contributed actively to parish life. Had the Atherton and Hussey families known each other? Both were of similar backgrounds but from different areas. Why had the Athertons moved to Overstone? Anyway, early in 1902, it was announced that Rowden, now aged thirty-seven, and Lilian Mary, the middle sister aged twenty-two, were to be married immediately after Easter.

Lent, that year, was a special time for them both, leading to Easter and to their life together, as it was for the parish they would serve. 'Lent,' said Rowden, 'is a blessed time for our souls if only we make good use of it. Let us try to be more definite, more sincere, more persevering in our spiritual life, more earnest in conquering our faults, in learning to understand something more of our faith, in keeping some rule of self-denial, in helping others and all the better if this is something hard and humbling. Lent is a time for giving time and thought and prayer to God.'

The previous year, Andrew Carr had left to run the Mission at Notting Hill and now, at last, he was to be replaced. Reginald Maxwell Woolley was a graduate of St. John's College, Cambridge, with a First-Class degree in Theology. He was heartily welcomed, particularly by Rowden, after the long gap with only one Assistant Curate, when the work of the parish really needed three clergy.

Easter was a great celebration and, as previously, the Free-will Offerings would be given to the Vicar. Just in time for the wedding!

The Easter Vestry was held on Easter Monday, 31st March, and on 1st April, Easter Tuesday, the Annual Tea and Parochial Gathering took place. The 6.00 p.m. Tea was followed by Evensong and, at 8.00 p.m., a large gathering assembled for the Entertainment, but also for the presentation to Rowden and Lilian. They received a handsome walnut plate chest with solid silver tablewear for eighteen places; two pairs of silver candlesticks and an illuminated white vellum album containing the names of the subscribers, over 500 of them! A wonderful gift and illustrative of the love and respect in which the Vicar was held and the welcome accorded to Lilian Atherton as his wife. The following day, the Young Men's Bible Class presented a silver salver and a framed illuminated address. Mr. William Kew made the presentation, an interesting choice, as he was later to marry Lilian's younger sister Jessie. The Choirboys gave a silver paper-knife and the Girls' Bible Class some cut-glass fruit bowls.

The following day, the couple and Lilian's sisters, departed for Hertfordshire, where the marriage was to take place in Great Amwell church, near Haileybury. Lilian's brother Richard was to give her away. Of Lilian's two sisters Jessie, the younger, married William Kew almost eight years later. His family had lived in Kingsley Park Terrace and he became the Town Solicitor. Elsie Marion Atherton, having seen her two sisters safely married, joined the Convent of St. Margaret at East Grinstead where she is remembered as a kindly, smiling person, gently teased by her pupils in the Convent School but really a very practical person able to organise efficiently and without fuss.

Both Lilian and Rowden were of similar backgrounds, from reasonably prosperous farming families, used to country life and the enjoyment of riding, but in other ways they were complementary. Rowden was a somewhat fussy person, despite a stern and determined character of strong principles. He had a smooth, pink and white complexion, which never really aged, but with stiff, rather unruly hair. He always got on well with his female parishioners, especially the older ones, though he had a very loyal congregation of men as well. Lilian was a strong personality, very practical; it was always Lilian who carved the joint when entertaining, and in later years, it was Lilian who learned to drive the car.

In the summer of 1904, there was the excitement of pregnancy, news of which was kept quietly within the family, and in September, the new Vicarage House was at last completed. The approval of the Ecclesiastical Commissioners was obtained and it was with excitement and some relief that Rowden and Lilian eventually moved across the Kettering Road. They were moving from a terrace house that confronted the road, to a detached house standing back in its own garden, with the church only yards away. A chance at last to spread their belongings and to have room for a nursery. A chance to have rooms for parish meetings and for entertaining their friends and relations.

The Building Fund had raised money and there had been grants, but there was still a debt to pay off and a Sale of Work was organised for January 1905 to raise more money.

As Rowden soon had only Reginald Woolley as his assistant, he was doubtless particularly grateful to have a better working base, though he was saddened to have to cut back on visiting which he felt was so very important. At least it was now easier for parishioners to come to him!

In February 1905, Lilian gave birth to twins, John Atherton was a weak baby and was baptised privately soon after birth; Dorothy May was baptised in church at the end of March. Sadly, however, both babies died in May, John at thirteen weeks and Dorothy at fourteen weeks of age. The nursery was to remain empty for a while longer.

6

The Church Overseas

The new Parochial Missionary Association had its quarterly meetings in the schoolroom. In June, the meeting was addressed by the Rev'd. John Neale, Rector of Harpole, who had been a Missionary at Hanghow in East China and spoke of the people there. In September, the speaker was the former Bishop of Zanzibar, who had also been invited to speak at the Children's Service at the Patronal Festival, when a collection was taken for Foreign Missions. Bishop Richardson talked mainly of the work of the Universities' Missions to East Central Africa, which had originally been the idea of Dr. David Livingstone. The first head, and later the Bishop, had been Charles Mackenzie. Bishop Richardson had been consecrated Bishop of Zanzibar in 1895. He said he felt there were two ways to help the Missions, to offer oneself and to offer one's prayers. The Bishop described the country but did not minimise the difficulties; he reminded his audience of St. Matthew's Gospel and the Lord's words, 'Go into the world and preach the Gospel.' In thanking the Bishop, the Vicar expressed his very strong opinion that *all* communicants should belong to the Missionary Association, showing that they had a real interest in Missionary work deeply in their hearts.

Meetings continued over the years at St. Matthew's, though the attendance never got much larger and, at times, actually dropped. There was a good attendance to hear Bishop Popham Blyth, the Anglican Bishop of Jerusalem, who was the speaker at the meeting during the 1905 Patronal Festival. He also spoke at a Sunday service. Bishop Popham Blyth spoke of the difficult nature of Missionary work among the Jews, but said there was evidence of rewarding results. The need was to represent the Anglican Church among her sister churches in the Mother City of Christianity and to make witness there.

The contact with the Bishop of Jerusalem and the inspiration of his talks made it possible for Rowden and Lilian to go to the Holy Land themselves in 1906. It was a first visit and they prepared to leave on 13th January, to be due back towards the end of February. This was to be a great experience and even more of an adventure than any of us today could imagine! There were seven in the group and they arrived at Haifa at the foot of Mount Carmel. In the Holy Land they travelled by carriage when the roads were passable or on horseback. It was very hot and the hotels were of variable standards, but despite the dust and squalor in many places, the countryside was beautiful and it was exciting just to be there. The Galilee region was another great contrast, with the beauty of the lake and dirt and fleas in Tiberias. A visit to Nablus showed them some of the important work done by the Medical Mission of the Church Missionary Society.

Their return was by way of Jerusalem, where they stayed with the Bishop, and explored the markets, the narrow alleys as well as the Holy places, including trips to Bethany and Bethlehem.

Their journey was a great stimulus to deeper devotion, every Bible reading became more meaningful and brought pictures to the mind's eye which would never be forgotten. An experience to be meditated upon, to be treasured and, especially, to be shared with all their friends in the parish to which they returned.

7

Back to St. Matthew's

In January 1904, Henry Fry had left to become Vicar of St. George's, Cullercoats, in Northumberland (he was later made a Canon of Newcastle), and he was due to be replaced by the Rev'd. Edward Allen Sydenham, a graduate of Merton College, Oxford who had trained at Wells Theological College. He had been six years at St. Mary's, Oldham, a big parish of 11,000 people. Unfortunately, just before he was to leave Oldham, he contracted typhoid fever and, although he recovered, it was a long and serious illness which left him weak and debilitated and unable to work, so Rowden Hussey and Reginald Woolley had to battle on without a second assistant. As his health improved, Edward Sydenham was sent to Bologna to recuperate. He stayed there for two months acting as English Chaplain. He eventually came to St. Matthew's in May 1905 and there was great rejoicing at his arrival.

Things never remain static and the overlap was barely a month when Reginald Woolley left to go to St. Bartholomew's, Smithfield, having been at St. Matthew's for three and a half years. He had been a hard worker and a loyal support, especially in the long period when he was the only curate. He was presented with a silver pencil case and various theology books as a leaving gift by a grateful parish. Over the years he wrote a number of scholarly books on Church History, so the presents were quite appropriate! In later years, he became a Canon of Lincoln Cathedral, but sadly he died comparatively young.

Rowden was obviously distressed to be left once more with only one assistant, and that one a young man only recently recovered from a lowering illness. Lilian was only just recovering from pregnancy and both of them were grieving for the loss of their twins.

In September, things looked rosier as the Rev'd. Noblett Henry

Cranmer Ruddock came to live in Church Avenue (later Collingwood Road). Dr. Ruddock was an experienced priest from the Church of the Holy Nativity, Knowle, Bristol, from which benefice he had retired for health reasons. Although not fully fit, he was able and willing to undertake some parochial duties.

This was the state of affairs when Rowden and his party set off for the Holy Land, doubtless encouraged by Dr. Ruddock who had been there himself and believed it a wonderful experience for anyone, but particularly for a parish priest. Rowden was fortunate to have been able to leave the parish in such capable hands.

The return from the Holy Land led almost immediately into Lent, with Ash Wednesday on 28th February, and on the following evening, Rowden gave a well-attended talk on the visit, illustrated by Lantern slides, taken and coloured by Messrs. R. & H. Chapman, who worked the Lantern for him. The profits of the collection went to the Mission in Jerusalem.

During Lent, Rowden's belief in the stimulation of visiting clergy was to the fore. He had invited the Rev'd. Arthur Ivan Greaves, Vicar of St. Mary's, Northampton, to preach on Ash Wednesday and the Thursdays of the following weeks. The talks were on 'The Spiritual Life: How it begins; Hindrances (sin); How it is Supported; Growth; and The Church, the Corporate Aspect of Spiritual Life'. For the Tuesday afternoon services, he invited the Rev'd. William Edward Terry, Vicar of All Saints, Wellingborough, to preach on 'Cross Bearing'. It was during this Lent that an experiment was introduced musically, using Merbeck's setting for the Holy Communion. This was an introduction to Plain-song, the music coming from the sixteenth century and being the first musical setting to the English Communion Service. It was hoped that, though the congregation would probably find it strange to begin with, it would be a help to devotion. Rowden was pleased to report that there were good attendances through Lent and an increased number of communicants.

In November, the Bishop was to hold a Confirmation Service in the church and classes were held in preparation. All who 'were come to years of discretion' and who were not already confirmed were urged to attend classes. Over sixty candidates were eventually presented to the Bishop and, although these were mainly aged thirteen to seventeen years of age, there were a number of adults, including two in their seventies!

It was this autumn that it was decided to start a parish branch of the Church of England Men's Society. The Vicar was made President, the other clergy and the Churchwardens were Vice-Presidents and the Treasurer was William Kew, who was later to marry Lilian Hussey's younger sister Jessie; there were ten others on the Committee. Meetings would be both educational and social, and there would be special Men's Services. Fifty-seven were admitted at the first meeting and others joined later until the membership was over eighty by the end of the year. The National Society had the Archbishops as Presidents, the Bishops as Vice-Presidents and the Bishop of Stepney was Chairman. Members and Associates undertook to pray daily and to do something to forward the cause of the Church. The first of a series of services was addressed by the Vicar on 'Is Christianity True?'

Nineteen hundred and seven brought sadness to the parish with the death of the older Mrs. Pickering Phipps of Collingtree Grange; she was the widow of the Pickering Phipps to whose memory the church was built and she had been a generous benefactor, particularly in her gifts of the East Window and the magnificent organ. She was seventy-seven when she died in March and her memory would be cherished for her generosity and for her quiet, Christian life.

In the Hussey family, however, a new life was being welcomed. Christopher Rowden Hussey was born on 25th February 1907 and he was baptised by his father a month later, on 25th March. This baby was thriving and was a joy to his parents, his doting aunts and to the parish.

It was back in June 1905, after the Vicarage was completed, that the need to pay off the debt called for much thought and prayer over the finances of the parish. After much consideration, the Churchwardens and the clergy came up with the idea of a Free-Will Offering Envelope Scheme. They called it 'The Instalment Fund'. To begin with, it was specially directed to pay off the debt on the Vicarage. Subscribers were asked to fill in a slip which showed their intended giving and which would be secret to the Secretary of the Fund. Envelopes supplied would be numbered and dated so that a check could be kept. The Churchwardens were greatly encouraged by the response, over eighty-four subscribers in the first year, with subscriptions from one penny a month to several pounds a year, promising a total of nearly £100. The subscriptions could be kept anonymous, though usually subscription lists were published in the Magazine; quite a few people availed themselves of anonymity so their contributions were only indicated by their number. The Churchwardens felt that, in addition to Sunday collections, this was the best method of giving support to the Church and its work. It was easy for all sorts of people, even children, and was in the principle of Christian alms-giving. The debt on the Vicarage was cleared by November

1907 but it was decided to keep the Instalment Fund for Parochial purposes.

One obvious need was for a Parish Room, particularly when the Day School was unavailable, though it would, of course, put the Parish into debt again. A committee was formed and after enquiry, accepted a tender from Messrs. F. Smith of London to erect an 'iron hut' for £141. 10s. 0d. for foundations and services, and a further sum for paths, fencing, etc., as well as furniture, totalling approximately £250. There was land along the Kettering Road, adjoining the Vicarage, which Mr Phipps suggested they could use.

The Instalment Fund had 137 subscriptions by this time, with amounts from 1d. a month to 3s. 0d. a week, but although this was encouraging, it only represented one quarter of the communicants. It was felt that *all* should make contributions and that everyone could probably afford 1d. a week.

The Parochial Accounts for 1907-8 showed the state of the parish finances:

The Church Account: The deficit of £107 had been reduced to £1. 4s. 1d. but only because £50 had been paid in from the Instalment Fund.

The total collections for the year were £470. 19s. 9d. and represented an increase on the previous year.

The Clergy Fund: the Balance was £12. 14s. 5d. but again, only because £50 had been transferred from the Instalment Fund. More subscribers were essential if the clergy stipends were to be paid.

The Parochial Instalment Fund: the Balance was £58. 5s. 7d.; £100 had been paid out as above and £15 for the repair and renewal of choir hassocks; £21 had been spent for lobbies at the church door. (Money was also received from various efforts during the year.)

Day and Sunday School Account: the Balance had been reduced to £11. 11s. 0d. as there had been various necessary repairs to the building (for which the church was responsible). Other payments were needed for lighting, heating, cleaning and so on, for when Church Meetings were held in the School building. There had also been books to buy for the Sunday School.

Parish Magazine Account: the Balance was 13s. 8d. Circulation of 500 magazines was attempted and there was need to sell more. For the last three years, the insert had been 'The Sign' and it was now decided to add 'The Living Church' which gave news from all dioceses and would keep everyone in touch 'with current doings of the Church both at Home and Abroad'. Despite the increased size of the magazine, its cost remained at 1d. a copy.

These accounts give some idea of the finances of the parish, just about solvent, but caring and conscientious parishioners must have had a difficult time allocating their giving between the various funds.

An occasion of importance in 1908 was a great Pan-Anglican Congress to be held in London in June. This was partly a Missionary effort but was mainly to discuss the Church's greatest needs, problems and difficulties. Every diocese (thirty-seven in England and Wales; 210 in the rest of the world) was asked to send representatives and was consulted in the preparation of the programme. Unlike the Lambeth Conference, this would be a public occasion and would be open to lay men and women, as well as all clergy. Dioceses were asked to collect money for a Great Thank Offering at St. Paul's Cathedral at the close of the Congress. There would also be a Living Offering of men and women who were ready to give themselves to the Church.

The Archbishop of Canterbury had said 'from our most distant colonies and Mission Fields, from the United States of America, from cities and plains of our Indian Empire, from the borders of the Arctic Circle and from the Islands of the Southern Sea, men and women will meet in London for counsel and prayer, with a view to set forward life upon earth, more vigorously than heretofore, the rule of the Lord Jesus Christ, over the daily life of those for whom He died upon the Cross.' 'Should we not,' asked Rowden, 'all like to have a share in this work?'

Special sermons were to be preached in all Northampton churches on 1st March. The Rev'd. Charles William Sherard, priest-vicar of Grahamstown Cathedral, preached at St. Matthew's, and there was also a special meeting at Northampton Town Hall on 25th May, when the speakers were the Bishop of Chota Nagpur and the Rev'd. Canon Westcott of Cawnpore. The contribution to the Thank Offering from the St. Matthew's congregation was £57. 7s. 6d. and this was sent to the Diocesan Treasurer.

Rowden Hussey was able to persuade the Bishop of Madagascar, Dr. G. L. King, and the Bishop of Likoma, in Central Africa, the Rev'd. Gerard Trower, to preach at the Patronal Festival, after they had attended the Lambeth Conference. (He had also hoped to get the Bishop of Bunbury in Western Australia, but in the end was unable to do so.) Father Stanton of St. Albans, Holborn, had again agreed to preach on St. Matthew's Day. He was a much loved priest who had lived and worked in Holborn for forty-six years. He was much admired at St. Matthew's and said that he found it heartening to visit the parish.

8

The End of an Era

In the background of the more exciting occasions, the normal life of St. Matthew's went on. The new Parish Hall was erected and the money for it had to be collected. A new cope was given at the Patronal Festival to complete the sets of vestments for the clergy to use. St. Matthew's had always used vestments though many churches did not. Dr. Ruddock, who had been such a rock for the parish since he had come three years before, was leaving the town at the end of 1908, to go to Edgbaston in Birmingham. His cheery kindness was much missed by everyone and Rowden, in particular, would miss his willing help and valuable advice.

Confirmation candidates continued to come forward and were presented to the Bishop. The monthly Guild Meetings were held regularly and many social events, widely enjoyed. A Needlework Guild was started to make useful articles for the poor. Attention was given to the Churchyard (not, of course, a burial ground) and the Vicar's Bible Class took on responsibility for its maintenance and planted flowers and bushes round the edges.

On 15th May 1909, John Walter Atherton Hussey was born, another thriving boy to round off the family. He was baptised on 12th June.

In November 1909, a meeting was held, to be addressed by Mrs. Clayton, the wife of the Bishop of Leicester who was also the Diocesan President of the Mothers' Union. It was decided to start a Parochial Branch and Mrs. Clayton explained how it was done. She also outlined the aims of the Union:

1. To uphold the sanctity of Marriage.
2. To awaken in mothers of all classes a sense of responsibility in the training of their children.
3. To unite in prayer and to seek by example to lead families in the purity and holiness of life.

Fifty women declared their wish to join and Mrs Montague Browne was introduced as the President of the new Branch.

In the early days of 1910, Lilian Hussey, recovered from her pregnancy and with her nursery established, turned her attention back to parish affairs. On 7th February, she invited, for 7.15 p.m., the mothers of the children attending the Sunday School. As far as she could she sent out personal invitations and asked any others to come too. Sunday School Helpers were also invited: 260 invitations were sent out. The District Visitors presided at the tables in the Schoolroom, the Vicar welcomed them all and they were then entertained with a concert. A very successful occasion went into the regular calendar.

A great shock came to the whole country when Edward VII died on 6th May 1910. On the day of the funeral many communicants attended the Requiem Services held at St. Matthew's at 7.30 and 9.30 a.m. and a Solemn Memorial Service at 1.00 p.m. In the following year when George V was crowned, another Special Service was held to mark the occasion.

The town of Northampton suffered a loss in the death of Matthew Holding, A.R.I.B.A., who died after a long illness on 2nd June, at the age of sixty-three. Matthew Holding had played an important part in the life of the town by designing many of the buildings. He was particularly noted as the Diocesan Architect and Surveyor and, during the period of the town's expansion, had designed Christchurch in Wellingborough Road; St. Mary's in Towcester Road; St. Paul's in Semilong; Holy Trinity in Balmoral road and St. Matthew's in Kettering Road. His name would ever be remembered in St. Matthew's since he had not only designed the old iron church and then the new church and the Vicarage, but he had designed most of the furniture and fittings. Matthew Holding was a loyal and devout Churchman, a Churchwarden of St. Edmund's, as well as a good architect, so his love of God and his devotion to the Church went into all his work. On the North wall of the side chapel of St. Matthew's, two Memorial Tablets were installed, recording the names of the late Mr. and Mrs. Pickering Phipps of Collingtree and also Matthew Holding. They were surmounted by an inscription, running the whole length of the wall, 'We also Bless Thy Holy Name for All Thy Servants Departed This Life in Thy Faith and Fear'. The work was done in alabaster, simple and effective, to record the names for posterity, of those who were most closely associated with the church's work and worship. Matthew Holding's son Edward was to carry on his work.

Further gifts came to the church, including an alabaster wall by the Chancel Screen, and stained glass windows in the transepts. The first glass was for the large window of the South Transept, consisting of two groups of three lights. It was to be dedicated on St. Matthew's Day. The left-hand group illustrated the Incarnation, using a tree of Jesse, with the figures of Jesse, St. Matthew and St. Luke. The tree leading to the head of the central light with the figure of the Blessed Virgin Mary and the Christ Child. The righthand window illustrated the Atonement, with Our Lord as the True Vine, branches leading to Bishops. At the base of the central light was placed St. John, flanked by St. Peter and St. Paul and, at the head of the central light, Our Lord Triumphant on the Tree of Glory. Brilliant sunshine showed the colours of the windows when they were unveiled and blessed by the Bishop.

In 1913 the North Transept windows were ready, these showing the Archangels and depicting the Annunciation. They were dedicated on the twentieth Anniversary of the Church's Consecration.

At Easter 1912, the Churchwardens had published a letter suggesting that another effort should be made to increase the permanent endowment of the Benefice. The then income, excluding the Easter offering, was under £200 a year. During the last three years £100 had been raised, mostly from the Instalment Fund. This, offered to the Diocesan Association, was met by an equal amount, another £100, from the Small Benefices Endowment Fund. The £200 was then offered to the Ecclesiastical Commissioners, who met it with an equal grant and the resulting £400 was invested at three per cent, bringing an extra £12 a year to the Vicar's stipend. The Churchwardens believed that if another £100 were raised, this could be repeated. Money was slowly collected but it was obvious that no real enthusiasm was generated!

On 11th January 1914, Rowden Hussey was celebrating his fiftieth birthday and also his twenty-five years ministry in Kingsley; great plans were made for everyone to celebrate with him. On the Anniversary Sunday, joyful services were held and congratulations showered from all sides. Canon Jones of All Saints preached at the Sung Eucharist and Bishop Lang of Leicester at the Festal Evensong. The whole district, said Canon Jones, thanked God for their church and the work and teaching of their Vicar. Bishop Lang reminded everyone of the days of the little schoolroom church, the iron church and now the glorious new church. Great celebrations were held on the Monday evening, when Mr. Pollock, the first curate, and Mr. Haviland, an early churchwarden, returned to join the party. Eight hundred and thirty-one people had contributed to a silver salver, a 'purse of gold' and a gold watch for Mrs. Hussey. These were presented by Mr. Pickering Phipps, together with an illuminated address, which he read aloud. The address desired 'to place on record our heartiest appreciation of, and our thankfulness for, your twenty-five years ministry to the spiritual needs of the parish. During this period your teaching has always been consistent with the principles and doctrines of the English Branch of the Catholic Church as laid down in the Prayer Book and for this loyalty to our Faith we are deeply grateful. We also heartily congratulate you upon the fiftieth anniversary of your birth. With these congratulations we associate the name of Mrs. Hussey who, during the large part of your sojourn amongst us, has been your truest friend and companion. We ask you to accept this address, together with a silver salver and a purse of gold, as an assurance of the true respect and love of your people, the warm place you hold in our hearts, and their earnest prayers that you may long be spared to continue your ministrations among them.' The names of the subscribers followed, bound in cream vellum with the monogram J.R.H. on the outside. There were also coloured views of the inside and outside of the church.

Rowden thanked them all in a much appreciated speech, and gave an outline of his twenty-five years. He said how little he had wanted to leave Belgrave but, in a letter, Bishop Magee had told him, 'You were not ordained to be happy but to do your duty where God called you', but had promised that he would be sent elsewhere after three years! 'And here I am, twenty-five years later!' 'It has,' he continued, 'often been difficult but it has never been unpleasant. 'God's call is a safer guide to happiness than our own choice.' Further speeches wished them well and hoped they would be celebrating again twenty-five years ahead!

But 1914 was a momentous and awesome year in Europe's history – 'a war to end wars' was ahead; was to engulf the world and affect the lives of everyone and, certainly, nothing would ever be the same again. This was truly the end of an era!

9

The Day Schools

The Kingsley Park Infant School had opened on 7th January 1889, with Miss Ethel Warren as Headmistress. From the first there were twenty children and in a rapidly growing district, the numbers increased very quickly. Very soon there were older children and the Managers decided to appoint Mr. William Westmorland to be Head of the Mixed School. He was very experienced and proved an excellent choice, proving his value to the parish as well as the school. From the beginning the clergy, who were on the Board of Managers, visited the school regularly, taking Morning Assembly and teaching the children. Rowden soon found that knowing the children was a ready passport to the houses of the parish.

An adjoining plot of land was purchased so that the school could be extended; there were soon over 500 children on the roll. After the Free Education Act of 1891 the parish voted to keep the school as a Voluntary Church School but this was to be a big financial drain on parish funds in years ahead.

When Rowden and Lilian returned from their honeymoon, one of the first places in the parish that they visited together was the Day School in Byron Street. The school was developing steadily but there were still problems. The January Report from the H.M.I.s suggested the need for a folding partition in the large schoolroom of the Mixed School and insisted that the lighting must be improved. The scholars were, it said, too talkative, though not really badly behaved! Spelling and composition needed to be better but the attendance was much improved.

The Balfour Act of 1902 was due to come into operation in October 1903 and from that date the working expenses of the school were provided by the Local Education Authority but the Act provided that 'The Managers of the Schools shall, *out of funds provided by them*, keep the Schoolhouse in good repair and make such alterations and improvements in the buildings as may reasonably be required by the L.E.A.' The Act reorganised Education on a Municipal basis and the School Boards, which had filled in the gaps of the Voluntary System, were set aside. They were replaced by 120 County and County Borough Councils which become responsible for both secondary and elementary schools. Each Local Authority had to appoint an Education Committee and had to control the Board Schools, now known as Provided Schools, and erect new ones when they were needed. They also had to control and be responsible for the secular instruction in the Voluntary Schools, now called 'non-provided'.

These non-provided denominational schools were now eligible for Rate-Aid, but the Religious Bodies were responsible for structural repairs and alterations. The Managers retained the right of appointing and dismissing teachers, subject to the approval of the L.E.A. Religious Instruction could be given but there had to be the possibility of withdrawal by parents. The new Act still retained the dual system introduced by the 1870 Act. It fostered local interest in the Voluntary School but provided administrative difficulties.

By 1913 many alterations and improvements had been made to the buildings, the lighting and ventilation were much improved and the playground had been asphalted, all necessary for the continued recognition conferred by the Board of Education. The cost of about £230 was defrayed from the Reserve Fund, including £15 from Miss Phipps; £30 from the Diocesan Association and £40 from the L.E.A. There was urgent need to build up the Fund again.

In the magazine Rowden Hussey pointed out that for twenty-five years the Church people of St. Matthew's Parish had supported their Church Schools because:-

1. they were morally bound to hand to posterity their trust for the future generations of school children;
2. when a child is baptised, the Church directs that he shall learn the Creed, the Lord's Prayer, the Ten Commandments and the Catechism and the latter is only taught in Church Schools;
3. our bounden duty is to see that children are taught the principles of the Church by believing teachers;
4. of the high standard of religious teaching in Church Schools.

'Please,' he said, 'continue to keep our schools for the future.'

10

The 1914–1918 War

The four years of the First World War were a traumatic experience for everyone, including the people of St. Matthew's Parish. Miss Gertrude Hollis in the book she wrote for the fortieth Anniversary described it as follows:

'The close proximity of St. Matthew's parish to the great war camp on the Northampton Racecourse made the church a centre for military religious observances. To view the Racecourse from the top of the Church tower when any manoeuvres were in progress was like looking down at an actual battlefield; occasionally, when there was a route march, the road past the church was filled with guns, horses and men in ceaseless stream from 7.00 a.m. until midday. The whole parish was a barracks, almost every house having its contingent of billeted men. The Welsh Division (wonderful singers they were!), the Gloucestershire and Warwickshire Regiments worshipped at St. Matthew's. Services on Sundays succeeded each other almost hourly, one thousand men marching in as another thousand left: sometimes as many as five military bands were stationed outside.

'There were many Catholic Churchmen among the soldiers, especially in the Warwickshire Regiment which had many parishioners from St. Alban's, Birmingham, who found St. Matthew'sa spiritual home. It was no uncommon thing to see a considerable number of men in khaki waiting to make their confession after the Saturday Evensong, or, when no server happened to be present at the daily Eucharist, to see a soldier leaving his place in the chapel to serve. Of course, many of the choir and servers of the church had gone, some, alas, never to return.

'The particular field of church work which most felt the war conditions was the Sunday School; the effect upon that for the time being was disastrous. The boys were undisciplined in the absence of their fathers; the girls were naturally excited and reckless. Mothers, with three or four soldiers in their houses to be provided for, found it impossible to get their younger children ready for school, and seemed to lose all control over their elder girls. A Girls' Bible Class of nearly eighty members dwindled away altogether; the number of children in the (Sunday) School lessened by several hundreds. The loss was inevitable, and no one could wonder at it while the Racecourse provided such absorbing sights. To the teachers the work during those years was heartbreaking indeed; many tears were shed over the apparently useless efforts. It was a really hard struggle to hold on in faith that some day the former conditions of order and discipline would be restored.'

Rowden Hussey himself had no personal decisions to make, he was over fifty and not eligible to be sent as a military chaplain and his two sons were only children. There was plenty for him to do in his parish and in the town of Northampton. His elder son Christopher was now seven and ready for school. Conveniently, Waynflete School, under Mr. George Lindsay Charlesworth, an Exhibitioner of Magdalen College, Oxford, and an ex-master of Northampton Grammar School (where he had taught Classics and History), had, in 1910, opened at 23 St. Matthew's Parade, nearby. It advertised that it prepared boys between seven and fourteen for Public Schools, with 'A Strong Staff, Modern Methods and Individual Attention'. This was just what was needed for Christopher.

Then there was a warning to the Northampton Yeomanry that the men would be expected to parade if mobilisation was ordered – and it was! In the ensuing panic, while the Territorials mobilised, those with money enough rushed to stock up food, candles, paraffin oil; it was reported that £100 worth of goods went to one house and that another family had ordered a ton of sugar! Even if the rumours were false or exaggerated, they were disquieting. Arrogant articles about the 'Knavish Kaiser' appeared in the newspapers and there came reports of Northamptonians arrested as spies in Belgium and Germany. There were many stories and rumours and spy scares around! The Government desperately sent out pleas to stop the panic, declaring that there were adequate stocks for all. There was a rush of recruits and fears of factory closures, until people began to realise that it wouldn't 'be over by Christmas' and also that orders for Army boots were pouring in. Red Cross Working Parties were formed, and there were appeals for nurses. Things began to calm down.

The Yeomanry were billeted for a week in the British Schools and then departed for Derby, but at the end of August there was tremendous excitement at the arrival of 16,000 soldiers and 7,000 horses of the Welsh Brigade, horse, foot, and artillery in Northampton. This was the start of the great Army camp referred to by Miss Hollis; the horse lines were on the Racecourse and so were some lines of tents, but most of the soldiers were billeted in private houses. The local authorities reckoned that there were 20,900 houses in Northampton, as well as some derelict factories which could be used. The Racecourse being near Kingsley, the residents were in great demand to take in the soldiers. Lodging and attendance allowances were paid for, as were the meals which had to be provided. The soldiers soon made themselves at home and helped in many ways, cutting the grass or even turning the mangle on wash-days.

The military bands were in great demand and the local children were to be found round the bands with their own toy weapons or musical instruments. The morning bugles were at 5.30 a.m. which roused everyone!

There were guns on the Racecourse used for training, which sometimes looked as if they would take off the top of the church spire! The ration trucks were around most days and the housewives lined up with plates to receive their allowance of jam, cheese and meat. Potatoes they carried in their aprons and loaves were tucked under their arms, as they returned to their chores. At 7.00 a.m. the soldiers did Swedish Drill in the streets for half an hour, often 'helped' by the children joining in! One can see what Miss Hollis meant by 'absorbing sights'!

The Sunday School Treats and other social events were abandoned for the duration, except those intended to raise money for the War Effort. Particularly, the Annual Luncheon at the time of the Patronal Festival was given up until after the Armistice.

In 1916, Charles Eastgate joined the parish clergy on a part-time basis, after his retirement from Ramsgate. On 19th September, when Waynflete School's Autumn Term began, young Walter Hussey joined his brother Christopher at the school. The house next door had been taken over as a Boarding House for the school, run by Mr. Osborne Lee, and although the two Hussey boys hardly needed to be boarders, it was convenient that they could join them on occasions.

The 1914–1918 War

The Patronal Festival was held in a spirit of solemnity. Bishop Frodsham, ex-Bishop of Queensland, Australia (known as the Bushman's Bishop), who was a Mission preacher of great power, was the chief visiting preacher. In October, the new Bishop of Peterborough, the Rt. Rev'd. Theodore Woods, conducted an Open-air Service on Sunday 8th October. He was an imposing figure, well over six foot tall, broadly built and with a powerful, deep voice, well suited to the open air. The parade of Volunteers and other bodies were nearly a mile long, and hundreds of local people turned out to see them and to attend the services. Later in 1916 the whole town was involved in a three-day War Bazaar in the Town Hall, to raise money for War Relief.

The National Mission, prepared for during the last months of 1916, began in St. Matthew's parish on Sunday 10th December, and continued for the following three days. On the previous Sunday, the church people of Northampton had united in a Procession of Witness. God always works from the inside, from the heart of things. The Mission was for the Church to inform the Nation that it was their responsibility; a Mission of Repentance and Hope; a call to be better and truer Christians; a chance to reconstruct the Nation on a Spiritual basis rather than a material one. Services should be continued out-of-doors so that all could easily attend, and also in factories; study circles, retreats, etc., should be arranged together with many united services. The Rev'd. Rowden Hussey was on the Committee set up to have charge of the work involved, which was chaired by the Vicar of All Saints, the Rev'd. L. T. Jones, who was also the Rural Dean. At Easter 1917, in his magazine message, Rowden regretted that the tide of intercession was receding and the promise of the National Mission had not been fulfilled. The war, he said, has great need for intercession and there should have been opportunity to teach the importance of joining Holy Communion with intention but 'nothing in the history of the Catholic Revival has proved more difficult'. 'Is it too late?' he asked; the men at the Front need the support of a great volume of prayer. 'This is perhaps the best service we can render the Nation at this time of crisis.' It was in 1917 that the Bishop of Peterborough conferred the eighteenth Canonry on Rowden Hussey (in 1913 he had been appointed as Master of St. John's Hospital, in Weston Favell). To have their Vicar made a Canon was a great honour for the parish as well as for him. But it all added considerably to his work load.

At the 1917 Patronal Festival, Rowden had persuaded the Bishop of Kingston-on-Thames and the Bishop of St. Andrews to preach at special services. In October, the Rev'd. Edward Tuson of Kingsthorpe announced that he was retiring early in 1918. It was from his parish that St. Matthew's had been separated and there had always been a special feeling towards him. He had been thirty-two years at Kingsthorpe, he had been ordained in 1872 and was now sixty-nine. He was well known for a magnificent voice and was regarded as an ideal parish priest. He would be much missed but had certainly earned himself a happy retirement.

During this period of the war, money was being collected for Church Army Recreation Huts; Memorial Services were held for those who had died. At this time seventy-four men from the parish had been killed or had died.

The curate, Gerald Thompson, who had worked very hard in the parish and was 'a most loyal and earnest friend and priest', was leaving to go to be Rector of St. Jude's, Wednesbury. He and his wife had been in the parish for the three years of the war and would be sadly missed. It is always sad when clergy change and inevitably people are missed, but a church's gifts remain ever the same, however those who dispense them may change! In the meantime, the Rev'd. L. E. Baumer, Senior Chaplain of the Forces, was able to help to some extent, though this was only until March 1918 when he was transferred.

There were increasing problems of shortages, of the need to conserve light and heat. Spanish 'flu caused much illness amongst the civilian population whose resistance was reduced. The illness often turned to pneumonia and many died. Children were much affected and the schools were closed for long periods. Despite everything, there was a feeling that the end was coming; the people were 'awaiting the end of the most appalling misery mankind has ever suffered'.

St. Martin's Day, 11th November 1918, was a day never to be forgotten. It was, strangely, the day the schools re-opened, there were still many absentees but it was a great day and they all had a half-holiday. The news of the 'Cease Fire' flashed round like magic; shops and factories closed as well as the schools; flags appeared everywhere and the town galvanized into life despite the dull skies and the dismal drizzle. Flags of red, white and blue were being sold by street traders. The gaily bedecked crowds sang and danced as the Church bells rang out. Thousands surged around the Market square as the Volunteers' Band played popular and patriotic songs. The young were full of energy and delighting in the promise of the future; the older people were more subdued, remembering the past and the sacrifices that had been made.

Services were arranged of heartfelt thankfulness to God. 'The Victory is from God. We can never repay those who have given their lives and who have regained a world's freedom. If there ever was a time in the History of men when it was their duty to acknowledge the good hand of God and to be thankful, can we doubt that this solemn and happy privilege is ours today?'

What had the future in store? The bells of St. Matthew's Church rang out in gladness but underneath there was thought of the cost. The parish had lost 126 young men in the cause of freedom and to others the cost was shattered health and broken lives. A cost which could never be forgotten and never repaid.

11

Post-War and the New Parochial Church Council

One of the first thoughts after the Armistice was to erect War Memorials to commemorate the Fallen. In the town of Northampton were lengthy discussions on both the forms such a Memorial would take and the position it would occupy.

In the parish of St. Matthew, a large gathering decided that the parish should separately commemorate the sacrifice of all who served and those who had given their lives in the serving. Mr. Phipps offered to pay for the enlargement of the Vestry to form a meeting room and, when that proved a problem, to erect a Church Room on a site to the north of the church, by Collingwood Road, as a Memorial to all who served. This was something the parish really needed and the idea was heartily approved.

The Memorial to the Fallen should be something provided by all the parish. Earlier during the War, a temporary shrine had been placed at the West end of the North aisle, as a focus for services and private intercessions. It was decided that a permanent chapel should be erected on the same site. The decision was circulated to all houses in the parish and, in time, about 1,500 subscriptions were received from all sorts of people, by no means all from Church people. Edward Holding, Matthew's son, was asked to design the chapel, though the final plans had to wait until they knew how much money would be raised. There were also snags in obtaining suitable materials and employing the right craftsmen, so the final Memorial wasn't ready until the Festival in 1921, when it was dedicated at the first Evensong by the Bishop of Leicester, Dr. Lang. 'The souls of the righteous are in the hand of God.'

The chapel is set apart by wrought iron screens and gates resembling

The 'Great War' memorial listing the 126 parishioners who died for their country.

those of the choir and baptistry. The carved oak reredos has a massive crucifix. The money collected, with accrued interest, finally came to about £1,000, and there were individual gifts of silver candlesticks, vases and altar linen.

Rowden Hussey had been appointed as the Rural Dean of Northampton Deanery which meant, of course, that he would have even more responsibilities outside the parish. He was instituted by the Bishop on 7th April. The Deanery issued a special 'Call To Prayer', a series of short services in various churches for united prayer. At St. Matthew's this was on Mondays at 8.15 p.m. after Evensong, the services to be held in the Lady Chapel.

Just before Easter, a Company of the Church Lads' Brigade was formed in the parish, the object being 'to train our lads, body and soul, on a spiritual, moral, social and educational basis', the hope being to retain some influence over the boys when they left school and became wage-earners. In June, a Company of Girl Guides was formed. The District Commissioner, Miss Hennings, explained the aims of the Movement and thirty-seven girls were interested to join; Miss Olney became their Captain.

Miss Olney remained as Guide Captain for seven years, joined in 1922 by Miss Allen as Lieutenant. She was succeeded by Miss Wood in 1927 and Miss Nora Banks in 1929. Nora Banks captained the company until she joined the Wantage Sisters; being followed by Ethel Dodd as captain and then into the Order. The Guides continued as a most successful organisation and in 1970 the Company, with Peggy Ward as Captain, celebrated their Jubilee.

Another great party celebrated the Golden Jubilee in 1980 – an event not visualised by those first Guides when they pioneered the company in those days so soon after the First World War.

The new curate, Alfred Seaman, joined the parish in July, living in Cedar Road, to help the Vicar and Charles Eastgate. The Sunday School Treat was reinstated and was much enjoyed.

The Patronal Festival of 1919 was an occasion for thanksgiving and the Bishops of Aberdeen and Birmingham were welcomed as visiting preachers. St. Matthew's Day being a Sunday added a special spiritual dimension but prevented the holding of the luncheon that had formed part of the celebrations pre-war. In this year the Commemoration of All Souls on 2nd November was of particular significance. Advent and Christmas concluded the first year since the Armistice and saw the restoration of many of the annual activities which had long been part of the St. Matthew's calendar.

On 7th November 1919, the Second Reading was given of the Enabling Bill in the House of Commons, and on 3rd December 1919 it received the Royal Assent and was placed on the Statute Book. This Act meant that the laity, both men and women, might now have a voice in Church affairs. This was a great opportunity, Rowden explained in the magazine, but also a great responsibility which would need both knowledge and patience and co-operation between clergy and laity. Those members of the Church who were over eighteen and had been baptised, should enrol themselves as Electors to be members of the Parochial Church Meeting. The forms had to be in by the end of March. This was the beginning of the Parish Electoral Roll.

The Parochial Church Meeting was to be held on Thursday 15th April 1920 in the new Church Room, which was to be opened on Tuesday 6th April, for the Easter Parochial Tea. Mr. Phipps had provided the Room but there was another £200 to be found for equipment.

The Church Meeting was to:
1. elect two representatives (communicants over twenty-one) to serve on the Ruri-Decanal Conference;
2. decide on the number to serve on the new Parochial Church Council;
3. elect the members of the P.C.C. for the first year (these also had to be communicants, over twenty-one and on the Electoral Roll).

It was decided to hold the P.C.C. meetings once a month and at the May meeting Parish Finances were reviewed. It was suggested that all Funds should be amalgamated under one account and that a preliminary budget should be prepared. The Organist, Charles King, was to have his salary supplemented by a grant of £40. In June, financial matters were again discussed, with particular reference to the debt of £400 on the Church Rooms, and a small Finance Committee of the Officers of the P.C.C. was formed.

The work of the P.C.C. gave its members a much wider view of their Church life, looking out at the Deanery, the Diocese and the Church in general; such matters were soon to appear on future agendas. It also lightened the load of decision for the Vicar and the Churchwardens and made delegation easier. Certainly the enthusiasm shown by the laity was strong and encouraging.

The Cathedral Restoration Fund was one subject for discussion. The importance to the Diocese of the Cathedral was something not so easily realised in Northampton, a long way from Peterborough. The first church on the site was built in 654 and burnt by the Danes in 870; the second church was dedicated in 972 and burnt in 1116 and it was after that that the present church was begun, a building of glorious Norman architecture. For the eight-hundredth Anniversary a sum of £25,000 was needed to restore the roof, choir stalls, bell tower and bells, and the flooring, as well as the need to improve the lighting and the fire precautions. The Bishop asked that every parish should make an offering on St. Peter's Day, 29th June; £31 was collected by the parish and sent by the Rural Dean.

The St. Matthew's Patronal Festival was also of concern this year to a wider range of decision-makers. Canon Hussey had persuaded the Bishop of Kimberley and Kuruman, Dr. Wilfred Gore-Brown, to celebrate on St. Matthew's Day, and, on the Tuesday, the Bishop of British Honduras, the Rt. Rev'd. E. A. Dunn (people sometimes wondered when he would run out of Bishops!), with Canon Hands of St. Laurence, Northampton and the Rev'd. J. A. V. Magee, the son of Archbishop Magee who, as Bishop of Peterborough, had appointed Rowden Hussey to the Kingsley Mission. For the first time since 1913 the Parochial Luncheon could be held, and in the new Church Room, though the tickets had gone up to 3s. 6d.

After Lent and Easter, the Second Annual Parochial Church Meeting was held and the P.C.C. presented the results of the year's work. The Accounts were submitted and accepted, the financial situation being considered satisfactory (though the various funds were still kept separate). Mr. Olney retired as a Churchwarden and was replaced by Mr. R. Bament at the Vestry Meeting. Thirty-two nominations were received for the twenty-five P.C.C. places and practically all were re-elected, with Mr. Charles King taking the place vacated by Mr. Bament.

In 1921, the House of Lords accepted the Archbishop of Canterbury's motion that the Parochial Church Council Measure should be recommended for Royal Assent. Parliament also affirmed that the Convocations of Canterbury and York, acting by canon, have powers to reform themselves. So the two Measures of the Enabling Act were finally accepted. The new legislation secured more representative Houses of Clergy in Convocation and gave the laity legal powers. Convocation would now contain more elected members though its resolutions would have to be accepted by the National Assembly before they became effective. The Parochial Church Council Measure gave the laity legal rights in their parishes which should make for increased efficiency provided the Vicar and the Council could work together. The possibilities were great, the opportunities immense, but so were the responsibilities. The future could be both different and exciting!

12

Mission

In his New Year letter of 1922, Rowden Hussey said that, 'we must not make the fatal mistake of allowing our outward work and material things to outpace the growth of our spiritual life. Nothing is more essential for us to remember than that we are absolutely dependent on God Himself, therefore let us all make this coming year a year of special dependence on God in prayer, in intercession, in meditation and in communion.'

The importance of the Sunday Schools was emphasised in the June magazine, they should be a 'remedy for the lack of personal religion and living faith' replacing the 'inadequate religious instruction' in State schools. Rowden felt that the future of the Church of England was in the hands of the Sunday Schools, in that the congregations, the people of God, of the future depended on the religious upbringing of the children.

It was in June also, that the Chapter of the Northampton clergy suggested a special effort from 30th September to 6th October, to declare the Church's message in a series of services. This was not intended as a Mission in the outreach sense, but a Mission to the faithful to encourage and to help their faith. As far as St. Matthew's was concerned, this would come immediately after the Patronal and Dedication Festival. It was to be a week of 'Instruction in the Church's Faith and Practice'. The Messenger to St. Matthew's was to be Father Paul Bull of the Community of the Resurrection at Mirfield, who was one of the best known and experienced of Mission priests. In a letter written by Father Paul, he said that he came with great joy and remembered his time as Chaplain to the Northamptonshire Regiment twenty-five years before. He asked that he should have the help of all communicants and that, between them, they should contact everyone in the parish, so that all had a chance to go to the meetings. 'I rely,' he wrote, 'on Communicants to bring other souls to hear God's message.'

In the following year, 1923, the Deanery Conference unanimously decided to make a further spiritual effort as a 'follow-up' to deepen the spiritual life of Northampton. This Church Mission was arranged for 16th to 26th November. It was decided that all the parishes were to have a simultaneous parochial mission each with its own Missioners. It was a tremendous challenge and nine months were devoted to preparations. It was asked that Church people should get together and co-operate; find comradeship and allow the love of God to fill their churches and stimulate the life of the Deanery. Committees were elected to help with preparations, including the mundane one of raising money. The Mission was to involve *real* prayer; *real* friendship and the need to wait on God.

The Missioner who was to lead the Mission at St. Matthew's was the Rev'd. Arthur Creyke England, Vicar of Hessle in Yorkshire; he was a Canon Missioner of York and took a wide interest in public activities. He was the Chairman of the Urban and District Council and a Country Magistrate for the East Riding of Yorkshire. He was to be assisted by the Rev'd. Francis Morse Windley, Priest-in-Charge of Dormanstown, Yorkshire. Canon England was to make his first visit in May to discuss arrangements. The first stage was for Corporate Prayer: prayer for the Holy Spirit upon the clergy of the Deanery for the Mission, prayer for the Missioners that they might be men of God's choosing, full of Spiritual Power, wisdom and charity, and prayer for the parish that love might be rekindled in everyone and that all might realise their need of Christ and His need of them.

Canon England visited the parish on 16th May, and gave a series of inspiring addresses, stimulating everyone in their preparations.

In mid-July there was a three-day Communicants' Convention for all the Northampton parishes, the services being held in the Church of the Holy Sepulchre, where there were addresses by the Bishop of Peterborough, the Bishop of Leicester and others. The programme was 'Witness for Christ'; Individual Witness and Corporate Witness. Back at St. Matthew's there was a parochial meeting when the programme for the Mission was discussed. It was emphasised that, although it was to be a corporate Mission, individual responsibility was all important, *all* were capable of some form of personal service.

In September, the programme was distributed, so that everyone could be prepared and ensure that they were free to attend the meetings and services. Everyone – clergy, laity; rich, poor; young, old – was asked to pray daily for the Mission; to pray that God would bless it and that it might be begun, continued and ended in Him and prove a blessing to all people.

The Missioners arrived on Friday 6th November, and all of them assembled in All Saints Church, in the town centre, to be commissioned by the Bishop of Peterborough, Frank Theodore Woods, and, the following evening, the Mission began simultaneously in all parishes.

In St. Matthew's Church, the Vicar laid his hands on the two Missioners and entrusted to them the spiritual charge of the parish. On the Sunday, Francis Windley preached at the Sung Eucharist and to the children in the afternoon, tracing, for them, the Spiritual Life from Baptism and through life. Canon England addressed several hundred men on 'The Alleged Failure of Christianity' in the afternoon and at Evensong preached on 'Personal Sin'. During the following weeks talks dealt with Contrition; Confession; the Life of Faith; Prayer; the Catholic Church; the Blessed Sacrament and Vision – all concerned with a life surrendered to God. On the Tuesday and Friday evenings special services were arranged for women, drawing on the stories and the characters of women in the Bible, showing how they accepted a life dedicated to God.

Opportunity was given throughout the Mission for people to make personal confessions and seek absolution; for people to seek advice or further instruction and sick people were visited in their homes. On the last Sunday, nearly 600 men attended an afternoon talk and, in the evening, Canon England outlined his vision of a life of service following Christ. On Monday were held services of thanksgiving and a last address on the Rule for a Spiritual Life and then the Missioners in copes presented 600 Memorial cards from the High Altar. The congregation sang 'Crown Him Lord of All' and the 'Te Deum'. On Tuesday evening there was a Sung Eucharist with full choir to conclude the Mission on a note of triumph.

The year of 1924 was made a Year of Prayer for the conversion of our country. Continuous prayers were said in all parishes that God would bless and further the revival that was taking place. Tuesday 4th November was to be a day of continuous prayer. It had been remembered that in Scotland in olden times, a Fiery Cross was passed to rouse the clans and that the Cross is the symbol of Salvation. So, a cross with the words 'God So Loved the World' was being passed from parish to parish on that day. The Cross was to reach St. Matthew's at 7.00 a.m. and Holy Communion would be celebrated at 7.30 a.m., with further celebrations at 8.30 and 9.30. Mattins would be at 10.30 a.m., Evensong at 6.00 p.m. Between the services there would be private intercessions and it was hoped that everyone would spend some time in prayer, so that there would be no occasion when intercession was not being made.

'What a joy,' wrote Canon England, 'this must be for the Vicar who had laboured here so long, and with such love and devotion patiently taught his people the great truth of the ever-present Christ. To few priests has been given more evidence of the fact that his teaching has been grasped, than he sees every Sunday morning. Nothing, in my experience, is so stimulating as to see that multitude of men and women at their worship, for in Eucharist, Evensong and Procession there is shown the same reverent devotion.'

13

Anglo-Catholicism

Missions are special occasions but Canon Hussey was a firm believer in a steady process of teaching, in sermons, evening or daytime meetings and in the Magazine. His doctrine was based on the Oxford Movement of the nineteenth century worked out on English lines to meet the Spiritual needs of the Church people of this country. Right from the beginning of his Ministry Rowden had laid great emphasis on the Eucharist and on the use of vestments. He had always emphasised the importance of Lent and Advent as preparation for the great festivals.

From the time the new church was consecrated in 1893, a Daily Eucharist had taken place at St. Matthew's with the laity encouraged to take part, and this at a time when many, possibly most, church people and many clergy, felt that once a week was enough or even excessive! Certainly there were times at St. Matthew's when only the clergy were present, but everyone in the parish knew that their priest was praying for them, even in their absence. In many churches the main Morning Service on Sundays was Mattins, but at St. Matthew's it had been Holy Communion since 1898, because this is the service commanded by Our Lord. It was celebrated by the Apostles and the first Christians and with every branch of the Catholic Church. Mattins is a service of prayer, praise and Bible readings derived from the offices said in Monasteries from the English Reformation; a valuable service but not the main one, Mattins can be said by a lay-person if necessary, whereas the essential parts of the Communion Service are the Acts and the Words of Consecration. Liturgies have been arranged and re-arranged and different sects may use different liturgies, but the Consecration is the heart of them all. Canon Hussey explained that the Vestments were to add dignity and beauty, and the colours are a reminder of the Liturgical Year. White is for Holy

Trinity and the Festivals of Our Lord's Incarnate Life; for Our Lady's Feasts; for Holy Angels; All Saints; the Conversion of St. Paul; the Nativity of St. John the Baptist and the Church's Dedication Festival. Red, being the colour of fire and of blood, is for Feasts of the Holy Spirit and the Martyr Saints. Violet, for mourning and penitence, for Lent, Advent and Rogation Days and for the priest when he hears confessions. On other occasions the colour is green.

The priest celebrated communion facing East, when with his back to the congregation he is speaking for them to God; when facing the people he is speaking to them in God's name. The Epistle is read from the South side, the side of goodness and light, because it is written for those who have already received God's word; the Gospel from the North, the side of darkness, because it is the good news to the heathen. The Consecration or Sacring Bell is rung during the prayer of Consecration.

Canon Hussey pointed out very firmly that one is not worshipping the Cross but using it as a Holy Sign. He also explained that the Lights on the altar, the candles, go back to the early times and are symbolic of the Divine and Human Natures of Christ. Wafer Bread and the Mixed Chalice, symbolise the unleavened bread and the wine and water of the Jewish Passover Feast, a custom from early days, as the Oxford Movement advocated the return to the early practices; these acts and customs come to us from the Apostles themselves.

The Holy Communion is one of the great occasions for the congregation to be one, the body of Christ. The Christian is incomplete until he is a member of the whole and has the responsibility to share in the whole. The Church of Christ is one, and all mankind must be brought into one great sacramental fellowship, which is the Body of Christ. This, Canon Hussey said, is the great challenge of Anglo-Catholicism to English religion.

Rowden was worried over the increasing secularism of Sundays, and, in a magazine article, discussed what Sunday should mean. 'It is the weekly Festival of Our Lord's Resurrection, a weekly rejoicing for His victory over sin and death. We must go back to the Prayer Book and see its true meaning.' Ideally there would be one Communion for everyone and all, except the sick, infirm and old, should go to Communion fasting.

In early October 1925, there was to be in Northampton a three-day Anglo-Catholic Congress, the subject to be 'The Message of the Church for the Common Life'. It was to be a teaching Congress to give a clear survey of the Christian Faith and its bearing on everyday life. On Sunday 4th October, there was to be a special service with full ritual, including incense, at 11.00 a.m. when the Rev'd. W. J. B. Crouch, the Secretary of

E.C.U., would preach. The Evensong preacher would be Father Wallis of the Cowley Fathers. Then on the Tuesday, the Bishop of Buckingham would preach. The ordinary meetings would be in St. Michael's Church Hall. Tickets were 1s. 6d. for the whole Congress and there was a Booklet available to buy.

The Bishop of Buckingham pointed out that it was strong conviction that supported the Oxford Movement and a similar conviction must support Anglo-Catholicism. These convictions must be in all our daily lives. There were many speakers including the Bishops of Truro, Monmouth and Woolwich. Afterwards there was a Thanksgiving Service at St. Matthew's at which the hope was expressed that the Congress had brought a wider spirit of fellowship to the churches of Northampton.

It was a year later, at the end of 1926, that a decision was made to introduce incense into the services at St. Matthew's. The 103 church workers in the parish were consulted. Thirty-three were against the introduction; twenty-six were 'not opposed' and forty-four signed a petition asking for incense to be introduced. At the P.C.C. meeting twenty-two were in favour and six against. The reasons put forward for incense were:

1. that it is Catholic and used in Catholic Churches worldwide;
2. that it is referred to in the Prayer Book and bears the mark of Divine approval;
3. that it gives honour to God and helps the worshippers to lift their hearts and minds to God;
4. that it is a mark of unity throughout the world.

Despite the fact that the majority in favour was not particularly large, it was used on Sunday 9th January and on 6th February 1927. Mr. Pickering Phipps presented a massive silver censer and matching incense boat and a pair of processional candle-holders, as well as extra cassocks and surplices for the servers.

It was not until 1930 that permission was obtained for the Reserved Sacrament to be held at St. Matthew's. Previously, the only church in the town so permitted was St. Lawrence's, and any priest sent for a visit to a dying parishioner had to go via St. Lawrence's Church. It was an important privilege, explained Canon Hussey, not only for the practicality of taking Communion to the sick who were thus drawn nearer to the main congregation, but also because the presence of the Reserved Sacrament manifests the presence of God at all times and in all places.

The services at St. Matthew's were firmly based on the Prayer Book with the Athanasius Creed used six times a year, at Christmas, Epiphany, Easter, Ascension Day, Whit Sunday and Trinity Sunday.

The Centenary of the Oxford Movement was celebrated in July 1933. At St. Matthew's there was an introductory Lantern lecture in February, given by Mr. Clifton Kenway. There were eighty pictures showing people and places which illustrated the History of the Movement. The Oxford Movement, or the Tractarians, believed that the Church of England is that branch of the Catholic Church originally planted in this island, derived by an unbroken succession from the Apostles; with the Book of Common Prayer as the best witness to its Catholic claims. 'The great work of the Tractarians was the revival throughout the English Church, of Supernatural Religion and Sacramental Truth.'

On Sunday 7th July at 11.00 a.m. there was a Solemn Eucharist and Procession with Bishop Fyffe, formerly Bishop of Rangoon, and, as preacher, Canon H.L. Goudge, Canon of Christ Church and Regius Professor of Divinity in the University of Oxford. 'Let the Centenary inspire us with an increased readiness to offer loyal and faithful service.'

14

The Hussey Family and Others

The two Hussey boys, Christopher and Walter, were growing up. They were fortunate in having their early schooling at Waynflete School; not only was it so conveniently situated but it was also a good and happy school.

In January 1921, a month before his fourteenth birthday, Christopher was sent to Marlborough College, back near his father's birthplace, and he remained there until Easter 1925. From there he went to Pembroke College, Oxford, obtaining his B.A. degree in Theology in 1929. He then spent a year at Cuddesdon College before being ordained Deacon by the Bishop of London at St. Paul's Cathedral on 4th October 1930. He served as a curate at St. Mark's Church, Noel Park, Wood Green in London, from where he was priested a year later. A clever, studious, young man whose glasses made him look particularly solemn, he continued to work in London at a succession of parishes, only returning to Northampton for special occasions and occasional holidays.

Walter Hussey, his junior by two years, went from Waynflete School to the Knoll in Woburn Sands, then followed his brother with a scholarship to Marlborough College in September 1922 at thirteen and a half, remaining there until Summer 1927. He also went to Oxford, but to Keble College, taking his B.A. in Philosophy and Political Economy in 1930. For a year he became an Assistant Master at a school in Seaford but, deciding to take Holy Orders, returned to Oxford to Cuddesdon, where Christopher had been. He was also ordained Deacon in London, serving his title at St. Mary Abbott Church, Kensington, from where he was ordained priest and also served as Priest-in-Charge of St. Paul's, Kensington for a while. It was from there that he returned to Northampton in 1937.

The two boys had been active at St. Matthew's when at home, frequently acting as servers to their father and to various visiting clergy at Patronal Festivals. They were well-known in the parish and the congregation followed their progress to manhood with interest and affection.

It was Easter 1922 that the Rev'd. Charles Wheeler announced his move to Littlehampton after a brief eighteen months at St. Matthew's. He had been efficient and popular and would be much missed, he was to be replaced by the Rev'd. Guy Trevor Brodie. He had been at Bremerton, near Salisbury (with its memories of George Herbert), and then at All Saints, Margaret Street, London, a sound background for his work in Northampton. He was to live at the clergy house at 12 The Drive, a house he soon christened Herbert Cottage!

Guy Brodie's father had been obstetrician and surgeon to Queen Victoria, and so he came from a rather privileged background. When he first came to St. Matthew's he was so thin that he was nicknamed The Spider, his girdle often fell off and was constantly being rescued! His house was run by a Housekeeper, a Mrs. Budden, who ran him too! She was an efficient but rather formidable lady known as The Duchess, who kept Guy supplied with delicacies to take to the poor. She must have fed him well because he became quite plump. He was a gentle, saintly man, much teased, particularly by the boys, though he took it all in good part and was much loved. 'An absent-minded saint.'

In September 1923 came the news that Frank Theodore Woods, the Bishop of Peterborough, had been appointed to the See of Winchester. He would be much missed, particularly at St. Matthew's where his sympathy and inspiration had been much appreciated. He was to pay the church a farewell visit on Sunday 4th November. On that occasion his sermon was a memorable one and, at the end of the service, he shook hands with everyone in the large congregation. At his request he was presented with framed photographs of the church.

His replacement was the Rt. Rev'd. Cyril Charles Bowman Bardsley, who was consecrated on 2nd February 1924. He was publicly received into Northampton on 27th February, with a service at All Saints' Church and a Reception at the Town Hall. He visited St. Matthew's on 20th March, to conduct a Confirmation Service for 218 candidates from five churches.

One of the new Bishop's first Diocesan duties was to supervise the division of that Diocese. The Diocese of Peterborough was created in 1539, when it consisted of the counties of Northamptonshire and Rutland. In 1839 the county of Leicester, which had once been a separate See but was then attached to Lincoln, was separated from Lincoln and attached to Peterborough. Always a huge diocese, the population had more than doubled. There were 700 clergy in 597 parishes, an impossible size to be overseen by one Bishop, even with help. The ancient See of Leicester was again to become a separate diocese of 260 parishes.

In June 1925, the Bishop was able to speak over the wireless due to the newly opened High Power Broadcasting Station at Daventry. In due course, the money for the Diocese of Leicester was raised and St. Martin's Church became the Cathedral. Bishop Bardsley, the relatively new Bishop of Peterborough, became the first Diocesan Bishop of Leicester.

On 25th March 1927, the Rt. Rev'd. Claude Martin Blagden was consecrated as the thirty-first Bishop of Peterborough at Westminster Abbey, being enthroned in his Cathedral on St. George's Day. He promised to preach at St. Matthew's on the Dedication Day.

In July 1924, the Church and the Church School were distressed to lose Mr. William Westmorland, who had been Headmaster of the school for thirty-two years. He was retiring to Bournemouth. His loss was great to the church and the parish as he had done a lot for both. His successor was to be Mr. E. W. Tucker, who came from Tolleshunt D'Arcy School in Essex. Miss Smith, the Head of the Infants' School, went to Cedar Road School the following summer and it was decided to combine the two departments under Mr. Tucker.

It was in 1926 that Lilian Hussey was made President of the Mothers' Union, following the sudden death of Mrs. Montague Browne, who had been President since the parochial branch was formed. It was the next year, 1927, that Lilian and Rowden celebrated their Silver Wedding. A presentation was to be made at a special service and party on 20th April in Easter week. It was a very happy family party, the whole parish being their family, the church bells were rung in anticipation.

In March 1928, a presentation was made to Charles King, who had completed fifty years as a Church Organist, thirty-two of them at St. Matthew's. Many Northampton people were at the ceremony, including the Mayor. Mr. King was given a cheque for £150 and an illuminated album. The whole of Northampton owed a great debt to Charles King for his contribution to its musical life.

Nineteen twenty-nine brought the sad news of the death of Andrew Carr, who had been Assistant Curate from 1898 to 1901. He was well remembered as a quiet man and devoted priest. He had given his services without pay at a time when the finances were low, and had given, anonymously, generous gifts to the church. He had started the idea of the

Endowment Fund and raised the first £1,000. His last parish had been in Worcester and he had been retired for some time. September 1931 brought news of the death of the Rev'd. Canon Reginald Woolley, another well-remembered assistant curate from 1902 to 1905, at the age of fifty-four. He had always kept in touch and was a frequent visitor to the Festivals.

In 1930, the clerical staff had become three again, a great relief as the population of the parish had doubled within the last three years. Edward Ion Carroll of Keble and Cuddesdon (like Walter Hussey) was ordained as a Deacon in Peterborough at Advent. He was much welcomed, although the parish had to raise extra money for the Clergy Fund.

It was in 1932 that the History of the Parish was written by Miss Gertrude Hollis, a small book but packed full of useful and interesting information, it celebrated forty-five years, being aimed to come out just before the Centenary of the Oxford Movement.

Two years later, in February 1934, Charles King died, having played at services up to 31st December. Thus he died in harness, as he would have wished, after only a short illness and with no real suffering. He had, however, not been really well for some time and in 1933 he had been 'sent' on holiday by friends in the congregation. He had served St. Matthew's for thirty-nine years, at all times giving of himself and his musical talents in his courteous, gentle and unselfish way. He was devoted to the Church, a true gentleman who could be cheery and humorous and interested in many people and things. He truly walked with God.

In the summer of that year, the parish lost Ion Carroll to the Overseas Missionary Service; he was being sent to the Korean Mission Field for a five-year term. Despite their sorrow, the parish was proud that he was to be a Missionary and would keep in touch. Ion Carroll had been most active with the Scouts which he had started in the parish and he had also been a most assiduous visitor round the parish, particularly on the new estate on the west of the Kettering Road; the Kenmuir Road area. He visited daily and often arrived with the furniture van to greet new arrivals! He kept a very detailed card-index of the parishioners and knew the district intimately. The new curate was Frederick Hugh Stallard of Pembroke and Cuddesdon (like Christopher Hussey), who joined the parish at Christmas. He remembers travelling by tram to the Racecourse from the railway station, though the trams were abolished soon afterwards, and thinking that St. Matthew's was unlike any other church and being impressed by the orderly ritual and the music. He lived in lodgings in Kingsley Park Terrace, rooms were dark and cold in those days, but he always got a good Sunday dinner usually cooked in the nearby bakehouse oven.

In 1934 the school was to be re-organised, the Board of Education having agreed to a proposal of the L.E.A. that St. Matthew's Church of England School was to be for Junior Mixed Children aged seven to eleven and that Kingsley Junior and Infants would take the children from five to seven. Children over eleven would go to other schools, these older children would be missed but at least those that remained would fit into the building. Mr. Tucker was resigning at Easter, after ten years as Headmaster, and was to go to a school at Deal. He had been a valuable Headmaster and had also been Superintendent of the Sunday School and Secretary of the P.C.C. There were eighty-seven applicants for the post, which went to Mr. E. G. Ashby, who had worked under Mr. Tucker and had recently been an Assistant at Kettering Road Intermediate School. The newly organised school had a good report from the Inspectors who congratulated everyone that the disturbance had not been too abrupt; this was a period of transition as the younger children remained, though no more under sevens were to be admitted. Mr. Ashby was said to be approaching his new post with 'zeal, tempered with caution'. The atmosphere of hard work, friendliness and good feeling was still there.

In 1935 Mr. Phipps decided to give the church the piece of land to the east of the Vicarage as an extension to the churchyard. Originally he had had it for sale. There were long discussions over the best way to enclose the land and to whom the conveyance was to be made. From the P.C.C. Minutes it seems that the P.C.C. took responsibility, certainly the papers were signed by the Churchwardens. At the same time, it seems that the conveyances of the two houses in the parish, 12 The Drive (or Herbert Cottage) and Windhoek on Collingwood Road, were also passed to the P.C.C., presumably under the control of the Diocesan Trustees. Windhoek was let to Mr Corrin for £85 a year.

15

Thirty-Sixth Northampton (St. Matthew's) Boy Scouts

It was early in 1931 that Ion Carroll, the assistant curate of St. Matthew's, suggested the formation of a Scout Troop. The troop was duly registered, under the control of the Vicar – Mr. Carroll received a warrant as Group Scout Master, and Mr. Ablett as Scoutmaster. To start with five boys were trained, so that they could be the first Patrol Leaders or Seconds. These boys were A. Pickhaver, R. Allen, T. Jones, A. Williams and R. Adams and they were invested on 14th April 1931, after which the troop was opened to any boys in the parish who attended church.

The four original patrols were Hawks, Woodpeckers, Peewits and Herons (later changed to Owls) and by August, when the first camp was held at Deene Park, the troop numbered between twenty-five and thirty.

The second summer camp was at Turvey; and in the third year, being more ambitious, the camp was held at Hamble on Southampton Water. It was a successful venture, and being further from home, there was plenty to see. The scouts inspected the training-ship *Mercury* and the liner *Berengaria*. To their delight they were asked to join in a Guard of Honour for the Chief Scout and Chief Guide, who were to sail on a cruise to Norway on the liner *Calgaric*. The Guard consisted of Guides, Brownies and Wolf Cubs, as well as the St. Matthew's Scouts. Lord and Lady Baden-Powell came to inspect them all; talked to them and took photographs; it was a marvellous experience for them all. The following year they again camped at Hamble, because Ion Carroll was leaving for Korea but decided to run the camp before he left. A Group photograph of the Troop was presented to him as a memento. Summer camps took place every year until the war.

The departure of Ion Carroll was a blow to the troop, as he had been acting as Scoutmaster as well as Group Scoutmaster, but Mr. Arthur Wilson was warranted as Scoutmaster with Mr. Sidney Baxter as his Assistant. Later, the Rev'd. Fred Stallard, the new curate, became Group S.M.

In February 1937, by which time the troop numbered forty divided into five patrols, P. L. Raymond Furniss was presented with his King's Scout Badge and All Round Cords. This meant that all the P.L.s had their King's Badge, a great record. Actually this was the ninth such badge won by the troop. On 12th April, the troop celebrated its sixth birthday with an evening for about eighty parents and friends. This also was the beginning of a regular event in the calendar.

Also in April, two of the scouts were able to join a county group to visit St. George's Chapel at Windsor Castle. There were about 1,000 scouts on parade and at the service. It was exciting to see the Royal Family so closely. In May, there was the Coronation; the scouts of the world had been allocated 1,000 places on Constitution Hill; fifteen of these went to Northamptonshire and two of these to St. Matthew's Troop. The lucky ones were E. Roberts and R. Sable.

By 1938 the troop had increased to nearly fifty and a sixth patrol, the Eagles, was formed.

The summer camp of 1939 was held near Skegness, just before the Declaration of War. The scouts were back home in time to help with the reception of evacuees, some of whom were welcomed at troop meetings, forming a new patrol. Meetings continued throughout the war, including air-raid practices and instruction in First Aid and Civil Defence. There was still opportunity for games and fun but it was decided that 'full' camps were inadvisable. However, they did manage some patrol camps and daytime hikes. Occasionally, ex-scouts, home on leave, would attend or even run meetings and it was exciting news when one won a bravery award, though sad when someone was reported killed or missing or a prisoner-of-war. By January 1942 six new King's Scout Badges were presented, so there was no let-up on standards!

In September 1943, a retrospective account, written at the start of a new log-book, gave the then total of King's Scout Badges won as 24; also, 29 First Class Badges, 2 Bushman's Thongs, and 2 Gold, 8 Red and White, and 25 Green and Yellow, All Round Cards.

In 1942, a patrol of Air Scouts was formed and won first prize for a scale model of a Blackburn Skua aircraft at a National Exhibition. Also, during the war, the regular monthly church parades were begun and the Vicar, Walter Hussey, was invited to become Group Scoutmaster.

On 23rd July 1945, twenty-two troops of scouts assembled for a rally on the grounds of the Boys' Grammar School, on Billing Road, with a tent-pitching competition followed by demonstrations of camp craft by each troop. In August, the summer camp was held at Wakefield Lawn.

With the end of the war, many ex-scouts were demobilised and returned home. Many visited troop meetings and Bill Reason became A.S.M., replacing Mr. E. J. Roberts, who was moving to Shrewsbury.

Nineteen forty-two saw the troops celebrating the twenty-first Birthday; the five original members all returned for the party and the Rev'd. Ion Carroll, the founder of the troop, was there to cut the cake. Although the troop was still very active, the numbers had dropped to thirty-four and the two sections, formed during the war, had re-combined, Senior Scouting had come into being in 1946, but it had been decided not to form a senior group. The Air Scout patrol had also ceased as a separate entity. The St. George's Day and Empire Day parades were still attended and the annual camps were highlights in the Troop's year. Bob-a-job week had been instituted, scouts were to do jobs for one shilling a job and were expected to earn at least three shillings in the week. People who provided jobs were given a sticker to prevent other scouts coming to the door! The money

The 36th. Northampton (St. Matthew's) Scout Group in 1948 with their Scoutmaster, Arthur Wilson, seated centre, second row.

The 31st. Northampton (St. Matthew's) Guide Company parading into church on St. George's Day, 1969.

went half for H.Q. funds; a quarter to County Funds and the remaining quarter to local funds.

A Coronation Camp was held in 1953 at Delapre Park, when the Chief Scout, Lord Rowallan, was the chief visitor. The camp was attended by 800 scouts and, for one day, 600 Cubs.

The Gang Show became an annual event and in 1956 the troop celebrated its Jubilee in suitable fashion.

The Wolf Cub pack had been started in January 1935, with fifteen boys aged between eight and a half and ten. Mr. J. W. Spencer was Akela; the Rev'd. Fred Stallard was Baloo and Miss Brenda Green was Bagheera. Outings were arranged to local places where games could be played and also further afield. The Northampton Cubs had one such outing to Whipsnade. Numbers grew steadily and during the autumn and winter meetings, the Cubs learnt knots and semaphore.

St. Matthew's Scouts and Cubs continued to flourish after the war, though numbers were never so large again and meetings and activities had to change with the times. Today, Thursday is Scout Night. Beavers, the newly formed 'colonies' for boys of six to eight years, meet at 5.45 p.m.

under Richard Stringer; Cubs meet later, under Alan Marsh and later still the Scouts meet under Ian Rivett. In 1991 the troop celebrated its sixtieth birthday.

16

Dedication Festivals

As the church had been consecrated on St. Matthew's Day, the Patronal and Dedication Festivals were one and the same. The Festival was kept from the year when the Foundation Stone was laid in 1891 and the Consecration of the new church in 1893 right through the years, even during the war.

Dedication Festivals are of ancient origin, dating from the time of St. Augustine, when it was ordained that every church should have a Feast of Thanksgiving. At the time of the Reformation, it was decided that this day should be the first Sunday in October, but later this was only kept for those churches which did not know the date of the dedication. The idea of a Thanksgiving Day was to include a Service in the morning and an afternoon of entertainment, a Feast with a play or a Fair. Basically the St. Matthew's Festival followed this plan. There were morning services of Holy Communion and everyone was expected to take communion at one of these services. The 'high spot' was the 11.00 a.m. Sung Eucharist to which a special preacher was invited and another presided over the Celebration. It was not usual for the laity to take communion at this service, but all were expected to attend. The congregation, under Canon Hussey, were very loyal to the traditions, even though it meant that many had to give up a day's work and a day's wages. The Festival was such an important event in the calendar that many, both clergy and laity, who had left the district made a point of returning for St. Matthew's Day. Mr. Pollock, who was the very first Assistant Curate, came back year after year until they began to think that they couldn't have the Festival without him!

The Festival was an occasion when local clergy and Northampton dignitaries were invited and Mr. and Mrs. Pickering Phipps, as patron, made a point of attending on every possible occasion. Mr. Phipps acted as Crucifier in the procession from the first when he carried the cross he had just presented. He would be followed by thurifier, boat boy, Master of Ceremonies, servers, choir and clergy; though usually there were two processions, the second one for the Bishops.

Although St. Matthew's Day was the most important celebration, other special services took place right through the Octave, the eight days. Right from the beginning, Rowden Hussey took care to invite visiting preachers who would make a mark on the congregation. As the years went by, he became more ambitious, asking clergy from further away, even those from Overseas who were in this country, and asking Canons and Archdeacons and Bishops! He developed a reputation for his persuasive powers and for refusing to take 'no' for an answer. Rapidly he built up a list of 'Friends of St. Matthew's' who returned on many occasions.

Most years the Bishop of Peterborough attended and on many, the Suffragan Bishop of Leicester. Later the Bishop of Salisbury came frequently. Bishops from Birmingham; Ely; Grantham; Guildford; Hereford; Ipswich; Kingston; Oxford; Southwark; Thetford; Taunton and Woolwich; of Argyll; Brecon; Dublin; Glasgow; and St. Andrews; Bombay; Honduras; Jerusalem; Kimberley; Madagascar; Nassau; Nyasaland; Trinidad; Waikato and Zanzibar are names one can draw from the records!

The morning Eucharist Service was usually followed by the Festival Luncheon, except during the war years and when the Festival fell on a Sunday, the Luncheon was usually hosted by Mr. Phipps and was like a great family party, always including a review of the past year by the Vicar and a series of amusing and serious speeches. In the afternoon there would be a gathering for Church Workers and members of the congregation who hadn't been able to get to the luncheon, and to this the Hussey family, the Phipps family, the chief guests, all made an appearance when they could. The Church School was always closed so that the children could take part.

The Festival Day was often the occasion to consecrate gifts to the church. In the early days, as we have seen, these were large and important, like the new organ and the stained glass windows and, in 1921, the War Memorial, on which occasion the Most Rev'd. the Lord Archbishop of Wales was the preacher. The following year the preacher was the Primate of All Ireland and, in 1923, it was the Primus of the Episcopal Church of Scotland. St. Matthew's congregation had no excuse for parochialism! In 1925, for example, there were gifts of a massive brass Alms Dish and eight white alms bags, to complete the series of liturgical colours previously given. There was also Altar linen and a large Altar Book. On every occasion there was a profusion of flowers for the Altar and all over the church.

An event which was much enjoyed at the Festival was the special Organ Recital; sometimes there were others through the Octave or there were special Choir Recitals or some other Musical performance. Many of the Organ Recitals, both at Festivals and other occasions, were by the Organist, Mr. Charles King, who gave over 600 such recitals during his time at St. Matthew's, but on many occasions other organists were invited to play and these added to the lustre of St. Matthew's musical reputation: Sir Walford Davies of the Temple Church and later of St. George's, Windsor; Dr. Alcock of the Chapel Royal and Salisbury Cathedral; Sir George Martin of St. Paul's Cathedral; Dr. Hunter of Bristol; Dr. Haydn Keeton of Peterborough; Henry Ley of Christ Church, Oxford; Dr. Perrin of Canterbury were just some of those who came, many several times. The music presented was a wide variety of schools and periods, but always some of the finest that has been written.

The preparation of the church for the Festival was the work of a large number of voluntary helpers. Mrs. Montague Browne had founded a Guild of those who helped to clean the church and a very important band were the Servers, some of whom did years of devoted work. It was all very much a combined effort.

The children of the Sunday School were always an important part of any Festival. There were special services but they were also expected to attend the 'adult' services, particularly if with their parents. The Sunday School was the 'nursery of St. Matthew's spiritual life' and some of the teachers served for years without a break (St. Matthew's seemed to attract long-serving helpers). The children were instructed in the Catechism, the Creed, the Lord's Prayer and the Commandments; in fact they were being steadily prepared for the day of their Confirmation. Older children who had been confirmed were invited to Bible Classes. In all cases it was the policy to teach boys and girls separately – as, in fact, it was still the habit with instruction classes for adults. The children were always present at the celebration of Holy Communion as the Vicar believed strongly that they must become familiar with the liturgy at an early age, for this reason he liked them to sit as near the front of the nave as possible. There were voluntary examinations on certain afternoons and, in any case, those who attended the Church School were well used to the Annual Diocesan Inspectors and their questions.

At Festivals, there was usually a procession of the Sunday School children, led by the choir, at the afternoon service. There were so many children, at least in the early days, that it took a number of processional hymns before all had reached their seats. There was great excitement when a child was selected to carry a candle. It has even been recorded that the odd doll or teddy bear was smuggled in!

The Sunday School Treat was still a highlight of the children's year, despite the increase in cars and public transport and family holidays; money for it was collected by the Sunday School teachers, and others, asking at every home in the parish, not a task they really enjoyed! The days of games, sports and races, with prizes of chocolate bars, as well as the TEA, was greatly appreciated. In the early days the children walked to the borrowed field; in those days this varied but by the 1930s THE FIELD as it was known, was behind a farm off the Kettering Road in Spinney Hill. Earlier, the walk was led by a band but by the thirties seven 'buses were needed. After the 1914/18 War, ice-cream became an important feature of the refreshments. On at least one occasion when the weather

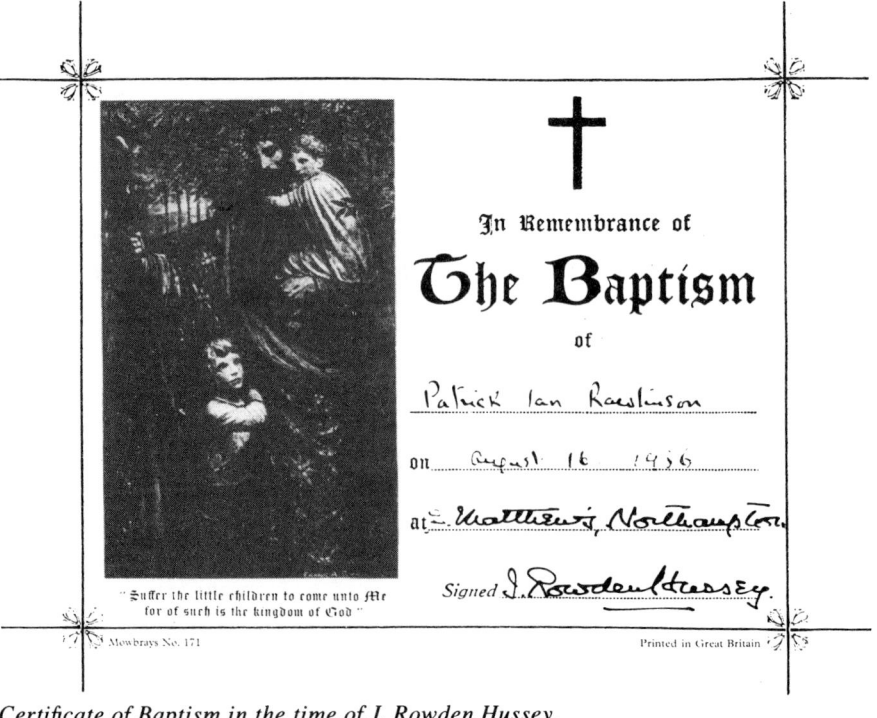

Certificate of Baptism in the time of J. Rowden Hussey.

was wet, the Treat adjourned to the Picturedrome! There were parties at Christmas and the children were usually in demand for entertainments and money-raising activities.

In the summer of 1928 the idea of a Childrens' Corner in the church was conceived. A Committee was set up consisting of the Vicar and Mrs. Hussey; the assistant curate; the Churchwardens and their wives, Mr. and Mrs. Agutter and Mr. and Mrs. Brooks; and Miss Hollis and Miss Lloyd representing the P.C.C. Offerings were asked for and received; the corner, near the west end of the South Aisle, was provided with child-sized chairs and prayer-desks and tables. Suitable books, pictures and statues were also provided together with instructional objects which were changed with the seasons. Mrs. Phipps gave some lovely figures for the Christmas crib. All was arranged so that the children would really feel it belonged to them.

Festivals were great occasions and involved the whole congregation. Adults and children; clergy and laity; all found the yearly Festivals exciting and a boost to their Faith and love of God.

'O Word of God above, Who fillest all in all,
Hallow this House with Thy sure love, and bless our Festival.'

17

Coming Retirement

'There will be a great need of courage, wisdom and loyalty during 1936,' said Canon Hussey in his New Year letter. One wonders how he managed to be so far-seeing! In January came the news of the death of George V and the proclamation of Edward VIII, causing the postponement of the usual parties; flags were at halfmast and special prayers were said in the Churches. The same year brought the news, more personal to St. Matthews, of the passing of Charles Eastgate. He was eighty-six and after his retirement in 1916 he had helped for some years in the parish. He was remembered with love and affection after a long life devoted to the service of God and the Catholic religion.

It was around March in 1937 that Rowden Hussey actually announced his impending retirement, in a letter published in the Parish Magazine he said: 'Many of you know that my health had not been good for several months and I have been warned to go slowly with regard to my work, and I think you ought to know that I have felt obliged to tell the Bishop and the Patron that it is my intention to resign my work at St. Matthew's in the early summer of this year.' Rowden had completed forty-eight years of devoted service to the parish and he was seventy-three years old. Lilian was fifty-seven and they had been married for thirty-five years. Rowden was leaving a flourishing church with an efficient P.C.C. and with the finances as good as they had been for some time. The churchyard had recently been extended and the stone wall and railings had been made to enclose it.

On 12th May came the coronation of King George VI, following the Abdication of Edward VIII; it was celebrated nationally with great joy and enthusiasm. At St. Matthew's the day began with a Sung Eucharist.

Later in May, it was announced that the Patron of St. Matthew's, Mr. Pickering Phipps, had offered the benefice to Walter Hussey, Rowden's younger son, who was Senior Assistant Curate at St. Mary Abbott's in Kensingston. Walter was twenty-eight, just three years older than his father had been when he first came to Kingsley and a little younger than his father had been when he was actually instituted as Vicar of the new church as its consecration in 1893. He would be returning to live in the Vicarage which had been his childhood home.

Rowden must have been proud to hand his loved parish to his son. Rowden and Lilian were to stay in Northampton in a new house on the upper side of Abington Park Crescent, a good-sized house close to the Borough boundary and looking down on the Park. The garden was spacious enough for Lilian to have her beloved roses. It was outside St. Matthew's parish but not too far, so it would be easy to keep in touch. Rowden continued to celebrate at Holy Communion on Wednesday mornings and Lilian remained President of the Mothers' Union until she died, but they managed to remain in the background except on special occasions.

Guy Brodie was also leaving, after fifteen years at St. Matthew's, to be Vicar of Brafield, and Denis Pouncey, who had replaced Charles King as organist, was off to Wells Cathedral and had himself been replaced by Philip Pfaff.

Canon Hussey was to leave the parish on 17th July, and in his Farewell Letter, said: 'No priest has ever been happier in his work than I, and it will be a hard wrench to give up the work which has been so full of happiness.' The fact that he was standing down for his own son, must have produced mixed feelings, but he commended Walter to the parish. He also said how much he owed to his wife who had been beside him for so long. It was because of her influence on her son that he based his confidence in the new Vicar!

The Interregnum only lasted a few months and the Sequestrators had the two Assistant Curates, Guy Brodie and Frederick Stallard, to maintain the services and other activities. A social evening was organised to say 'Goodbye' and make presentations to Canon and Mrs. Hussey. The Church Room was packed and there were many speeches.

The Festival was in the short Interregnum, a wonderfully sunny day, and the services were as well attended as ever. Bishop Lang celebrated at the main Eucharist and Mr. Pollock gave the final speech.

Friday evening, 1st October, was the day when the Bishop of Peterborough instituted John Walter Atherton Hussey as the second Vicar of St.

Matthew's benefice and the Induction by the Archdeacon gave him the possession of the living. The church was packed with the normal congregation and all the visitors from St. Mary Abbott's, the Vicar of that parish presented him to the Bishop in the absence of the Patron, who was too ill to attend. The long service was followed by a joyful gathering in the Church Hall. On 5th October he chaired his first P.C.C. and promised to carry on the traditions of the church.

On 8th October only a week after the Institution, came the news of the death of Pickering Phipps; strange how he had lived to see the church he had built launched on its second phase! Mr. Phipps had been the Church's founder and a most generous benefactor – a regular worshipper and a faithful Christian. On 11th October his body was taken to the church and received by both father and son, the past and present vicars, remaining before the altar for the Requiem at 7.30 a.m. and the Funeral Service at 11.00 a.m. The church was crowded and many more watched as the cortège left for the burial at Pitsford. He was seventy-six. The parish grieved with his widow and children; and for their own loss. In due course, a commemorative plaque was put into the Lady Chapel to enshrine his memory, to be followed by others in later years. Though the memory of Pickering Phipps and his family will remain as the church remains. 'Phipps' Fire-Escape' the church was sometimes called, in gentle amusement, but one might think that no one needed a fire-escape less! In October 1938, it was announced that Mrs. Phipps had transferred the patronage of the benefice to the Diocesan Board of Patronage, as a gift, the Board would, therefore, appoint future Vicars.

Walter Hussey was a modest man, not given to entertaining, though he could be effervescent and witty at parties and was good at making friends. He was not a natural, spontaneous speaker, and a slight stutter could sometimes be detected when he was under pressure. Like his father he could preach a good sermon but was nervous in anticipation. He was really a very private person, elegant and attractive (despite his pipe!) but capable of public display when necessary. He hated giving interviews but was good at drawing out the diffident. He ranged the parish on his pushbike, always stopping to walk with someone if time allowed. He treated everyone alike, with no feeling of class distinction or snobbery.

The easiest way to go forward was to go on as before, to maintain all as his father had done. Walter approved of his father's methods but he was young and new and inevitably had plenty of ideas of his own. The Young People's Fellowship was one new idea, for those who had been confirmed and were between sixteen and thirty. They met on Tuesday evenings, with outside speakers or discussions led by one of the clergy. The meetings were very successful and some serious discussions took place. Later, when the war came, and many of the young men joined up, those remaining sent regular parcels to them, with knitted comforts and other things to relieve the monotony of Forces' life.

In May it was announced that Fred Stallard was to be married and the congregation was glad to welcome his bride and take her to their hearts. Their new home was at 12 The Drive. Fred Stallard's salary was raised, enough to cover the rent. Their first child was born in August 1939. The other good news was that Malcolm Methuen Clarke was to join the parish after being ordained as a Deacon on Trinity Sunday. He had been a schoolmaster and had then trained at Cuddesdon College, Oxford. Cuddesdon was the Prayer Book Catholic College and all the students had good degrees. It provided a sound, disciplined foundation for ministry. The era of the 'Cuddesdon Curates' at St. Matthew's started in the 1930s with Edward Carroll and he was followed by others; between them they covered nearly a quarter of a century of Cuddesdon and St. Matthew's history!

There were three staff again and Walter divided the parish roughly between them: regular visiting was expected. Walter held staff meetings on Monday mornings and expected his Assistants to attend all daily services, unless it was their 'day off'; to attend Morning Prayers at the school and to make a regular practice of attending all other meetings. It was an exciting parish to work in but it was never short of things to do! The whole parish life was built on the daily Mass.

An early decision was to erect a permanent Church Hall in memory of Mr. Pickering Phipps. The War Memorial Church Room was showing serious signs of wear. Mr. Phipps had already donated a double frontage of land at the corner of Kettering Road and Collingwood Road, across from the church. An architect drew up plans and various money-raising activities were thought up.

Over the whole of 1938 there hung the threat of a European crisis, another war was looming, or was it? Hopes were raised and dashed. Neville Chamberlain talked of 'Peace in our time'. After an uneasy year, it became clear that war was inevitable. Once more the World was plunged into a conflict which was to affect everyone.

18

War

Christmas 1938 had a particularly beautiful Christmas Tree in the church, a symbol of the Family; the Human Family, the Holy Family and the Family of the Church – perhaps especially poignant as families were so soon to be disrupted. The Munich Agreement of September 1938 had brought the promise of 'Peace in our time', a promise few really believed, though they welcomed the interlude and the hope it gave.

In Northampton, the A.R.P. (Air Raid Precautions) Posts and Ambulance Centres were being set up and house to house enquiries were being made to prepare for the billeting of children should evacuation be necessary; National Service notices were circulated. Kingsley Hall, now given to the Borough, was to be used as an A.R.P. storage depot.

In March 1939, the German Army occupied Czechoslovakia and marched into Prague, and in April, the Italians invaded Albania at Easter weekend. In May, a jumbo-like barrage balloon loomed over the Racecourse, as a great attraction to children and adults alike and as the centre of a Recruitment Campaign. Then, in August, after a lovely hot summer, came the news of the invasion of Poland and on 3rd September war was declared!

During these months, Walter kept the normal liturgical calendar, following its regular pattern. Services were well attended, as people prayed that the outbreak of war would be averted. On Good Friday there had been an Ecumenical Procession of Witness in the town. There were five processions down the five main routes to the Market Square, for a simple service of hymns and prayers and an address by the Bishop of Ely. The Kettering Road procession left St. Matthew's at 7.15 p.m. and followed down Abington Street to the Town Centre.

The summer outings were enjoyed in the lovely summer. The Sunday School children went to Moulton Park; the Scouts to Skegness (with Mr.

Carroll who had started the Troop in 1931); but from the glories of the holidays, they all returned to the finality of 3rd September and the silence of the church bells. The School returned to find eight air-raid-shelters on the playground, each intended to hold fifty children and staff. Unfortunately at least two of them were water-logged and one was still roofless! The school was a Billeting Centre and the teachers and the curates were busy trying to place children and mothers with babies, in suitable homes, a tiring and somewhat heart-breaking job. Evacuation of schoolchildren had started promptly and children from London, mostly Willesden and Kilburn, later other areas, poured into the town. Mothers and babies also arrived and later, the students and staff of the L.C.C. Art College. The houses of the parish were once again being used as billets, this time mostly children and teachers. The Church opened for Special Sunday Schools for the London children on Sunday afternoons, with different arrangements for those under seven. Re-organising of classes at schools was necessary, sometimes two shifts, extra lessons out of doors, special 'outings' or in borrowed rooms including the Church Room and even the Church itself. Air-raid shelters had been built in many streets, in fact the school had to overflow into the one in Byron Street during practices. The playground was also under water after rain, until the damage to the drains, when the shelters were dug, was rectified! Over on the Racecourse, trenches were dug. School re-started in October in a moderately organised way.

Walter Hussey, Fred Stallard and Methuen Clarke, the clergy of the parish, were all young men and so offered themselves to the Bishop for Overseas or any Army Service as Chaplains, if he thought they should go, but the Bishop told them to look after the parish, particularly the evacuees, at least for the present. Some evacuee children settled well, though many had to have their billets changed. Some were soon playing with the local children and were seen on the Racecourse teaching them the Lambeth Walk! Others were homesick and miserable, children and foster-parents did not always agree, the Londoners had different habits and they did not even understand each other's dialects! Clergy and teachers had a busy job trying to sort out unhappiness and misunderstanding. Many children went home for Christmas and stayed there, but more came when the bombing of London started.

Buildings in the town were well sand-bagged, everyone carried their gasmask in its uncomfortable cardboard box, rationing was beginning, things were in short supply, khaki was everywhere, it was frightening, exciting and unreal! The expected air raids did not immediately materialise, the 'Phoney War' was in progress.

In his New Year letter of 1940, Walter said, 'Perhaps few will be sorry to see the end of 1939. It has seen so much sorrow, anxiety and evil come upon the war, facing a future of which none dare prophecy. Yet every sincere and thinking Christian must be more than ever convinced that his faith offers the one way of escape from tragedy.' A cold winter with deep snow was ahead, with all its hazards. Knitting parties were organised, squares for blankets and 'comforts' for the Forces, balaclavas and sea-boot stockings; and there were parties for the evacuee children and for the soldiers in the town. Names of men and women of the parish serving with the Forces were collected so that Newsletters could be sent out and Intercessions said daily at 6.00 p.m. mentioning them by name in rotation.

May 14th brought the formation of the Local Defence Volunteers (later the Home Guard – 'Dad's Army'), an opportunity for older people, women as well as men, and the older teenagers, to 'do their bit'. Blood donors were sought, Salvage Drives proliferated, 'Dig for Victory' included the Racecourse as well as gardens, the A.T.S. girls, living there in huts, were busy tending vegetables among their training programmes.

Nineteen forty-one also brought the problem of Church Fire-watching; the church needed a rota whereby some people were on duty all through the hours of blackout. Stirrup pumps were purchased, buckets of sand and water placed at strategic points. Sixty Watchers aged sixteen and over were required. Walter claimed that it was worse than any crossword to arrange a rota to suit everyone! There was also need of Fire-watchers for the School; the teachers all took part but more people were needed to make a longer rota. In the church, the little lobby beneath the Vestry was already an A.R.P. Post and now the Choir Room was used as well. The Watchers slept on a camp bed in turns unless there was an Air-Raid Warning.

In 1941, came a new assistant Curate to replace Fred Stallard, who left to become a Forces Chaplain after five years at St. Matthew's. David Stewart Smith was to be ordained deacon in September, he had been educated at Marlborough College and at King's College, Cambridge, and then at Cuddesdon, as had most of St. Matthew's curates. He joined on the eve of St. Matthew's Day. He was to have his special district near the Golfcourse and Kettering Road, to which area many people had moved from the town centre; many found St. Matthew's rather intimidating. Methuen Clarke had the other half of the parish, which now totalled about 12,000, the aim was to visit all, though the sick and bereaved took priority. Unexpectedly, the parish was offered the stipend of a third curate for three years. This was to be Mr. Fred Whittle, who was ordained deacon in

Fred Stallard (curate) at his farewell party in 1940.

Advent. He was also from Cuddesdon College and had done very well despite his handicap of blindness. He and David Stewart Smith were to live at 2 Broadway, until David's marriage.

St. Matthew's parish, as the whole of the civilian population, was settling down to life in wartime, coping with shortages, rationing, the blackout, Fire-watching, Home Guard duties, bad news and sleepless nights, as well as daytime work in home and factory. Women in particular were shouldering extra jobs, on the 'buses, as postwomen, in fire stations, in factories, as well as running homes, often without their husbands, and joining queues! School children, and their teachers, were inoculated against diphtheria; German Measles was rife, but everyone battled on. The Home Front was as important as any battlefield. Strange uniforms were seen in the streets and strange accents heard. It was fast becoming a way of life, the war seemed to have been going on for ever!

The clergy still visited the School, now packed with evacuees, to take Assembly at 9.00 a.m. The young deacons found this quite intimidating, especially as the children were often yawning from late and disturbed nights, double summer-time didn't help them to sleep! The St. Matthew's

Fellowship (of eighteen to twenty-five year-olds) was more encouraging as keen, young, church people, though they were being drawn away to warwork and the Forces. Confirmation classes continued, usually in the curates' homes, girls and boys still being taught in separate classes. The classes imparted and tested facts; the rote learning of the catechism, the Creed, etc., and the importance of worship; the importance of the fasting communion at 8.00 a.m. and the Solemn service, to give thanks, at 11.00 a.m., was emphasised. There was still a feeling that St. Matthew's was the best and that other churches and chapels didn't really count!

19

1943 – Jubilee Year

Christmas 1942 lacked many of the luxuries and decorations usual at that season but for once the bells were allowed to peal out. The blackout seemed rather less of a deterrent as the services were well attended. The dark church lit by just candles on the altar was deeply inspiring; a small light in a world of darkness; the light of Bethlehem in a world of sin. There was a tree, bigger than ever; the Crib in the Children's Corner and the wreaths of holly on the Chancel Screen. On the Sunday there was the usual gift-service and, on three nights before Christmas, Methuen Clarke and a group of Carol Singers braved the dark and raised £13 to be divided between the Red Cross and the Church Hall Fund, visiting selected houses in the parish.

Nineteen forty-three was to be a Special Year for St. Matthew's, the church would be fifty years old on St. Matthew's Day in September. At the Annual Parish meeting it was announced that the various Church Funds were in a healthy state and that, despite war-time difficulties, services were well attended and all the Youth Organisations were flourishing. Plans were already in hand to celebrate the fiftieth Birthday.

'We must be grateful,' said the Vicar, 'that we have suffered so little but we must beware of complacency. A parish to be fully alive must make progress.' He hoped that the Jubilee Celebrations would include a vigorous evangelistic effort.

The aim of the Jubilee celebrations was spelt out by Walter:
1. to give thanks to God for our church and all our blessings for fifty years;
2. to dedicate ourselves anew to the service of God;
3. to bring others to share and join the family of the church.

Walter Hussey had always had a great interest in music and the arts. At school he had played the trombone, though he himself said that he had few talents but a great deal of enthusiasm. When in Kensington as a curate, he had found time to visit the London Art Galleries and had managed to collect several good paintings as a basis for his own collection. He had also been to a number of concerts and said that he used music as a background to thought, as when composing a sermon. He remembered how, in years past, the Church had so often commissioned music and paintings and sculpture, and he had a great longing to do the same. Here in the Jubilee year was an opportunity which he could grasp. He had, he said, 'a wild and ambitious dream to include five projects:

1. to get a special piece of music written for the occasion;
2. to get a first-rate organist to give a recital;
3. to get a fine soloist to give a recital;
4. to get a symphony orchestra and conductor to give a concert;
5. to commission a work of art, painting or sculpture, for the church.'

As a composer, he hoped to get a relatively young man who had not yet established a great reputation, and his first thought was William Walton, but he refused. A second choice was Benjamin Britten. After some delay, he got into correspondence with Britten, who agreed to compose an anthem for the Jubilee Festival. Benjamin Britten visited Northampton to hear the choir and judge its capabilities. Eventually he decided to use some of the words of 'Rejoice in the Lamb,' recently published, by the eighteenth-century poet Christopher Smart. Christopher Smart was a deeply religious man but with a strange and somewhat unbalanced mind; some parts of the poem are chaotic but there are also flashes of genius. The passages chosen by Britten, showed the drawing together of all Creation in Praise of God; a strange poem but strangely moving. A booklet was prepared to give facts about the Church and to give details of the Festival Cantata. There were to be ten sections, the first setting the theme; the second giving examples of Old Testament personages joining with an animal in praising God. The third and final sections are Hallelujahs, while the others illustrate nature praising God, using a cat and a mouse; flowers and musical instruments. Britten himself conducted the final rehearsals and the first performance. The question of a fee was raised, but Britten said that he would get his rewards from later performing fees and the sale of sheet music. A fee of £25 was agreed.

Michael Tippett agreed to write a fanfare for the entrance of the Bishop and this was adapted to be played by the Northamptonshire Regimental Band. On St. Matthew's Day the preacher was to be Dr. E. S. Woods, the Bishop of Lichfield, and the brother of Theodore Woods, who had been Bishop of Peterborough. The service was to be followed by the first performance of the new Cantata. It was a fantastic occasion of great reverence.

At 3.00 p.m. there was the Children's Service and Procession. All processions were carefully practised and strict standards imposed. The choir boys wore black cassocks with white ruffs, they had to wear black shoes; as they approached the chancel steps they had to maintain a steady pace and go up the steps slowly so that no one wobbled. It was important not to crowd the crucifer. The choir members processed in matching pairs, carefully arranged, with arm's-length gaps. The choir practised three evenings a week in the 'dungeon' under the Choir Vestry. New choir probationers, mostly ten-year-olds, were enrolled from the Church School but only just over half actually qualified as choristers.

At Evensong on St. Matthew's Day the Lord Bishop of Grimsby, once the Vicar of St. Mary's, Far Cotton, was to preach. Despite the war, it was decided to hold the luncheon, and there had been urgent requests for 'points' to buy food, or for tins of suitable meat. In the Church Room 200 people enjoyed their meal and the guests included five former curates. It was almost like old times!

To parallel the celebrations, an Exhibition was held in the Church Room to show how the Church had grown and to show how all the organisations had developed: the displays arranged by the various church groups – 'The Church Arrives'; 'The Church as Builders'; 'The Church and Music'; 'The Church and Art'; 'The Church and the Prayer Book'. Over 700 people visited it and it was well commended, the visitors being from other churches, as well as the Anglican ones.

Canon Hussey made a suggestion of a practical way of celebrating, he thought that all the congregation could collect fifty coins towards the Church Hall Fund, fifty pence, fifty shillings, etc., as far as people could go; the money being put into War Savings until the War was over and a new Hall could be built.

Three Organ Recitals were arranged; on the Sunday in the octave, 250 people heard Dr. Thalben-Ball give a memorable recital and on the Saturday 2nd October the B.B.C. Symphony orchestra, who were based at Bedford under Sir Adrian Boult, gave a concert. This had been very difficult to organise, and Walter only succeeded after many letters and visits, and his absolute refusal to take 'no' for an answer. Eventually, St. Matthew's church was used as a 'studio' from which the concert was broadcast.

Later in October, there was a recital of vocal and piano music by Benjamin Britten and Peter Pears, the tenor; the Cantata was performed again on that occasion. On Sunday 31st October the B.B.C. broadcast 'Rejoice in the Lamb' on the Home Service, the first in a series on 'Church Music of Today'.

The last of Walter's projects was to provide a work of art for the church. This was to be a statue of Madonna and Child by the sculptor Henry Moore. The statue was to be the gift of Canon Rowden Hussey, though the idea was really Walter's. Walter had seen drawings of Henry Moore's work in 1942 and had been impressed by them. He discussed the idea of commissioning from him with Harold Williamson, the Principal of the Chelsea College of Art, which had been evacuated to Northampton and was based on the College near the Racecourse. Harold Williamson was able to introduce Walter Hussey to Henry Moore and after much correspondence and various visits, drawings were produced and small clay models prepared. There were various possible variations on the basic design and Henry Moore suggested carving it from a two-ton block of brown Hornton stone to be obtained from Banbury quarry. It would take six weeks of hard work and would cost from £300 to £350 depending on the costs of delivery.

Walter showed the clay models to his father and then to the P.C.C., and opinions were obtained from Sir Kenneth Clark, Director of the National Gallery; Eric Newton, the writer, and Dr. Bell, Bishop of Chichester. Walter was not prepared to have his idea stymied by some Diocesan Authority who knew nothing about modern art! Surprisingly, the P.C.C. agreed almost unanimously to accept the gift and on which model they preferred. The commission was to find fulfilment!

During the weeks of carving, Walter was able to visit Henry Moore's studio and was even able to chip off a few pieces of stone himself.

It was January 1944 when the carving was completed and the unveiling was arranged for Saturday 29th January. For various reasons this had to be postponed to 19th February. The great day arrived, cold and rather dreary, the congregation assembled, including various local dignitaries, the organist and the choir, the Bishop and Canon Hussey, and the clergy of St. Matthew's. The statue was duly shrouded and everyone waited eagerly for it to be unveiled. The unveiling was to be done by Sir Kenneth Clark, followed by a service of Dedication by the Bishop, Dr. Blagden. There

The Henry Moore 'Madonna and Child' (1944) framed by the magnificent wrought iron screen surrounding the Lady Chapel.

had been bombs on London the night before and the Euston Line had been blocked. The London party, Sir Kenneth and Lady Clark; Mr. and Mrs. Moore and Mr. and Mrs. Graham Sutherland, were seriously delayed; the train, unheated and corridorless, was shunted into a siding for three hours, and they didn't arrive until 3.30 p.m., very cold and hungry. The congregation, also getting colder, had listened to an organ recital and then to a performance of 'Rejoice in the Lamb', earlier in the programme than had been intended. The Bishop, who was not really much in sympathy with the occasion anyway, got cross and impatient with the delay, and Methuen Clarke had to use all his soothing powers. As soon as the visitors arrived, the service began. The statue was unveiled after Sir Kenneth had given an inspiring address; the Dedication ceremony took place and, despite all the delays, it all went off reasonably well. A great many people viewed the statue that day and on the days following. The reaction was *not* always favourable!

20

Criticism

People flocked to the church to see the statue and it soon became the talk of Northampton and further afield. Probably the people of St. Matthew's had their reservations, it seems likely that Rowden himself, and certainly the Bishop, were a bit doubtful about it. It seems rather surprising that the Faculty was granted to put it in the church. The chairman of the Diocesan Advisory Board was Bishop Norman Lang and those who knew Walter trusted his judgement and believed his suggestion that regular viewing would bring a deeper understanding of the work.

People who were not of the congregation, maybe not even churchpeople at all, had very definite ideas. Letters began to pour into the offices of the local paper, the *Northampton Chronicle and Echo*. Many were distinctly hostile to the statue; many obviously felt threatened by it and many were quite hysterical in their protestations:

'An insult to our intelligence. I always thought of the Madonna as a plain and a gentle woman.'

'An insult to every woman, this will disgust thousands of right-minded people.'

'A grotesque portrayal. It warps a mental picture of an ideal which has remained unchanged for 2,000 years.'

'I cannot understand any sane artist devoting time and trouble to the making of an image out of all proportion and perspective. To my normal mind it is revolting.'

'A nightmare creation.'

'We think of the Madonna as an ordinary but noble specimen of womanhood and not as a physical freak.'

Though others said that 'courage and judgement' were shown in the choice of the statue.

An article by Tom Driberg in *Reynolds News* ended: 'as was no doubt foreseen by the courageous and intelligent clergymen concerned, some of the worthy burghers of Northampton were more disturbed by the true originality of this work than they would have been by a pretty, conventional, plaster statue painted in blue, white and pink!'

It seems unbelievable today, that people could have felt so strongly that the work was crude, even disgusting, and that it degraded a sacred subject. One wonders what they would have thought if they could then have foreseen some of Henry Moore's later works! Despite the opinions of many art experts, which were published in articles, the ordinary person felt that their opinion was the correct one, as, to them, it was. One wonders how many changed their minds and if they later wondered at their own first impressions. Only four years later, speaking in a European broadcast, Sir Eric Maclagan described the statue as 'the finest religious work of art of our time'.

Whatever people's opinions, St. Matthew's had acquired a masterpiece which was recently the centrepiece of a London Exhibition of the works of Henry Moore, all due to the far-seeing 'ambitious dream' of Walter Hussey and the generosity of Rowden Hussey to his much loved church.

21

The End of the War

As the excitement of the Jubilee and the establishing of the Madonna and Child statue began to subside, St. Matthew's returned to wartime drabness, though there was a silent hope that the end of the war might be in sight. When D-Day arrived and the invasion was launched on 6th June 1944 there were fresh hopes; then the United States Forces and the Free French invaded from the Mediterranean and, despite set-backs, the Rhine was crossed, Paris and the Low Countries liberated and, eventually, the Armistice signed in May 1945, followed by the surrender of the Japanese in September.

Although peace was a great occasion for rejoicing and thanksgiving and there was much excitement with flags and decorations and street parties; the bells could ring and the lights were on again and those in the Forces would be coming home; it wasn't like 1918, when people really believed that a 'world for heroes' had been won and that things would return to their pre-war state. Just as the Second War had come gradually, so the end was gradual, it was months before some came home; rationing did not eventually end until 1954. The atomic bomb had probably been the immediate cause of the end of the war in the east. At first there was a feeling that it had been necessary, then people began to think about the horror of the forces thus unleashed. Peace was not to be easy, nothing would ever really be the same again.

Plans for a St. Christopher's Memorial Home for Old People were being discussed even before the war ended. The idea was to build a series of cottages in a garden, with a chapel and a small nursing home for the sick. A site near Spinney Hill was thought possible, though in the end, Abington Rectory was the nucleus of the project. This was a project for the whole of Northampton and each parish was to raise part of the

£100,000 envisaged. St. Matthew's set itself to raise £1,500, the cost of two cottages and a scheme of 2s. 6d. a month was started for this purpose.

St. Matthew's Day was to have Bishop Carpenter-Garnier, Bishop of Colombo until 1938, who had since been Principal of St. Boniface College, Salisbury; the Dean of Peterborough, the Very Rev'd. Noel Christopherson was to preach on the Sunday; he had been Archdeacon of Colombo when the Bishop was there. The Bishop of Lincoln, the Rt. Rev'd. H. A. Shelton, was to preach at the Sunday Evensong. The 1944 Festival was to have a motet composed by Edmund Rubbra, a setting for 'The Revival', a poem by the mystical seventeenth-century poet Henry Vaughan. The poem bids us open our hearts to the Light and Spirit of God, that as the sun and warm air of spring revive the trees and the flowers, so the Light may bring new life and love. Edmund Rubbra was born in Northampton in 1901 and had been taught by Charles King on the organ of St. Matthew's Church. Later he had gone to the Royal College of Music and studied under Gustav Holst. Another honour for St. Matthew's and another young, up-and-coming composer!

There was also to be played, by Mr. Barker and the Northampton Regimental Band, *'Salvum fac Populum Tuum'* by Widor, for organ, brass and tympani, to greet the procession of Bishops. On St. Matthew's Day, there was to be a recital by Peter Pears, the tenor, Benjamin Britten, pianist, and Norina Semino, on the 'cello, and the choir was to sing once again 'Rejoice in the Lamb' conducted by Benjamin Britten.

Despite war-time conditions the church was decked with red and white dahlias, gold chrysanthemums and Michaelmas Daisies. The Festival was more relaxed and the congregation was delighted that Canon Hussey was there once again.

This year, for the first time at St. Matthew's, there was to be a Midnight Eucharist on Christmas Eve, the first celebration for Christmas to be at midnight, the service to be preceded by a Procession and the Blessing of the Crib. The communicants were told that they must prepare themselves prayerfully and not come straight from a party, and they were expected to fast for at least five hours beforehand. There were over 300 communicants at the service, which persuaded Walter that the innovation was justified.

The Armistice in June 1945 was signed just before the Summer Fête. A Victory Social was a great success and the fête was much enjoyed despite the rain. It had been hoped that when the war was over, Mr. Pfaff would return as Organist, but he decided to resign. Charles Barker and Charles Bull had done a magnificent job during the war years but it was decided that a more permanent appointment should be made and, from January

Jack and the Beanstalk pantomime, Christmas 1948. Jack and Jill were played by Marjorie Guilbert and Joy Teasdale respectively.

1946, Alec Wyton was appointed. He had been Organ Scholar at Exeter College, Oxford and then sub-organist at Christchurch, Oxford. He had great ability and experience and was a strict disciplinarian. Mr. Pfaff became Music Tutor Organiser to Lindsey and Holland Rural Community Council in Lincolnshire.

It was marvellous to have no more blackouts or fire-watching and to have evening activities without problems; Church bells could be rung, but it was found that the ringing apparatus needed attention and it was decided that the bells needed to be re-cast and re-hung at a cost of £2,000, in the meanwhile a single bell was used. The heating system also needed renewing at still further cost! It was also sad when the last of the evacuees returned to London. They were much missed and many returned again to visit friends and 'foster parents'; some even returned to make Northampton their home.

Walter had given a talk on the B.B.C. European Service on 1st March in which he talked of the attempt to reforge the ancient link between the Church and the Arts and the success of the fiftieth Anniversary Celebrations and, particularly, the installation of the Henry Moore Madonna and Child.

At that time he had started a voluntary fund for financing further such projects; this had been growing steadily, his mother had given a generous donation and he already had another ambitious project in mind.

Among the party who had had that long, cold journey from London, for the unveiling of the statue, had been Mr. and Mrs. Graham Sutherland. When visiting Henry Moore, Walter had raised his idea of a painting for the South Transept. Henry Moore had thought that Graham Sutherland would be a good choice for such a painting. At the unveiling, despite the lack of time, Walter managed to get Sutherland into the empty church and to broach the idea, suggesting 'The Agony in the Garden' would be a suitable theme to balance the Madonna and Child in the North Transept. Sutherland showed interest and thought that he could paint such a picture for £300 to £350. After much correspondence and several meetings, he decided that it would be a challenge to paint a Crucifixion; that most tragic of themes but with the promise of salvation.

Walter decided to test his idea on the P.C.C. and after much talking, he could be very persuasive when he wanted, it was decided that such a picture should be commissioned. In August 1946, Graham Sutherland visited Northampton, studied the church and decided to accept the commission, though he pointed out the practical difficulties in obtaining materials, particularly in obtaining canvas or hardboard of sufficient size and of making a stretcher and a frame of such dimensions. Nevertheless, he continued to think about the picture, made many sketches of thorns and, in September, produced a large sketch to show Walter, photographs of which were brought back for the P.C.C. There were reservations over some aspects of the sketch and a long discussion. Opinions had also been sought from a number of experts. Sir Kenneth Clarke wrote: 'the large sketch made a great impression on me. I thought it quite worthy to be placed with Moore's Madonna and having the same relation to the great art of the past. Just as Moore's Madonna, although entirely modern, was obviously in the tradition of Romanesque sculpture, so Sutherland's Crucifixion is the successor to the Crucifixion of Grunewald (the Isenheim Altarpiece) and the early Italians.'

The P.C.C. decided to go ahead. Sutherland was able to obtain suitable board, though he needed to rent a garage to accommodate the eight-foot by seven-foot painting. It was necessary again to obtain a Faculty from the Diocesan Advisory Board. When the Faculty for the Madonna was obtained, the Chairman of the Board was Bishop Lang, a great friend of

Graham Sutherland's 'Crucifixion' painting, hung in the South Transept in 1946.

Canon Hussey and of St. Matthew's. By now, the Chairman was Lord Spencer, who was known not to like 'Modern Art'. However, he evaded the issue by declaring that a movable painting didn't need a Faculty. This was not correct but by the time this had been resolved the painting was already in the church. The Chancellor allowed the painting to stay while a Faculty Citation was pinned to the Church door and, as no objections were received, the picture stayed!

The unveiling was fixed for 16th November 1946. The painting arrived on the 5th, accompanied by the artist who spent six days, behind screens, ensuring that the tones were correct for the lighting of the church. Once more Graham Sutherland enjoyed staying at the Vicarage, spending evenings in conversation with Walter, and generally being fussed over by Mrs. Cotton, Walter's loyal and efficient housekeeper, whose husband helped to keep the Vicarage garden in order.

This time the unveiling ceremony went off smoothly and, although there were public comments, there was nothing as traumatic as in 1944. Interestingly, when the picture was finally revealed it was found that some parts, which had caused reservations at the sketch stage, had been omitted by Sutherland in the finished picture. In many ways people found the picture shocking and distorted, but since the war had ended they, like Sutherland himself, had seen pictures of Belsen and other Concentration Camp victims and so the shock was seen as appropriate to the subject. Christ experienced human suffering and most people had never seen suffering of the holocaust level before. Graham Sutherland said that he wanted the picture to be *real* and to show the agony and suffering of war in the agony and suffering of Christ.

There was some feeling among the congregation that the children would find the picture frightening, but this proved to be an unnecessary fear!

Eric Newton writing in the *Sunday Times* said: 'Turning back from the Crucifixion to Moore's serene Madonna, one realises how eloquently these two artists have made paint and stone speak of things that are so little connected with the material world of the eye.'

The aim of Art in the Church should be to adorn God's House with a worthy offering of Man's creative spirit, while conveying some aspect of Christian truth.

This was what Walter Hussey hoped to achieve at St. Matthew's and time seems to be agreeing that he has done so.

22

People

Lilian Mary Hussey, who had been such a loyal support to her husband Canon Rowden Hussey, and then to her son, as Vicars of St. Matthew's, throughout her forty-five years of married life, died on 30th October 1946, aged sixty-six. She had been ill for some months and now her suffering was over. She lived long enough to hear details of the fifty-third Festival but not long enough to hear of the unveiling of the Crucifixion, though Walter told her all about it during his daily visits. Lilian loved St. Matthew's as she loved her home and her family. She was quietly unobtrusive and some people found her difficult to know. She had a strong sense of justice and right, but she had a sense of humour and had great sympathy with those in trouble. She was an expert gardener and had acted as a judge at the Chelsea Flower Show; she was a Fellow of the Royal Horticultural Society. Her love of flowers and her garden, a love she passed on to Walter, was shown in the flowers she arranged in the church and the care she had shown in the efforts to make part of the churchyard into a garden. Her garden at 66 Abington Park Crescent was a picture at all times.

She was survived by her husband, her sons and her two sisters, though her brothers had predeceased her. The funeral at St. Matthew's was well attended and was taken by the Archdeacon of Northampton, the Venerable C. J. Grimes, who was assisted by the Rev'd. Methuen Clarke; with Alec Wyton at the organ. She was cremated at Milton Crematorium and her ashes placed within the Lady Chapel of the church. Later, Canon Hussey gave oak kneelers for the chapel in her memory. In her will she left £1,000 to the church, as later, did her husband.

Mr. and Mrs. Fred Whittle left St. Matthew's in February 1947 to go to West Molesey. In June he was replaced by John Wolfe Walker, coming from Cuddesdon College after ordination at Peterborough.

The parish had not seen much of Mrs. Alice Phipps since the death of her husband in 1937, though she had continued to show interest and was always generous to appeals. Recently, she had moved to live nearer the church, at the corner of The Broadway and Park Avenue North, so she had been able to attend some services, although essentially housebound; she looked forward to visits from the clergy and particularly Canon Hussey in his retirement. Now eighty-six years old, she died in November 1948 and, after a moving service, was buried with her husband at Pitsford. She had always been a most generous benefactor of the church built as a memorial to her father-in-law.

Canon Rowden Hussey survived his wife by three years, and died, aged eighty-five, on 23rd February 1949. A huge congregation was in the church to say 'Farewell' to one of the most outstanding figures in the diocese. At the Requiem, said by the Vicar, his son, the coffin was covered with the pall and his Canon's crucifix and stole; the funeral service at 10.30 a.m. was 'not to mourn but to give thanks'. There was a full choir and many clergy from other parishes, as well as representatives from many local interests. In the Spring sunshine, the Archdeacon; the Rev'd. Christopher Hussey, his older son, and the Rev'd. Methuen Clarke accompanied the Vicar to the Crematorium. Rowden's ashes were placed next to those of his wife in the Lady Chapel.

It was over sixty years since Rowden Hussey was ordained and for sixty of those years he had lived in Northampton. He had great vision and the ability to inspire others, and he had a tremendous capacity for hard work. Since his retirement, he had raised money for a Church House in Northampton; for a chapel at the hospital and had endowed a second minor canonry at Peterborough. He had made friends all over the country.

In May, Walter Hussey was installed as a Non-Residentiary Canon of Peterborough Cathedral, into the same stall his father had occupied. It was a well-deserved honour. In 1950 he, like his father, was made Rural Dean for Northampton.

More changes were in store. In November 1949, Methuen Clarke, who had been with Walter practically all of his time at St. Matthew's, was off to be Vicar of All Hallows, Wellingborough; he preached his farewell sermon on 20th November and Alec Wyton had accepted the post of the first Director of Music at the Cathedral School at Dallas, Texas, U.S.A.

On 5th November the new Bishop of Peterborough, the Rt. Rev'd. Spencer Leeson, was enthroned at the Cathedral. The new Bishop had been called to the Bar, been a Private Secretary to the Parliamentary

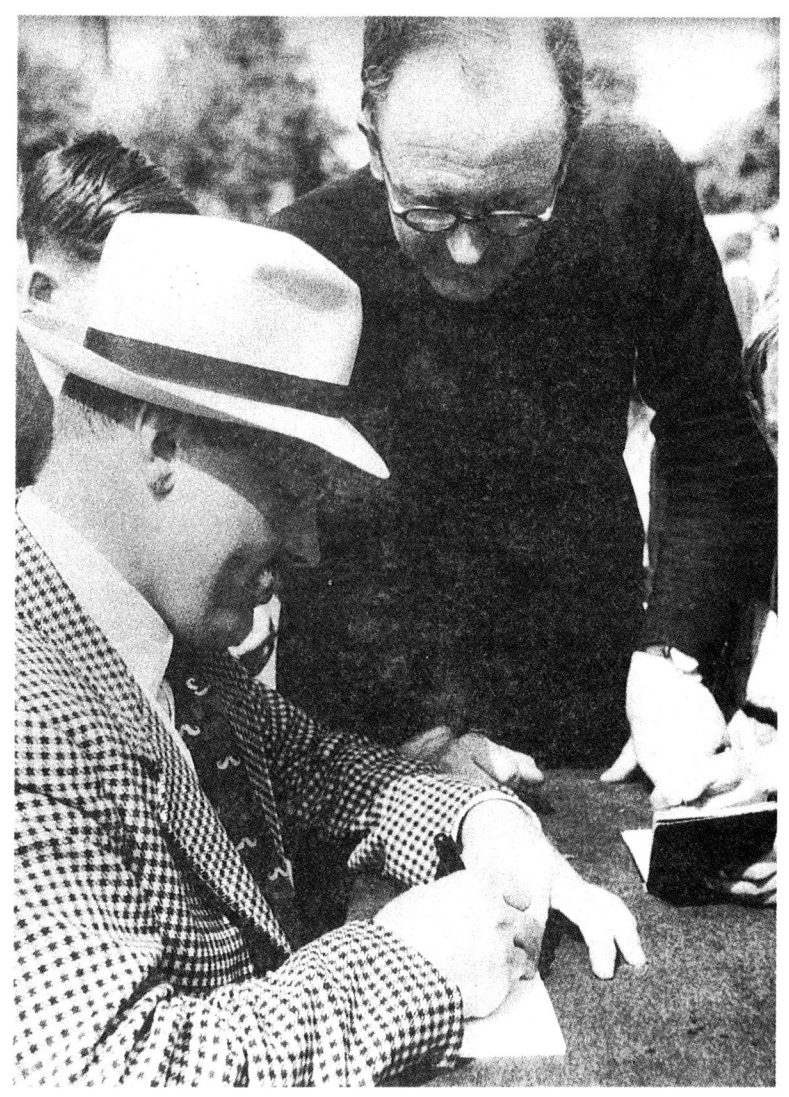

Walter Hussey having his autograph book signed by comedian Jimmy Edwards, who opened the church fete in 1947.

Secretary to the Board of Education, Headmaster of Merchant Taylor's School and then of Winchester College. He had been ordained in 1939 and had later been Rector of St. Mary's, Southampton. He was fifty-six, highly intelligent and a good mixer, stating, as a priority, his intention to visit all the parishes of the diocese in his first year.

In June 1950 came the new curate, David Jenkins, to join the other new boy, Robert Joyce, who was only twenty-two but had the highest qualifications and recommendations for the post of Organist and Choirmaster. David Jenkins was from Cuddesdon, like most of his predecessors, had been to Rugby School and Corpus Christi, and then served as a sub-lieutenant in the Royal Navy. He was at St. Matthew's for four years and then went to be Chaplain at the Woodward Foundation School at Hurstpierpoint in Sussex. He was replaced by Hewlett Thompson, a grandson of Canon Donaldson of Westminster Abbey, and the son of the Medical Officer at the Duke of York's School at Dover.

After his ordination, Hewlett Thompson was driven back from Peterborough by Canon Walter Hussey in his Riley car, and lodged at 41 The Vale with Mrs. Langley. The next day at the staff meeting, he was told to start at the first house in Kettering Road and work along door to door. He did this for twelve months, an interesting and instructive experience! However, curates usually found it better to visit one house in each terrace, so they got known and to know the area! In September, he experienced his first Festival, acting as Deacon at the Solemn Eucharist, which was to Schubert in G. Then he sang Evensong. Canon Hussey was a perfectionist, but it was a lasting experience for the future, as was the experience of meeting the visiting Bishops and other distinguished visitors. After the Festival he was able to go north to Westmoreland and marry Joy Taylor. They returned to live at 12 The Drive. The Mackintosh family who had rented it during the war had now left and the house was again free to be used as a curate-house, the rent being £50 a year!

Also in 1954, on 11th December, the parish was saddened to hear of the death in Watford, aged ninety-two, of the Rev'd. Leonard Pollock, who had been the first curate of St. Matthew's from 1893 to 1896. He had been a regular attender at Festivals and had attended the Diamond Jubilee Festival the year before.

It was in April 1955 when Walter Hussey was appointed Dean of Chichester Cathedral. It was impossible to think of St. Matthew's without a Canon Hussey, Walter had been there for eighteen years as Vicar. In his book *Patron of Art* he confessed that he 'had always felt that the most desirable job in the Church of England would be Dean of an ancient and beautiful Cathedral, preferably not too far from London'. He was encouraged to accept and received a very warm welcome there.

In the Magazine, Walter recorded his last plans for St. Matthew's, hoping they would be completed before he left. Firstly, new albs for the servers, with apparelled amices and girdles; secondly, a Crib designed and made by Gordon Pemble, a young artist recommended by John Piper and thirdly, a set of vestments designed by John Piper.

His going was a great shock to his parishioners and even to his curates, Hewlett Thompson had only been with him for nine months, but despite personal fears, they all shared the joy of the appointment.

Walter was to leave for Chichester in June, accompanied by Mr. and Mrs. Cotton, who would continue to look after him there. He was to be installed on 30th June and a coach-load of St. Matthew's people went down for the great occasion. A farewell party took place in the Church Room, when Walter was presented with a large cheque and he was to have a painting of the east end of the church painted for him by John Piper.

His last sermon as Vicar was on Sunday 19th June 1955 and he talked of the Sung Eucharist being the centre of the life of the church. That the 'purpose of coming together in the service was the worship of God, and to that everything else should be subordinated. What was done through eye and ear to help the worship had to be the best possible, always striving to improve.'

'All praise to God for the blessings He gives to this place.'

Once more, this was the end of an era!

23

Music at St. Matthew's

(This chapter owes a great deal to the book by Michael Nicholas,
Muse at St. Matthew's – to whom I am greatly indebted,
– which I recommend everyone to read.)

In 1890, the first organist, in the iron church in Byron Street, was John Eads, and he it was who started the musical tradition, but throughout most of Rowden Hussey's time, the organist and choirmaster was, as already explained, Charles King. Charles King died in office in 1934, only three years before Rowden retired. The great feature of Charles King's time, in addition to the growth and the growing experience of the choir, was the series of Organ Recitals, many by Mr. King himself but others by well-known organists.

Denys Pouncey came to St. Matthew's in June 1934 from being Deputy Organist at St. John's College, Cambridge. At first he was hesitant to accept as there was a lot of work needing to be done on the organ, which had not been cleaned since 1915. The organ was originally given by Mrs. Phipps, widow of the Pickering Phipps in whose memory the church was built. Throughout her life, she paid for its tuning and for any other expenses, and, after her death, her eldest daughter had continued to meet the organ expenses until she too died, in 1926. There had been problems since 1922 when it was first electrically powered. After consideration, he decided to accept the post, and lent the money to the parish for the organ to be restored to its normal excellent state. He only stayed until October 1936 when he was appointed to Wells Cathedral, but during his two years he founded the Bach Choir. There was a reference to such a choir in 1922, when the P.C.C. gave permission for it to use the Church Room for practices, recognising it as a 'parish organisation'. But the group was formed from within the Church Choir by Charles King and was 'to give periodic renderings of Bach's music in church'. The new Bach Choir, as founded by Denys Pouncey, was restricted to thirty to begin with, and held the first concert on Palm Sunday with a varied programme which was a great success. It was altogether more ambitious and had a wider scope. Although young, Denys Pouncey had very high standards and was quite an exacting taskmaster, his re-organisation of the choir was not appreciated by all and some choir members left. The problem was taken to Canon Hussey who, though not a musician himself, loyally supported his new choirmaster, though the stress did not help the heart problems from which he was beginning to suffer.

Philip Pfaff replaced Denys Pouncey, also coming from Cambridge. He took over both the Church Choir and the Bach Choir, which usually gave its concerts in the Carnegie Hall (now the Local Room in the Central Library) or the Guildhall in Northampton, and a Bach Orchestra was assembled in October 1937 at which Malcom Arnold was the solo trumpeter. Unfortunately, Philip's good work came to an end when the war came and he joined the Royal Air Force.

Soon after his appointment Rowden Hussey retired and was replaced as Vicar by his son Walter Hussey, and it was under Walter that much more variety was introduced into the Recitals for which the church was already famous. In 1940, Harold Craxton gave a piano recital and in 1941 Alfred de Reyghere played a concert of violin sonatas with Harold Craxton accompanying. In the following year, Guy Weitz's Organ Recital was broadcast.

The great highlight came in the Jubilee year of 1943 when Benjamin Britten wrote 'Rejoice in the Lamb' as a Jubilee Cantata and, as already explained, other concerts were arranged with the B.B.C. Symphony Orchestra, under Sir Adrian Boult, and Recitals were given by George Thalben-Ball, Peter Pears and Benjamin Britten.

The great success of the Jubilee Festival started the tradition of obtaining a special composition or recital for subsequent Festivals and, after the success of 1943, many composers and performers were very ready to offer their services.

In 1944, Edmund Rubbra, in Army uniform, conducted his newly composed motet 'The Revival' as an introit. In 1945, the composer of the Festival Anthem was Lennox Berkeley, a work described by him as portraying 'the desire for eternal happiness' with a hymn of praise to God; words from a Latin hymn and poems by George Herbert and Henry Vaughan. This was described in *Muse at St. Matthew's* 'as a work with many beautiful moments and a treble solo of delightful and succulent simplicity'. It was still being performed forty-five years later. Lennox Berkeley was a great friend of Benjamin Britten and the two became great friends of St. Matthew's!

Throughout the war, Charles Barker and Charles Ball did most valuable work and the choir, despite the problems of wartime (they had practised in the room under the Vestry, also used as an A.R.P. post and by the firewatchers, which was dark and rather scruffy), had risen to many occasions, even giving a broadcast recital in 1945.

When Philip Pfaff resigned, Charles Barker decided he would prefer to be assistant organist, so Alec Wyton was appointed. Alec had been at Northampton Grammar School and was well known to many, including Charles Barker. He had gone to Exeter College and later had become assistant organist at Christ Church, Oxford. He was a strict disciplinarian and had a real flair for choir training as well as being an excellent organist. The boys were still recruited mainly from the Church School and the standard rarely passed more than half the probationers into the actual choir.

Early in 1946, Alec Wyton took the choir to St. Bartholomew the Great, at Smithfield, to sing three commissioned anthems and also Britten's Festival 'Te Deum'. His first Festival was another great occasion. At the Sung Eucharist the choir began with Vittoria's 'Ecce Sacerdos Magnus'; the service was sung to Ireland in C and was followed by the new Prelude and Fugue on a Theme of Vittoria, for Organ solo, composed for the day by Benjamin Britten; then by Finzi's 'Lo, the Full, Final Sacrifice', a large-scale anthem with words taken from Richard Crashaw's free translations of two ancient Latin hymns. Then, after the Festival luncheon, there was a programme of 'Holy Music and Poetry', when W. H. Auden's 'Litany and Anthem for St. Matthew's Day' was read by Valentine Dyall (known to most as the Man in Black); his wonderful voice was listened to by a fascinated audience, even the choirboys were enchanted! Other poems were by Jeremy Taylor, George Herbert and others. The choir sang 'Rejoice in the Lamb' (becoming a tradition of its own) and Britten's Festival 'Te Deum'. In November of that year, the choir gave another broadcast recital.

The Bach Choir, started by Denys Pouncey, was revived by Alec Wyton and, in June 1946, a concert was given and he announced his intention of the choir performing, in time, all Bach's major works! The Christmas Oratorio, with C. D. Cunningham at the organ, was performed in December and the St. John Passion on Palm Sunday, 1947, with the re-assembled Bach Orchestra.

A rehearsal of the Northampton Bach Choir conducted by Alec Wyton (nearest the camera), who was also organist and choirmaster.

Alec Wyton also assembled a small group of men and women, the St. Matthew's Singers, to sing Bach's 'Choral Preludes' from the Minstrel's Gallery of the church. 'The St. Matthew Passion' was given in the next two years.

Carol Concerts given by the Bach Choir from 1948 were justly famous in Northampton, the standards were high and special soloists were employed. These concerts were also great fun and enjoyed by 'house-full' audiences.

In Holy Week 1947, the choir performed Rossini's 'Stabat Mater' and in the following year, Pergolesi's 'Stabat Mater' and Fauré's 'Requiem'. Brahm's 'Requiem' was sung in July 1948, with Jean Buck (soprano) and Kenneth Tudor (bass) as soloists. A series of broadcast organ recitals brought distinguished organists to the church and brought the church to the attention of the wider world.

It was in 1946 that Walter Hussey first wrote to the Norwegian soprano Kirsten Flagstad, asking if she would sing in the church. The letter eventually reached her and in her answer (written *en route* for America) she said she would be glad to do so. A letter from her Manager quoted her usual fee as 300 guineas but enquired what could be paid. Walter Hussey guaranteed 100 guineas! Eventually a programme was selected and she declared herself happy to be accompanied by Harold Craxton; he was a friend of Methuen Clarke, and had given other recitals at St. Matthew's, and he only charged a nominal fee!

Kirsten Flagstad flew to London on 1st July 1947 and arrived in Northampton the following day. The enthusiasm of Methuen Clarke in selling programmes produced a full church, although her name was not then widely known in this country. Her programme was greatly appreciated, ending with 'Ocean, Thou Mighty Monster' from *Oberon* by Weber, which Walter had persuaded her to sing. This was a concert, not a service, but it was not the custom to applaud in church; Kirsten Flagstad ended her performance with a restrained bow to the audience and everyone spontaneously stood, silently, and bowed back.

Mme. Flagstad endeared herself to her audience and also to Walter's housekeeper, Mrs. Cotton, who found her very friendly and ready to do her own ironing, so they had pleasant chats in the Vicarage kitchen. Mme. Flagstad returned in 1948, exactly twelve months later, to give a second

Walter Hussey (vicar), on right, welcoming the operatic soprano Kirsten Flagstad in 1948.

concert, again accompanied by Harold Craxton, when again she sang the *Oberon* aria, the last time she ever sang it! Another achievement for Walter and St. Matthew's.

In 1949, as already mentioned, Alex Wyton left for the United States of America, a post leading soon to his being organist at the Cathedral Church of St. John the Divine in New York. A great loss to St. Matthew's but the inevitable result of employing such highly talented musicians.

Robert Joyce replaced Alec Wyton. He was already making his mark as an organist for B.B.C. recitals and, at his first Festival in 1950, there was a special setting of the 150th Psalm by Malcolm Arnold 'Laudata Dominum'; and an Organ Recital by Boris Orde from King's College, Cambridge.

Nineteen fifty-three was Coronation Year and also the Diamond Jubilee of St. Matthew's. John Piper designed a new magazine cover, using 'an angel with the face of man', the symbol of St. Matthew, from a medieval church window. At the Festival Solemn Eucharist the setting of the service was Mozart's 'Coronation Mass in C', accompanied by Robert Joyce on the organ, and a full orchestral accompaniment as written by Mozart, by the Boyd Neal Orchestra, conducted by Clarence Raybould. Later there was an orchestral recital, with Colin Horsley at the piano.

Robert Joyce taught music at Cherry Orchard School when it opened in 1955. He also taught many individual pupils both piano and organ. He was very popular and so everyone was disappointed when he was appointed to Llandaff Cathedral in 1958, though, of course, they were delighted for him. He was replaced by John Bertalot in November, the gap being covered by Charles Barker. John Bertalot was to remain for six years.

In his book *Muse at St. Matthew's* Michael Nicholas points out four distinguished features in John Bertalot's work. One, his work with the choir and his schemes to train the boys. Then, the enlargement of the Bach Choir, so that large-scale works could be undertaken. Thirdly, he re-founded the St. Matthew's Singers and encouraged the Laurence Lloyd Singers (formed by Michael Laurence Taylor and Stephen Lloyd Meakins); and fourthly, he organised concerts in church, forming them into an annual subscription series so that a loyal following was built up. He was described as a 'ball of fire' – he taught part-time at Trinity High School and had a great flair for choir training. He had a part to play in all the musical activities of the town. He organised a performance of the 'Messiah' with about 300 singers, and he took the St. Matthew's Singers all round the country. He left in 1964 to go to Blackburn Cathedral.

Michael Nicholas came to St. Matthew's in 1965 and wrote *Muse at St. Matthew's* for the seventy-fifth Anniversary; the book should be read for the detail and detailed comment on the musical traditions of St. Matthew's.

24

A New Vicar – 1955

The interregnum was short but gave time for everyone to speculate about a new vicar, someone they did not know, a strange position for St. Matthew's parish which had had father and son only for over sixty years; for a generation and more!

It was said of Canon Rowden Hussey that when he returned to the parish after even a brief absence, he would do seven home visits before he could rest! Canon Walter Hussey had put St. Matthew's 'on the map' and brought a pride of achievement, particularly in music and the arts, and in the high standard of services. In the new Vicar, the parish gained a pastor and a missioner, described by his curate as a radical traditionalist.

Charles Gerard MacKenzie, M.A., O.B.E., was Vicar of St. John the Evangelist in East Dulwich. He had been at Selwyn College, Cambridge and then at Ely Theological College; he had been ordained deacon in 1937 to the Pembroke College Mission at Walworth and, in 1940, as a priest, had gone to his present church as Assistant Curate, but the war had taken him as a Chaplain in the R.A.F. and then, after the war, with the O.B.E., he had returned to Dulwich as Vicar. The church had been damaged during the war, so he had shouldered the task of having it rebuilt and building up the congregation again. He was due to be instituted to St. Matthew's in September, but first, on 20th August at Windsor, he was to be married to Joyce Fox, so it was as a newly married couple that they came to live in St. Matthew's Vicarage in September 1955.

Tuesday 13th September was 'Scrub-Day' and willing hands set to work to remove every spot from the church. Then at 7.30 p.m. on Thursday 15th September, Charles MacKenzie was instituted Vicar by the Rt. Rev'd. Spencer Leeson, the Bishop of Peterborough and inducted to the benefice by Archdeacon Grimes. Before the excitement of all this had died down, it was time for the Annual Festival, basically organised by Walter Hussey; the Bishop of Southampton, who had been consecrated in 1951, was to preach at the first Evensong, he had been Archdeacon of Lincoln and had worked in South Africa. The Bishop of Leicester, consecrated as recently as 1953, was to preach at the Solemn Eucharist and the Bishop of Bedford, who had been much in the Holy Land, being Archdeacon of Palestine and Transjordan, and had also been consecrated in 1953, was to preach on the Sunday of the Octave. The Rev'd. Marcus Morris, who was on the staff of Hulton's Press and the Editor of *Eagle*, *Girl*, *Swift* and *Robin*, was to conduct the special Children's Service. With the Bishop of Peterborough, the Festival lived up to its reputation and gave Charles MacKenzie a good 'baptism'!

In his first Magazine letter, Charles thanked everyone for his warm, if rather breathless, welcome, and said that the Institution and the Festival had been inspiring occasions. His aim pastorally, he said, was to visit and to get to know the people. The population of the parish was around 12,000, so this was obviously a long job (in fact both Rowden and Walter had found it impossible with smaller populations to cover) but he hoped to start by visiting the regular members of the congregation and asked that they would supply him with cards saying when it would be convenient! The dominant note of his ministry, he continued, would be Evangelism; there was a need to develop the congregation by prayer, example and service, and he called on everyone to play their part. The daily Eucharist, he said, was something he particularly valued and he would even return from a meeting or a Conference to celebrate it, when that was at all possible. A church dedicated to St. Matthew should be at the forefront of Evangelistic work. 'Start,' he suggested, 'with the Harvest Festival, the celebration of God's annual miracle, bring someone with you who does not usually attend church.'

Charles MacKenzie was rather of the 'Roman' rite, with high collar and biretta, and he expected the clergy to be addressed as 'Father', while under the Hussey regime they had been 'Mister'. He was what was then known as a Prayerbook Catholic.

The congregation found him friendly and enthusiastic, and a good preacher. He had been used to a Vicarage being 'Open House', different from Walter Hussey, who had made his contacts outside or in church and rather cherished his home privacy, and it took quite a time for the parishioners to come knocking at the Vicarage door! Joyce MacKenzie was quieter, less involved and concentrated more on her home and the two children who were born to her during their years at St. Matthew's, the first in 1957, baptised on 24th March, a few months before Hewlett and Mrs. Thompson's son Andrew, baptised on 11th August.

Quite early during his time in the parish, Charles joined the Kingsley Road Working Men's Club, as he was determined to interest all sorts of people in the church. He was a good mixer and popular at the club, though he scandalised some of the more conservative members of the congregation.

In his New Year letter for 1956, the Vicar outlined the problems facing the parish, as he saw them. There was need to increase the staff, but he saw little chance of obtaining a deacon for that year. However, he was delighted to welcome Deaconess Sankey to the parish, in an Honorary, part-time capacity. She had been assisting at Kingsthorpe but as she lived in St. Matthew's parish she now felt that she could not continue to travel out to Kingsthorpe. She would be particularly valuable in visiting parishioners. She lived at 27 Park Avenue North, sharing with her friend Miss Phyllis Oldaker, the Diocesan Adviser on Religious Education, but they later moved to Windhoek, 67 Collingwood Road, the corner house which belonged to St. Matthew's. There was much discussion over the future of Windhoek, an attempt to raise the rent had not been accepted by the tenant. In October 1957 the tenant, Mr. Corrin, senior, died and his widow left early in 1958. This was when the house became available for Deaconess Sankey, who rented the ground-floor flat with Miss Oldaker for £175 plus rates. The idea was to divide the house into two flats and the Misses Hennings were interested in renting the top flat for £200 plus rates. At this time too, work was put in hand at the Vicarage to improve the kitchen and to separate off a flat which could bring in extra income or provide a base for a curate. There was also the beginning of negotiations to buy the land between the Vicarage and St. Matthew's Nursing Home.

Deaconess Sankey was licensed by the Bishop to work in the parish, which went some way towards solving the staff problem. The Order of Deaconesses was a life-long order, administered by the Bishops and revived in the nineteenth century.

The second important problem was the constant one of finance. Costs continued to rise and it was difficult to balance the books. Bishop Spencer Leeson had campaigned to raise clergy stipends and, by April 1956, £630 per annum net was to be the minimum (this also meant that clergy had to have a house which was free of rates and dilapidations) and even with a grant from the Diocese, this was difficult to achieve. The Treasurer foretold a 'substantial deficit'! The Church Finances still depended very largely on collections, which varied with the weather! There were also various funds to which regular parishioners contributed but it was all very haphazard. It had long been apparent that some more organised scheme was needed and Charles MacKenzie suggested the weekly envelope scheme which was being, or had been, introduced in many churches. This scheme was to be introduced later in the year. The possibility of building the new Church Hall seemed even further away, it was felt that it would cost at least £15,000 (of which £6,000 had been collected over the years). Also, once built, it would require a substantial sum to maintain and there would still be Capital Expenditure needed for the heating systems and the lighting, as well as maintaining the fabric of the church.

For Lent, the Vicar advocated the adoption of a Lenten Rule; to go each day to Mattins and Evensong if possible, at least to say one's own prayers both night and morning and to take Communion every Sunday. For the first three Sunday evenings of Lent, he had invited the Rev'd. L. Douglas-Jones, the Vicar of Rushden, who had been a Senior Chaplain in the Desert Air Force, to preach; and there were to be services on Wednesday evenings when the Vicar would give Addresses on the Ten Commandments. Fasting must include real self-denial and Lent Boxes in aid of the Society for the Propagation of the Gospel were there for regular alms-giving throughout Lent. He also suggested that, as well as giving money, people should give of their time by visiting the old or the lonely.

It was on Friday 27th January 1956 that news came of the death of the much loved and respected Bishop Spencer Leeson. He had been ailing for a year or more but was still working hard. The Rt. Rev'd. Robert Stopford, then Bishop of Fulham, was enthroned on Saturday 29th September 1956 – a Bishop with an unusual background and a wide experience.

By the first anniversary of his Induction, closely followed by the Festival, the Vicar was regretting that he had still many parishioners to visit. The Festival lived up to its reputation and the preachers included the Bishop of Matabeland, the Rt. Rev'd. W. J. Hughes and the Lord Bishop of Dorchester, who was the Bishop-Designate of Lincoln. There was an Organ Recital by Sir William Harris of St. George's Chapel, Windsor, who had taught Robert Joyce, and a new anthem, specially written by David Barlow, who had been one of Robert Joyce's pupils. David Barlow had been born in Rothwell and educated at Kettering Grammar School and was a lecturer at Newcastle. The anthem was from Psalm 24, 'Who shall ascend into the hill of the Lord'. The music of the St. Matthew's Day Solemn Eucharist was written in 1818 by Carl Maria von Weber, a Mass in E flat major, written for the Chapel of the King of Saxony and known as 'Missa Sonata'.

A New Vicar – 1955

The sermons heard at the Festival had emphasised the need of the Church to proclaim the Gospel to those who were uncommitted, whether these be in Central Africa or in Northampton itself. As a follow-up the Vicar and the P.C.C. decided to have three special services on the Sunday evenings of 7th, 14th and 21st October on 'The Key to Happiness', 'The Key to Enter' and 'The Key to Keep'; the service to be Evensong with well-known hymns, and every house in the parish was to be circulated with details. The Vicar asked that every member of the congregation should attend and try to bring friends and neighbours with them. 'Let us show,' he wrote, 'the people of our parish that we want them, that our faith is the key to our lives and that we have a strong, united family spirit which welcomes and wants others to join us.' The response was remarkably good and the clergy worked hard to follow up by visiting the homes of as many as they could.

Charles MacKenzie was aiming to deepen the spirituality of the people of the parish and showed his wide humanity and sympathy for the problems they faced. He was always a realist and kept in touch with contemporary affairs by newspapers and television – he was a keen viewer of 'Any Questions'! He had a quiet sense of humour – once when Hewlett Thompson slipped back in the liturgy one Easter Day when he was celebrating, his kneeling vicar, savouring the moment, chided gently with 'I've done that already, chum!'

It was in December of 1956 that a letter was sent to every member of the congregation, outlining the financial state of the parish. Many people thought of St. Matthew's as a rich parish, but there were no donors of large amounts and no investments. In fact the parish had led a hand-to-mouth existence, financially, all through its seventy years! The P.C.C. had devised a new scheme, to be inaugurated in January 1957, and to be called God's Due. Everyone was invited to join. The form invited everyone to estimate what he or she could afford to give weekly. The form would then go to the Vicar who would be the only one to know the amount promised. Each person would be given a number and a year's supply of numbered envelopes. These should be put into the collection bag each Sunday, or as soon as possible. This scheme would replace all the other piece-meal schemes which had obtained in the past, and there would be no 'special collections' except for the Choir Fund, Welfare dues and the Easter and Whitsun offerings for the clergy. This would, of course, only work if enough was given in the envelopes and people were asked to assess honestly the amount which was God's Due from their income. Remember the quotation from 1 Corinthians 16, v.2., 'Upon the first day of the week let every one of us lay by him in store as God hath prospered him.' This meant an assured income so that expenditure could be budgeted properly and in advance. Covenants for seven years would ensure that the income would be larger as tax could be reclaimed.

So came the end of Charles McKenzie's first complete year at St. Matthew's, and though much remained to be done, a start had been made.

25

1957 to 1960

Nineteen fifty-seven dawned in the middle of the Suez crisis and saw the resignation of the Prime Minister, Anthony Eden, but St. Matthew's was in 'good heart'. The number of communicants had increased and the congregations were good. The Youth Fellowship for both girls and boys had been restarted by Hewlett Thompson and was flourishing, as were the Sunday Schools and the Women's Fellowship.

The finances had been reorganised into one main fund, God's Due, and promises to this were up to £1,200 a year plus another £240 for overseas work. The 1956 Christmas Sale had raised £400 for the Heating Fund and they were to raise a similar sum in 1957.

There was still need for further Evangelism and a great need to increase the opportunities in the Church School, which had 350 pupils. Deaconess Sankey was now to be seen round the parish, readily identifiable in her uniform, a welcome visitor at many houses where she was a ready listener, particularly to the problems of the women. One of her early engagements was to speak to the Mothers' Union, the first of many such addresses to various parish organisations, and she soon undertook the organisation of the flower rota!

After Lent, the church was visited by Father Graham of the Community of the Resurrection at Mirfield, a community of Mission Priests and Lay Brothers founded by Bishop Gore in 1892, under vows of poverty, chastity and obedience; and established at Mirfield in 1898. Bishop Gore was an Anglo-Catholic who was the first head of Pusey House in Oxford and he was successively Bishop of Worcester, Birmingham and Oxford. Bishop Gore had said, in a book written fifty years before this time, 'It still remains for us to restore the Eucharist to its central place as the chief, if not the most largely attended, act of Sunday worship.' Father Graham stayed at the Vicarage, though the members of the congregation were encouraged to invite him to their houses. His first address was to be on Palm Sunday. He spoke each night of Holy Week, the talk followed by Compline; and also conducted the Three Hours at the Foot of the Cross on Good Friday; ending with Easter Sunday night Evensong. On Good Friday evening, the choir sang 'The Passion of Our Lord According to St. Mark', arranged by the Very Rev'd. E. Milner-White, the Dean of York, and set to music by Charles Wood, the Professor of Music at Cambridge who contributed so much to Church music before his death in 1926.

David Jenkins joined the clergy for the Easter celebrations, at which a new set of white vestments were used for the first time.

As always, Easter was followed by the Parish A.G.M., preceded by the Vestry to elect Churchwardens. The previous year's Accounts were presented, P.C.C. elections took place and the Vicar discussed the staffing of the parish; the architect's report on the church; the possibility of a new Church Hall and plans for further Evangelism.

Charles MacKenzie's desire for an efficient heating system was to come to fruition by the winter, while the church stonework was to be cleaned and, in some parts, replaced. The cost was to be around £2,200, of which £1,000 was still to be found. The cost of the heating was paid off within twelve months, but by then it was realised that much more needed to be done to the fabric, and that the church needed to be re-wired and the roof re-tiled.

The third Festival of Charles' ministry at St. Matthew's was celebrated on the usual pattern with an interesting recital of 'Old Music with Old Instruments' between lunch and tea on St. Matthew's Day. Marshall Johnson and his wife, Cecily Arnold, presented vocal and instrumental music of the sixteenth and seventeenth centuries, including works by Byrd, Gibbons and Purcell. The instruments were the treble viol, lute, viola da gamba and harpsichord, as well as the organ, with Robert Joyce playing. At the Solemn Eucharist in the morning, the preacher was the Lord Bishop of Brechin and the music was the 'Missa Brevis in B flat major' by Mozart, composed in 1776. At Evensong, the Choir sang 'Let Their Celestial Concerts All Unite' from Handel's Oratorio *Samson*, and at the Sunday Evensong, they sang Parry's 'I was glad'.

Once again, the special services were held in October; Charles hoped they would be a regular part of St. Matthew's Calendar. He felt that the world was in a 'shocking mess' and wanted the October services to declare, especially to non-churchgoers, the meaning of the Church and what it stood for – God in His Justice, Love, Strength and Holiness.

The following year a group was trained to visit before and after the services.

In June 1958 came the addition to the staff of David Griffiths from Worcester College, Oxford and Lincoln Theological College (the age of Cuddesdon students was over). He was already married with a young family and was to be ordained deacon on Trinity Sunday. David had been attracted by the letter Charles had sent to his college: 'I am looking for a deacon next summer. I enclose a copy of our parish magazine.' Very different from the usual wordy letter! David set off to Northampton to investigate and, liking the look of the church and its notices, called at the Vicarage, and was asked to lunch. Afterwards, he was sent round to talk to Hewlett Thompson before any decision was made.

The Parochial week had a daily Mattins at 7.00 a.m., Communion at 7.30 a.m., followed by a Meditation in the chapel until about 8.20 a.m. and a daily Evensong at 6.00 p.m. As Deacon, David Griffiths had to open the church, re-set the chimes of the clock, ring the bell and officiate at Mattins. Mattins was only attended by the clergy but both Holy Communion and Evensong were quite well attended. A Staff Meeting took place on every Monday from 9.30 to 12.30 in the morning; this involved checking on the Sunday communicant numbers and then discussing various matters, some serious, some amusing; the week's pastoral problems; the Youth Fellowship; the School; all spiced with anecdotes from the past – a very good training for a potential parish priest! Charles taught his curates that a priest should spend at least forty minutes a day in praying and that time must also be found for reading. He expected his staff to work long hours, with a free day and reasonable holidays. We worked, said David Griffiths, like Trojans! But Charles worked as hard as anyone else.

It was in 1958 that the P.C.C. revived the idea of a new Church Hall. Land was finally purchased between the Drive and the Kettering Road between the Vicarage and the St. Matthew's Nursing Home, the conveyance was signed in October and negotiations were put in hand to sell the part by the Vicarage to the Nursing Home, leaving the rest open to The Drive, for the new Parish Hall. The architect, Mr. Scorer, was to prepare drawings and it was hoped that building would begin in 1959. The site of the Church Room would be sold towards the probable cost of £12,000. Unfortunately, as time went on delays occurred and the money was needed even more for the Church School, so it was decided to retain and do up the Church Room.

The lighting system of the church was switched on in October. The old system had been without proper earthing, the fittings were rusted and it was only surprising that there had never been an accident; clusters of bulbs were suspended from the roof by iron piping. Tom Shaw, the verger, hack-sawed the pipes into six-foot lengths, which served for many years as garden stakes. The cost of the work was £1,066 and this was to be raised from the Summer Fête and the Christmas Sale. Following this improvement, the kitchen of the Vicarage was to be improved.

At the end of 1958 it was reported that the cost of running St. Matthew's was £55 a week – including stipends, heating, lighting, communion wine and bread, and the Diocesan Quota. God's Due had 186 members together contributing about £34 a week, while cash collections had to bridge the gap. Actually there was usually a deficit of £8 a week, so more subscribers were needed. Obviously there was no spare for emergencies or maintenance, it was more a case of muddling along!

When Hewlett Thompson left to go to Wisbech, the P.C.C. decided to sell 12 The Drive, the money to be invested for the time being. It also decided to extend the church lawn to cover the allotments and so improve the appearance for the benefit of the neighbourhood.

Two important topics were discussed at the July session of the Church Assembly, which were also considered by the P.C.C. The requirements for having one's name on the Electoral Roll were; to be seventeen or over, baptised and to declare oneself a member of the Church of England. At the Assembly, an amendment was put forward proposing that the applicant should have attended public worship for six months unless prevented by illness *or other sufficient cause*. What was such a 'sufficient cause'? The amendment was rejected. The second topic concerned the expenses of a clergyman working in a parish, he was supposed to pay them from his stipend but this was becoming increasingly difficult with telephones, longer distances to travel, and so on, and could make for inefficiency. This was something St. Matthew's P.C.C. needed to think about. There were still those who thought clergy should be paid a bare minimum in case the wrong men applied.

With 1960, problems of finance were paramount. A Church Restoration Fund was essential. Luckily it was started with a generous legacy. The late Mrs. Elsie Linthwaite had left £3,000 for the clergy fund, £500 for the new Church Hall and her house at 73 Park Avenue North, as well as £1,500 for St. Christopher's Home, in the name of St. Matthew's. The house later fetched £2,653. There had also been an anonymous donation of £250. The Curate's house in The Drive had by now been sold, but as a new curate was needed, suitable accommodation was required. A curate's salary in the Peterborough diocese, was £8. 2s. 0d. a week (just over £400 a year). The endowment for the benefice had not increased and the new minimum for a vicar was likely to be £650 a year, well in excess of the endowment. The only extra the Vicar got was the Easter Offering; as the curate got, or shared, the Whitsun Offering. Something needed to be done!

Commissioned music I 'Justus quidem tu es Domine' composed by Peter Dickinson for John Bertalot and St, Matthew's Choir: (i) Cover; (ii) Original Manuscript.

JUSTUS QUIDEM TU ES, DOMINE (HOPKINS)

PETER DICKINSON

In 1960 too, the early Sunday services were re-organised. Mattins was said at 7.40 a.m. followed by Communion at 8.00 a.m. and again at 9.00 a.m., with the usual Sung Eucharist and Sermon at 11.00 a.m. The total number of communicants had increased considerably and it seemed that the 9.00 a.m. service had met a real need, particularly in the cold, dark mornings of winter. This was to be kept until Easter when the 7.00 a.m. service would be restored and the 9.00 a.m. discontinued. The schedule of preachers and topics for all services was prepared six months ahead.

David Jenkins, between jobs, was to return for three months, and this was particularly valuable as the clergy were helping out in other parishes.

The Festival of 1960 was special in that Walter Hussey, Dean of Chichester, was to attend. There was to be a reception for him after Evensong on the Eve of the Festival, after he had preached. The Bishop of Gambia was to preach on St. Matthew's Day, to be followed in the evening by the Master of the Temple. The organ recital was to be by Dr. Harold Darke, recently senior Professor of the Royal College of Music. The special Festival Anthem had been written by Peter Dickenson, to a poem of Gerard Manley Hopkins, based on Jeremiah 12, v.1 and 2; at the end of it, the men speak in Latin while the boys sing in English. Mr. Charles Barker was to be the accompanist. Peter Dickenson was a friend and contemporary of John Bertalot and had been to the United States of America, on a scholarship, and had met Alec Wyton there. The network of St. Matthew's was widespread! The Communion service was to be Purcell's, recently published, and the Creed would be sung to a sixteenth-century setting by Thomas Tallis.

A new church organisation was the Over-Twenty Club, aimed mostly at the under-thirties, it was quite formal with emphasis on discussions and play-readings, popular with many young people who were working in the town and living in digs.

The October Nights emphasised the constant need to bring those outside inside; to show the need to challenge every single person in the parish with the Christian Gospel and all it involves. St. Matthew's, said the Vicar, was not built for a select coterie but for everyone. It was during October that the parish was visited, at the suggestion of David Griffiths, by a group of students from Lincoln Theological College, so that they saw a parish in action and could assist in the work. They stayed with various parishioners and at least three young men were seriously interested in being considered for the next vacancy. Also in October, there were a series of tea and coffee parties for clergy and laity to socialise, to get to know each other and to make new friendships.

26

1961 – A Momentous Year

In one magazine, Charles MacKenzie admitted that his ministry at St. Matthew's was the hardest he had ever experienced. Later he said that Evangelism was the passion of his life, so that he would never be satisfied until every single person in the parish had been challenged with the Christian gospel. He had certainly worked hard since coming to St. Matthew's, and had been described as a firebrand, maybe nowadays we would have called him a workaholic. He had been confronted with a number of problems and, as his experience had largely been in London, he sometimes found it hard to adapt to Northampton life. He was a chain-smoker and often found himself awake for long hours worrying about current problems, so he probably suffered from some degree of hypertension.

One problem that continued to haunt him was that of the Fabric of the Church building; it had been built in 1893 and was coming towards seventy years old. The heating and lighting had been improved and made safe but the stonework was deteriorating. The building was the largest Anglican church in Northampton and one of the largest in the diocese, almost a young cathedral, as it has frequently been described. Sometimes the Vicar and the P.C.C. wished it were smaller and easier to maintain. They were faced with the need for at least £10,000 over the next few years, a sum that could not be raised by fêtes or sales or raffles. To cope with this problem, professional advice was invited from Stewardship Campaign Advisers. It was also realised that the Day School desperately needed modernising, though they hoped for a seventy-five per cent grant from the Ministry of Education and some Local Authority support towards the work to be done. This was all in the context of knowing that many Diocesan churches, especially those in small villages, needed similar financial help, as did the Christians of countries overseas.

Charles MacKenzie and the P.C.C. knew that St. Matthew's had been making do for far too long and putting off all but essential repairs – the situation had been tided over recently by the more organised 'God's Due Fund', but the finances had been haphazard and casual for many years. The time had come to appeal to the whole parish and not just to the congregation.

The Christmas festivities which led into 1961 were happy and successful but serious decisions were ahead. As an innovation at this time, not altogether unconnected with the financial crisis, a series of quarterly *parish* meetings was begun. At the first one, a liturgical experiment was discussed. The 9.00 a.m. Communion service, re-introduced for the winter months, was to introduce more *lay* participation on alternate Sundays, instead of the priestly monologue! Each communicant would place a wafer in the ciborium, signifying that they wished to receive; the Epistle would be read by a layman (the gospel by the deacon). The congregation was to join in the prayers of Humble Access, Oblation and Thanksgiving, as well as in other prayers.

The Director of the Stewardship Campaign was Major John Robinson, he was given an office in the Church Room and began the campaign on 2nd January 1961. There was a Campaign Prayer which the congregation was asked to use daily; 'O God who has called us to be fellow-workers with Thee, grant that as we have freely received, so we may freely bring to Thy work, all the good things we are and have; for Jesus Christ's Sake. Amen.'

There were to be two Loyalty Dinners in the Town Hall (two because no hall was large enough for the numbers hoped for) on 25th and 26th January. Intended as parochial occasions to welcome old friends and former clergy, they were also occasions during which people could be persuaded to join the Stewardship Campaign and make their pledges. Inevitably, there was criticism!

Symbolic of that momentous year, a new magazine cover was in use, designed by David Johnson, a young artist, who explained: 'The swirling curves and rectangles represent the presence and energy of the world unseen, crystallised in the angel, symbol of St. Matthew, and manifested in his gospel. Behind the gospel stands the cross with the crown of thorns, symbolic of the narration of Christ's incarnation and sacrifice, while in front is a chalice, representing the duties and privileges of the church.'

John Piper's picture of the church, given to Walter Hussey when he left, was now, with their permission, being sold as a coloured postcard, together with cards of the Madonna and the Crucifixion.

A brochure for the Stewardship Campaign was produced and a lively fellowship effected. No longer just the Vicar's responsibility, but for everyone a corporate witness to be fostered and deepened. Teams of men were out in the parish calling for the pledges of the parishioners, while sixty-three ladies were asked to call on 600 families within ten days, inviting people to the Loyalty dinners. Over 500 people accepted; £3,000 over three years was pledged from a small number of families, even before the dinners, and by March, £20,676 over three years, had been pledged by 354 families. This meant that the work of the church could go forward. As important as the financial promises were the new contacts made and the revelation of the amount of interest and affection there was. 'One must trust in God, for the harvest is there' – and to Charles' delight, more people began to call at the Vicarage!

With the financial situation in hand, for the time being at least, the Vicar turned his attention to other matters. He considered the newly revised Catechism and advised it for Lenten reading, and he gave talks on it on the Wednesday evenings during Lent.

The P.C.C. listed out many social problems which should be the concern of the Church and all Christians; they included marriage problems and the need for Counsellors; the problems of work and leisure, particularly concerning married women who worked, and their children; the temptations of advertising, gambling and hire purchase; the use and abuse of television and radio.

In March the New Testament section of the New English Bible was published, 350 years after the Authorised Version of 1611. The Revised Version of 1881-1884 was normally read at St. Matthew's. Charles MacKenzie thought that this new version, the result of long co-operation by a team of scholars, should be given a warm welcome because it was written in good, contemporary English.

In August, David Griffiths was to leave for his work for the S.P.C.K. and it was announced that Humphrey Prideaux, of Corpus Christi, Oxford, and Lincoln Theological College, would join the staff at Michaelmas. Deaconess Sankey was to retire, but would continue to live at 67 Collingwood Road and would retain her Bishop's Licence, so she would still worship at St. Matthew's and her advice and experience would still be available.

The ordination at Peterborough was on Sunday 24th September and was unusual for St. Matthew's as Alan Wakelin was to be priested and Humphrey Prideaux ordained as a deacon. A large party from the parish was there to support them both. The following day the helpers for the

October Services had a meeting at which they were briefed and, a week later, Charles MacKenzie took a funeral.

After the following Sunday, Charles and Joyce, with Mr. and Mrs. Abel, went to Christchurch for a late caravan holiday. To the great shock and sadness of everyone, Charles had a sudden thrombosis, while playing cards, and died.

The Lord Bishop of London, Dr. Stopford, who had left Peterborough earlier in the year, said that Charles 'was a wise parish priest, with a deep understanding and real concern for the evangelistic task of the church, his wisdom in dealing with people, all contributed to make his Ministry at St. Matthew's an outstanding one. It is hard to understand why a man in the full flight of his powers should be taken away in the midst of so successful a ministry. We can only believe that God, in His infinite wisdom, has some other plan for him and some other work for him to do. We, for our part, can only thank God for the inspiration of his ministry; for the influence of his friendship and his infectious good humour and for all he did for the Church of God.'

A funeral service for the late Vicar was held on 18th October, a simple but moving service with a packed church and others lining the streets outside. The sermon was preached by his friend and colleague, the Rev'd. Bazil Marsh, Vicar of St. Mary's, Northampton, who said that the news had been a great blow, followed by real pain. Many found their vision of the service sheet blurred by tears. Bazil Marsh continued,

'We who knew him were impressed by his bouncing vitality. We talked with him; laughed a great deal with him; worked with him; quite often quarrelled with him. We look forward to the constant surprises which his rich and colourful personality was always preparing for us.

'Death, as Charles himself often told others, is only an incident in a continuing and expanding life.

'It is at the altar that we must humbly put ourselves at God's disposal so that He may have men and women in whom He can continue the fruitful work which He did in the life of Charles MacKenzie, whom we love.'

27

An Interregnum and a New Vicar

The first of January 1962 saw the new Bishop of Peterborough, the Rt. Rev'd. Cyril Eastaugh moving into the Palace at Peterborough, with his wife, Lady Laura, and their three children, Laura aged twelve, Elizabeth aged ten and Andrew aged seven. A new year and a new beginning for the Diocese.

The congregation learnt that the Rev'd. Philip Turner had accepted the living of St. Matthew's and would be instituted in May. Philip Turner was thirty-six, he had been born in British Columbia in Canada; had been to Worcester College, Oxford and Chichester Theological College, after being in the Fleet Air Arm as an Aircraft Engineer. He was married with two sons, aged six and eight, and had been in charge of St. Peter's, Crawley New Town, Sussex, for the last six years, being previously in Armley, Leeds. He was well known as a writer of religious drama, particularly for *Christ in the Concrete City*, based on experiences in Leeds. He was known to be of somewhat High Church tradition and deeply interested in Ecumenism and in Sunday School work. In a letter to the parish at Easter, he said that he was looking forward to becoming part of St. Matthew's. He said he believed that God wanted him to move; that he was aware of his own incapacities but believed that with prayer, trust and love, priest and people together, in corporate activity, God's work would be done.

It was not a very easy interregnum and Humphrey Prideaux, who had come so soon before the death of his Vicar, and had found it difficult to come to terms with the resulting problems, was leaving to be curate of St. James', Portsmouth, so when Philip Turner was instituted by Bishop Eastaugh and inducted by Archdeacon Goodchild in the presence of a vast concourse of people, he only had Alan Wakelin as his curate. There was a reception to welcome the new Vicar and his wife and family; while, on the following Sunday, the Youth Fellowship provided breakfast as another occasion to get to know the family.

Philip Turner was of a very different temperament from Charles MacKenzie, a quieter, shy, sensitive, academic man, particularly interested in plays and books; he was not a musician, though anxious for the musical tradition to be maintained. Probably he was more in a modernised Hussey tradition. He was a fine preacher. In his first letter in the magazine, he thanked the parish for its kind welcome and asked for patience while he found his way around and got to know people. He was realistic enough to realise that this could not be done quickly. Love, he said, must be the basis of parish life, he was not there as a revolutionary, though he rather thought some people regarded him as such!

Philip Turner was not in an easy position, the parish was still recovering from the shock of the loss of his predecessor, who had left many of his ideas in mid-air. The congregation tended to split between those who valued the old ways and clung to them and those who wanted the church to appeal to the less well educated, the unartistic and those less musical, and thus looked for changes. They all waited to see how the new vicar would react. Philip took what he felt to be the middle way – changing the High Mass to a service where everyone could communicate but keeping many of the musical traditions under the leadership of John Bertalot. John was a fine musician and, coming from an evangelical background himself, he was aware of the need to compromise.

One of the things Charles MacKenzie had intended was to arrange a Parish Mission. Philip Turner decided to follow this and invited Father Denis Marsh, of the Society of St. Francis, to preach on 23rd September, the Sunday of the Festival Octave, with a view to arranging a Mission in 1964. Bishop Eastaugh preached at the High Mass on St. Matthew's Day and the Provost of Southwark at Evensong on the Eve of the Festival. The October nights, begun by Charles MacKenzie, to widen the out-reach of the parish, would be continued and taken by the new Vicar. He invited everyone interested to a meeting so that every house in the parish would be visited. Invitations, posters and arrows were designed, so that no one could possibly not know of the talks. After the three October Sunday Nights, he hoped to arrange Evensong sermons concerned with the general topic of 'Faith in the Twentieth Century'.

The follow-up in November and December was to be by visiting experts:

1. Tradition, Education and Faith, by the Rev'd. Philip Willmott, Chaplain of Winchester College.
2. Christianity and the Soldier, by the Rev'd. Andrew Bradley, Vicar of St. Peter's, St. Alban's, recently Warden of Bagshot Park. R.A.C.D.
3. The Gospel and the Mass Media, by the Rev'd. David Skinner, Secretary of the Church of England Radio and Television Council.
4. Into All the World, by the Rev'd. F.N. Davey. Director of S.P.C.K.
5. Christ and the Industrial Man, by the Rev'd. Prebendary Stephan Hopkins, General Director of the Industrial Christian Fellowship.

One follow-up from these talks was The Monday Club, in the Church Rooms at 2.15 p.m. on Monday afternoons. This was especially for the elderly and retired men and women of the parish and was run by the co-operation of the Mothers' Union and the Women's Society of the Methodist Church.

Christmas Services followed the usual pattern, though there was an extra Children's Service on Christmas Eve at 5.30 p.m. and Midnight Mass was to start earlier at 11.30 p.m., following Solemn Mattins at 10.45 p.m. Philip Turner recommended a three-hour fast before Communion but said it was more important to come ready for Communion.

Nineteen sixty-three saw St. Matthew's with, still, only the Vicar and Alan Wakelin as clerical staff, but Miss Phyllis Oldaker was recruited as a Lay-worker.

An innovation in 1963 was the Cellar Club – a practical use of a cellar at the Vicarage, which had been used as a pantry and a wine-cellar; then as a coke-cellar; while Philip Turner had used it to make home-made wine! The Youth Fellowship had cleaned it out and decorated it; three walls were painted black and one yellow; the ceiling was yellow and seats for twenty were provided, together with the facilities for making coffee. It was intended for socialising and for 'putting the world to rights'.

Alan Wakelin, writing in the magazine during the interregnum, had reminded everyone that, though the Stewardship Campaign of 1960 had been a great boost and a great effort by the laity, the money raised had been used mostly for essential repairs to the Church building. It was now necessary to think of others. In 1961, the P.C.C. had been able to give

£750 to sixteen charities; including the Northampton Mission to the Deaf; the S.P.C.K.; Inter-Church Aid and Oxfam. This charitable giving must go on and be improved. Giving is also about service and individual ministry, with everyone giving of their time and talents as they are able. Philip Turner was anxious to increase the ministry of the laity. He said 'The Church has been praying for years for an increase in the number of priests. Numbers have increased very little. God is therefore answering our prayers. He is saying NO! The Church has for too long regarded the laity as second-class Christians.' It is on responsible lay people that the future of the Church rests.

A Stewardship Renewal Campaign was planned for 1964, using the Diocesan Stewardship Department, thinking, not only of the stewardship of money, but of time and skills. 'Be generous and realistic before God.'

Reorganised – the Ministry of the Laity more established and with every hope of developing – with the services made simpler and more friendly, Philip Turner's first two years had been busy but satisfactory. He had really begun to settle in.

An exciting year ahead, he predicted, a chance for St. Matthew's to realise itself as a loving community.

28

1964 to 1966

In 1964, the Stewardship Campaign was uppermost in everyone's mind. On Sunday 2nd February, the campaign was to begin; the Archdeacon was to preach and the Bishop would commission the Visitors; afterwards there would be tea at fifty houses near the church.

The Needs of the Parish were summarised as:
1. to care for the old and lonely of the parish;
2. to visit the sick;
3. to welcome new arrivals;
4. to teach the children in the Sunday Schools;
5. to run the young people's organisations (seven of them);
6. to take care of the church and grounds.

The Finances of the parish were:
£60 per week in wages, heat, lighting, etc;
£15 per week for God's work in the diocese;
£14 per week for the needs of God's World;
PLUS the need to maintain the building in good condition.

The Stewardship was to be directed by Julian Hall and 500 invitations went out, Sixth-formers were enrolled to run a crèche for the time of the service (one to be in the crèche was baby Jane from the Vicarage).

The Campaign was very successful and, as well as money promises, Time and Talent cards were returned. Possibilities of a car-service, church maintenance, baby sitting and the care for the sick and elderly were all to be considered. There was an attempt to organise a baby-sitting service, so that parents could both go to Evensong occasionally, or to have an occasional evening out; and there was an attempt to form a car-pool to take the infirm to church or to medical appointments. The following year there was an attempt to organise a common car-pool among the six adjoining parishes, though there were many complications and it was never completely successful. In 1965, the period of Lent centred on problems of homelessness and the needs of one's fellow-men for education, medicine, food and so on.

In February 1965, a Caring Church Scheme was introduced, using Oliver Street, Cedar Road, Highfield Road and Raeburn Road as a pilot scheme, intending this as a supplement to the work of District Visitors. Later came the inauguration of the Fish Scheme, hopefully to be followed by many parishes and ecumenically. It was inaugurated by the recently formed Northampton Council of Churches, an Ecumenical Council. The Fish Scheme was intended as a caring service for the whole of the town. Each Parish Organisation, the Christian Churches in the area, were to provide the backing for Street Wardens and Area Representatives. The parish would organise the necessary transport, emergency support, visits, etc., when needs were reported by the Street Wardens. The Area Organisers would receive training. An inaugural service took place at All Saints Church on 14th October 1966. The report of one Area Representative said how important it was to look and listen, so that the real needs were perceived. The main problems seemed to arise from the disabilities of arthritis, and the need for Home Helps and Meals on Wheels could be pinpointed and passed to the relevant authorities. Often there was little the Wardens needed to do other than listen and then convince everyone of the needs and to alert the Welfare Services. Frequently the person needing the most convincing was the sufferer. Often the solution to problems or dangers was simple, like the provision of a fireguard. Lonely people needed someone to talk to and sometimes a solution was to invite them to join the Monday Club. It could be rewarding work.

The other major subject of discussion at this period was the Anglo-Methodist Report, originally published in 1963. This had followed a sermon by the Archbishop of Canterbury at Cambridge in November 1946, on Church Relations. Representatives of the Anglicans and the Methodist Assembly had met during the 1950s and this report was the result of all these meetings and the deliberations of the Methodist Assembly and the Convocations of York and Canterbury. The Report suggested that there should be two stages; the first one should allow the two Churches to enter upon full communion with each other, while retaining a distinct life and identity . . . this would help them to grow together and to learn how to achieve the final goal of unity. At St. Matthew's, Study

Groups were set up under Gordon Dalziel, Laurie Fallows and Christopher Elliott-Binns. It was necessary for everyone to decide what was to be done. To follow the guidance of the Holy Spirit might well take one from the security of the present to something unknown. Reunion, it was said, would be a matter of faith, hope and lots and lots of charity!

Co-operation between churches was something dear to Philip Turner's heart, and St. Matthew's was already trying to co-operate with Kingsley Park Methodist Church – over the road. For Lent, there was co-operation with St. Alban's Church, and the Vicar, Father Stubbs; the Lent courses were to consider the idea of a family worshipping, learning and serving together. There was an introductory service on Ash Wednesday and the Lent Meetings were in the Parish Room so that film strips could be used. There was also a Children's Course, 'Johnny and the Dreadful Giants', on Saturday mornings. Father Benedict Green of the Community of the Resurrection was to lead Holy Week.

Philip Turner worried at the lack of concern of the laity, and even of many clergy, for the theological issues involved; he tried to ensure that this was not true of his own congregation. It was hoped by those who had written the report that there would be Inter-Communion by 1965, but as time went on this was obviously unrealistic. The two local churches combined certain services, had simultaneous Harvest Festivals, St. Matthew's gave the Methodists bread and grapes from their own Festival, and the distribution of the gifts was a combined effort. There were legal complications that needed to be resolved and no one really understood what was involved in the Service of Reconciliation which was envisaged.

The May 1965 Synod of the Methodists gave general approval to the main proposals but did not consider this decisive. It was felt that much more time was needed and suggested another report in three years' time to explain all the modifications needed. It seemed obvious that the two Churches were not yet ready to accept 'Phase 1'. It was thought that it was better to start by locally getting together; to plan local Christian Mission, *not* to discuss Bishops, Communion wine or Confirmation! Joint collections for Oxfam went ahead; for Save the Children Fund; Christian Aid Week. The result was friendly activities between the two churches, the congregations and the clergy, but to some extent, it was all rather artificial.

Philip Turner went on record to say that he thought the ideas should go ahead and that he was disappointed and sad that so many people, both Anglicans and Methodists, preferred to stay as they were.

Inevitably, through these years changes took place, particularly in personnel. In 1964, the sad news had come of the death of Guy Brodie. He had been curate of St. Matthew's from 1922 to 1937, a much loved priest who had rarely missed a Festival.

In December 1964, Bazil Marsh became Archdeacon of Northampton. He was a Canadian, who had been Vicar of St. Mary's, Far Cotton, and who had spoken at Charles MacKenzie's funeral. He was Rector of St. Peter's, near the Railway Station, but as Archdeacon, he lived in The Drive, in St. Matthew's Parish. His sons acted as servers there and he usually celebrated there on Fridays.

Earlier than this, Sydney Gould and his wife, Mary, came to the parish, Sydney was to be ordained in Trinity Sunday 1964 and priested a year later. They were to live at number 72 Oliver Street, bought by the parish, and later known as St. Matthew's House. Sydney Gould had been well known to Philip Turner in Crawley, and he had always hoped to enter the church. Philip had encouraged him and he was eventually ordained to a title at St. Matthew's. The hope was, that living in Oliver Street and with a background that was not of public school and University, he would be able to do evangelical work among the people on the 'poet' side of the Kettering Road. Mary Gould found life in Oliver Street hard work too, there was no proper bathroom and, although the Vicarage was open to them, it didn't make for an easy time. Sydney was a prolific visitor in the parish and was particularly concerned with the school and, thus, the parents. He took an active part in the monthly school Eucharists, one of which was broadcast for Epiphany 1966. The children sang the hymns. Parts of the Prayer Book Service were modified appropriately for the younger children to understand.

Philip Turner continued to write. He produced a Christmas play which was presented on 17th December. In 1964, he had written a children's book and had contributed to 'Lift Up Your Hearts' on the Radio. He was most distressed when this programme was taken off in June 1965 and replaced by 'Ten-to-Eight'. The claim was that this was no longer a Christian country, and Philip found this a defeatist attitude. He won the Library Association's top award, the Carnegie Medal, for his children's book, which was reckoned the outstanding book of the year in this field.

On Good Friday 1966 'A Song for Cavalry' was broadcast; this had been written by Philip, and he and Laurie Fallows, the Church School Headmaster, were the Readers. The harpsichord was played by Michael Nicholas, with Brian Ager, Vaughan Meakins and Roger Blank singing 'The Lord of the Dance' and 'There is a Green Hill Far Away'. The programme was intended for young listeners and was recorded in Birmingham for the Midland Home Service.

Philip Turner told the parish that he would be spending August in the United States and Canada, where he was to serve on the staff of two drama schools; 1966 was seeing the departure of Jeffrey Bell, and it was unfortunate timing that, having agreed to spend August abroad, Philip Turner was to be appointed Religious Broadcasting Organiser for the Midland Region of the B.B.C., starting on 5th September.

Before he left, Philip Turner had suggested the idea of a portable nave altar to make ordinary services more intimate and more practical. St. Matthew's he pointed out,

> 'was built at the high water mark of the nineteenth-century Gothic revival and the form of worship which truly interprets this Victorian vision is a non-communicating Sung Eucharist with magnificently ordered ceremonial and music, in the Sanctuary and the Choir, reverently attended by a vast congregation, who had already made their communion at an 8.00 a.m. service, so they participated by listening and watching.
>
> 'A church like St. Alban's (built on Broadmead Avenue in 1938) is twentieth century Georgian and the priest, choir and people are together in a corporate Eucharist, which is more relevant to the second half of the twentieth century, than is St. Matthew's. So there is need to compromise.'

'The 11.00 a.m. Sung Eucharist,' he continued, 'attempts to marry the insights of the Tractarians with those of the Parish Communion Movement. The 8.00 a.m. service remains unchanged.' It was to help this problem that a portable nave altar was suggested, the idea being shown in model form for everyone to see. It would be experimental and could easily be moved for Festivals or concerts or any other occasions.

Philip Turner loved the church and was anxious that nothing irremediable was done, he had resisted suggestions to remove the Chancel Screen or the Clergy Stalls. He was deeply moved by the Henry Moore Madonna and Sutherland's Crucifixion. He had found, he said, 'that the best way to appreciate great art is to live with it, if you can kneel before it day by day, never tire of it, and see more in it each day, then it is great work.' The church he found particularly impressive when he unlocked it each morning and locked up each night. 'In the varying lights of summer and winter, the beauty of the interior is breathtaking.'

29

Overseas Contacts

St. Matthew's had always been interested in Overseas Missions and in the 1960s had a number of personal contacts to focus attention on specific areas. In 1963 Celia Frazer went out to Nigeria where she helped to train teachers in St. Monica's College, Onitsha. She was also Headmistress of the Girl's Grammar School in Alor. Equipment was short and there was a great need for books and magazines. The congregation of St. Matthew's collected books and magazines and also sent new hymn books, which were much appreciated.

Descriptions were sent of the work done at the Grammar School and there was one letter, published in the magazine, describing the celebration of Easter in 1966. After the Good Friday service, the girls went to help in the Rural Health Centre of Alor, going to the homes of the sick or the blind, or planting yams, helping with babies and so on. On Easter Day they got up at 5.00 a.m., assembled carrying lanterns and processed to the Market Square singing Easter hymns. There was a service at 9.00 a.m. with another procession and a Eucharist afterwards, at which 400 people took communion; as there was only one priest, these services were lengthy!

Nigerian problems were many and the country was involved in revolution, though Alor remained relatively unscathed. It ended up in the breakaway State of Biafra and it was with much relief that contact was re-established with Celia in 1967.

In 1963 too, Margaret Byard went out to teach at Codrington High School for Girls in Barbados, a relatively stable island at that time, with an economy based mainly on sugar cane. Near the school was Codrington College, run by the Mirfield Fathers for West Indian and other theological students. As the church of Holy Cross was adjacent to the school, the priests and deacons had to come up the steep hill for the church services. Thus the staff of the school and the students from the College met frequently. Margaret met Alan Heslop and it was from Alan that she sent back to St. Matthew's an account of an Islandwide Stewardship Campaign organised by a Director from England helped by local Directors in the twelve parishes. Cards and invitations were sent out and the Bishop visited every church. A feast, the Lord's Own Feast, for 25,000 people was held on the Savannah or Race Course near Bridgetown, the main town. There was a central Bishop's altar, and twenty-two side altars; it started with an hour of hymns and then the Mass lasted from 8.00 a.m. to 10.15 a.m. A fantastic occasion.

Margaret and Alan returned to Northampton to be married at St. Matthew's in 1965 and then went to Bartica in British Guiana.

In April 1964, the church had an even closer contact when the Rev'd. Festo Gakware, from Rwanda Urundi, came to join the staff for a month. He was in England for a two-year course at St. Augustine's College, Canterbury, and part was to obtain first-hand experience of the working of an English parish! Festo was married with six children and he was particularly interested in meeting lots of people in their homes, so there was plenty of opportunity for a two-way exchange of ideas and information. In December, the congregation were invited to help to buy him a car. He had been made Archdeacon of half Rwanda (10,000 square miles) with the care of 300 churches, he had to walk or cycle many miles. Originally £200 was provided but later, when it was discovered that more was needed, £350 was sent.

Nineteen sixty-four also saw Marian Hughes off to Addis Ababa, a very different sort of place as the hospital where she was to work as a physiotherapist, under the V.S.O. scheme, was near a dual carriageway and modern flats, though many families lived in mud houses and were poor. The Princess Zenebewark Memorial Hospital was working with leprosy. A few years earlier there had been nearly 2,000 people there, with leprosy or diseases so diagnosed. At this time there were about 300 patients, though there were beds for only 200. The hospital was planned as a centre for training.

Another hospital in which St. Matthew's people were concerned was that of St. Stephen's in Delhi, in India. A plea for help from Dr. Ruth Roseveare was published. The hospital had been founded in 1867 and had 130 beds and eighty cots; it had a high reputation particularly in maternity work. It served an area of very high population and the patients included Hindus, Sikhs, Muslims and Christians, many very poor and suffering from malnutrition and anaemia. There was desperate need for more qualified staff as well as for money and the care and prayers of all caring people.

The Mission in Nkozo, Pondoland, South Africa had been helped since the 1940s, when a cross, candlesticks, vestments and money had been sent. In 1966 it was heard that they had been saving for a new church, which was to be 60 feet by 25 feet, rounded at the East end, where was to be the Sacristy and Sanctuary; and square at the West end. It was to be built of brick and white-washed inside. It was to be dedicated to St. Giles.

A project which was put forward by the Diocese was for a tiny diocese in Africa, where money was needed to build classrooms at Buhiga Secondary School for Girls. The Diocese of Peterborough hoped to raise £2,500. The Bishop of the area, the Rt. Rev'd. Yohana Nkunzumwami, had recently been in England. St. Matthew's P.C.C. sent half the money raised at the 1967 fête to the fund.

In May 1969 there was news that Sister Nora Banks was elected as the Rev'd. Mother Provincial at the Convent of St. Mary, Panch Havd, in Poona.

Ex-members of the congregation of St. Matthew's, Northampton, were certainly spread around the world!

30

Another Interregnum and a New Vicar

Sydney Gould was somewhat overcome to be left, quite unexpectedly, in charge of the parish. He soon found that an interregnum produces a strong sense of fellowship and that many people offered their help. Philip Turner had prepared, as far as he could, up to Christmas and Phyllis Oldaker and Deaconess Sankey were around to help in various ways. The Festival went well with John McCabe's anthem 'A Hymne to God the Father', from a poem by Donne, as the year's commission. The Bishop of Peterborough presided and preached on St. Matthew's Day with Hewlett Thompson there to celebrate. All was followed by a buffet supper. There was a Festival Concert the next day and, on the Sunday, the Eucharist was sung to Willis' 'Missa Eliensis', with the Rural Dean preaching, while the Provost of Coventry preached at Evensong.

One problem that Sydney Gould had was that he had no car, but various members of the congregation were prepared to act as chauffeurs and others helped with Evensong services.

Christmas activities and services followed the usual pattern. It was at Christmas that the name of the new Vicar was known. Charles Moxon was to be instituted on Saturday 4th February 1967.

Charles Moxon was fifty years of age, married to Phyllis, a teacher who had trained at Peterborough. He might have come to St. Matthew's when Charles MacKenzie died, but had agreed to go to Weybridge. He said that he had known St. Matthew's for many years and had always hoped to be its Vicar! He declared that he had no fixed plans or policy but wanted to get acquainted with the parish problems and then build on the foundations that were already established. Changes would, if necessary, come later. He believed in the value of weekly communion and the value of tradition.

Another Interregnum and a New Vicar

Charles Moxon's ministry began with Lent and he announced that the 9.00 a.m. service would be introduced again. During Lent, he was to preach on Prayer at the mid-week services and the Lent Evensong sermons would be on God's Mission. Lent boxes would collect for 'Shelter' and for the school in Nigeria where Celia Frazer was Headmistress.

The 6th of April brought the Annual Vestry and Parish General Meeting. As the Vicar had only been in the parish for two months, he paid tribute to all those who had coped so well during the interregnum, and thanked everyone for the warmth of their welcome. He talked of the value of a regular worshipping community, with its sense of service, fellowship and opportunities. These were particularly presented by the Fish scheme. The tradition of St. Matthew's was important and must be an inspiration to everyone. A new chapter was beginning: 'We must not, though, rest content bathing in the tradition of the past, but seek every opportunity to see that St. Matthew's serves all who look to her as their Parish Church, that she is in very truth, a real spiritual home and the handmaid of God whose children we are.' The Treasurer pointed out that the income from Stewardship-giving had declined and that another Stewardship Campaign was essential. Unfortunately many had failed to realise the real needs and, contrary to what they seemed to think, money was needed if the church was to do God's work.

In July it was announced that Sydney and Mary Gould would be leaving for Worthing in September. It seemed to be a series of farewells! Phyllis Oldaker was to become full-time but the departure of the Goulds would leave many gaps and willing helpers would be needed. Sydney Gould had been particularly welcome in the parish because of his experience of life and of people in the time before he was ordained and because he showed true Christian love in all he did. He helped to close gaps; between the two sides of the Kettering Road; between the Methodists and the Anglicans; between the regular Church people and those less regular. Living in Oliver Street, he was known by many people who said, 'He's just like us!' Mary, too, had played an important part in the life of the parish, in the widest sense of that word. Worthing, everyone thought, was lucky! Farewells were sad, presentations were made from the church, the school and the organisations. Sydney and Mary would be particularly missed by the elderly and the children. They were leaving before the Festival but would be there for the Fête!

The Autumn Term – a beginning in the world of school – marks a beginning in many other ways too. Charles Moxon started it by a strong reminder of the financial truths shown in the Accounts at the A.G.M.: the need for more income. The Stewardship Campaign was to begin with a Buffet on Monday 6th November and brochures were given out. In the three weeks that followed, everyone would be visited and invited to make pledges. All we possess comes from God and to Him we must return time, money and our talents. We must give time to corporate worship; to use our abilities in the service of God and a realistic portion of our money must be given to the church for God's Work to be done.

From the Campaign, there were 250 pledges but the income from these failed to meet the needs. There was not enough to pay the Diocesan Quota nor to give money to missions and charities, even including the money given in cash collections. Congregations were also falling; Sunday's 8.00 a.m. service had from 40 to 50 communicants; 9.00 a.m. had 25 to 35 (this was to be discontinued) and the 11.00 a.m. Sung Eucharist had 80 to 100; at Evensong there were usually about 100 in the congregation. That made about 300 (from a population of 9,000) going to church on a Sunday. Four years before, the pledged income had been £95 a week; seven years ago it was nearer £100. It cost £90 a week just to keep the church going and any extras to basic maintenance had to come from collections, rents and interest. It was therefore impossible to employ a curate. Finance was a constant problem as it had been from the earliest days of the parish! With hindsight, it was obvious that the big, elaborate building, without adequate endowments, was bound to suffer financial problems. It is somewhat surprising that Pickering Phipps did not foresee the need to invest more of the money he spent on the church so that the interest would be there for future generations.

Another point of interest and discussion was the publication of the New Service for Holy Communion, Alternative Series II; it was approved and was to be experimental for the next four years. Charles Moxon wanted to try it, hoping it would appeal to more people, especially those without a heritage of Anglican worship. The Book of Common Prayer had been used since 1661, with some possible changes at 1928. The new version had new words but the same beliefs. He decided to use it for a service mainly intended for the P.C.C., who could then discuss it. Copies were available for sale. After much discussion, it was decided to introduce the new service in Lent 1968, after suitable preparation and explanation, for a period of not less than twelve months, the situation to be reviewed in 1969. Inevitably there were many opposed to the new service, but Charles Moxon begged them to give it an unprejudiced trial.

At Christmas, Charles introduced a Gift Service and Blessing of the Crib for Christmas Eve, in the afternoon. Christmas Eve was a Sunday that year, the Nine Lessons and Carols was to be at 6.30 p.m. and the Midnight Mass to begin at 11.30 p.m.

So ended Charles Moxon's first year at St. Matthew's, during which he had, with perseverance and endless patience, introduced some possible changes to bring St. Matthew's further into the twentieth century.

31

The Seventy-Fifth Anniversary Year – 1968

The new service of Holy Communion was used from Ash Wednesday. Charles Moxon formulated an Order of Service for three months; then some permitted changes would be introduced for the following three months. To use one form for three months would enable the congregation to become familiar with the text and, to make this as easy as possible, ceremonial changes were to be as few as possible. It was hoped that this new service would make the congregation feel more involved. Worship is something we should do together and the old service left the congregation almost as passive spectators. Comment and criticism would be welcomed but not until the new services had had a fair trial.

In July the P.C.C. gave approval for the use of the new services for Baptism and Evensong to be used for a trial period. Many of the congregation were resistant to the changes but Charles was determined that they should be used and not rejected out of hand.

It had been decided that despite money problems, a curate was essential, and Haydon Llewellyn Jones, curate of Towcester (as Charles had been before him), was to join the staff in September.

This was also the year when sides*women* were elected as well as sides*men*, a real move forward for St. Matthew's!

On 9th May the Duchess of Gloucester opened the new Diocesan Retreat House, Ecton House, once the old Rectory and situated opposite the church. Work had been going on to prepare the house and appeals had raised the necessary money for the alterations. Residence was being provided for twenty-four people and there were facilities for meetings in rooms of different sizes, including a large lounge as well as kitchen and dining room. There was also a chapel and a library. It was a facility which had long been needed, Bishop Blagden had suggested it in 1931.

The Festival of 1968, which would mark the seventy-fifth Birthday of St. Matthew's Church, was to be a great occasion. Gordon Crosse was commissioned to write an anthem, a work for Choir and Organ, two pianos and percussion. It was to use the words of the Chester Miracle Play – God's Covenant with Man after the Flood – and to be called 'The Convenant of the Rainbow'. It would be performed at Evensong on the Eve of St. Matthew's Day, a most interesting work but not altogether practical to perform!

Herbert Howells had composed a new communion motet for St. Matthew's Day, to be sung by unaccompanied choir, with words from Psalm 24, 'One thing have I desired of the Lord'. Benjamin Britten's 'Rejoice in the Lamb', first sung twenty-five years ago, was to be the anthem at Evensong on 22nd September. Trumpets and trombones sent forth the fanfares from the Minstrel's Gallery.

During the Festival Week, there would be three concerts; the English Chamber Orchestra; a concert by Johnny Dankworth and Cleo Laine and others, the Dankworth Ensemble, a fantastic introduction to jazz; and thirdly, the Northampton Bach Choir to sing Bach's B minor Mass, with professional soloists. There would be an Exhibition to illustrate seventy-five years of the Church and Parish and, after the Festival, from 3rd to 6th October there were to be a Flower Festival and a Concert by the St. Matthew's Singers. On 10th, 11th and 12th October there were to be major dramatic performances of T. S. Eliot's *Murder in the Cathedral* produced by Catherine Clarke. At the same time, David Gommon arranged an Exhibition of paintings and sculpture in the University Centre in Barrack Road, to illustrate 'The Church and Art', to include some of the works owned by Dean Hussey.

It was in 1968, too, that the P.C.C. finally decided to build a new Parish Hall. The idea had been around for many years and plans had been shown to Charles Moxon while he was still in Weybridge. In the past it had never seemed to be quite the right moment, but now the decision was taken. The land, between the Vicarage and the Nursing Home, had already been acquired and £13,000 had accumulated in the Memorial Hall Fund over the years. By selling the land in Collingwood Road where the Church Room had stood for so long, there should be enough money for the building. In time, this land was auctioned for £15,000 and a sale of 'bricks' was arranged to raise the money to equip the building when it was built. The contract was signed on 17th June, the job to take sixty weeks. It was to have three halls, one large, two small; a kitchen, choir room and, above, a flat. Entrance was to be from The Drive, through a parking area.

The Festival was a memorable occasion and the lunch graced by the presence of the Mayor and many friends and former curates. It was a splendid meal with, once again, particular thanks to Gwen Smith and her helpers.

For Michael Nicholas and the choir of St. Matthew's, Northampton

THE COVENANT OF THE RAINBOW

Commissioned Music II 'The Covenant of the Rainbow' composed by Gordon Crosse for Michael Nicholas and St. Matthew's Choir.

At the services, the ceremonial was most impressive and the Choir, under Michael Nicholas, impeccable. The main preachers had one theme, the need to go out and to be agents for Christ. All the music was recorded, with mountains of equipment in the Choir Vestry! Fred Stallard, Fred Whittle and Methuen Clarke were to preach at services during the month of October. A second grand-daughter for Charles and Phyllis, Emily Jane, tried to upstage the whole show by arriving on 20th September, St. Matthew's Eve!

The Flower Festival was unbelievably beautiful, with wonderful displays, some of which seemed to defy gravity. There were most ingenious arrangements, including musical instruments at the windows. Nearly 3,500 visitors came to see and there was a profit of £190. On 9th October a great stage filled the crossing of the church and went down the nave, ready for the great experience of *Murder in the Cathedral*. A great deal of work but a magnificent celebration.

It was in 1969 that the idea of a Choral Evensong, once a month, was mooted. This was to be at 3.30 p.m., to last forty-five minutes, to have no sermon, but to give the Choir a chance to sing a Cathedral-type service. There would be an anthem and the opportunity to use different settings for the Canticles.

To celebrate the end of the seventy-fifth year came the Opening of the new Parish Centre. The keys were handed over to Keith Locke on 10th July; the old Parish Room had been burnt on 13th May, so for the summer there was no Hall and the organisations had to use the School Building, when it was available. During this time, much thought was given to the best use of the new rooms. The Church School would use it for School Dinners and some other activities, and this would provide some useful income. It must be used for the good of the whole parish; for the organisations that met in the evenings and also day-time groups. It would also be used for the Sunday School. It was important that the Sunday School groups should meet at the time of the main Sunday Eucharist but it was also necessary that the Teachers should be able to make their own communion. The times of the Sunday services were therefore under careful consideration. It was thought that a 9.00 a.m. said Communion and a 10.15 a.m. Sung Eucharist would be most suitable, the latter giving time for coffee in the Centre after the service. The problem was given plenty of time for consideration and, of course, there were people for and against the suggestion as well as plenty of alternative suggestions! It wasn't until July that a decision was finally reached by the P.C.C. and then only after it had been agreed to add an 8.00 a.m. service in the summer months if clergy were available. The new times were approved by 17 votes, with 2 against and 6 abstaining. It was agreed that a crêche for under fives would be available for the 10.15 service.

At the beginning of July, Mr. and Mrs. Pitcher, from Leicester, moved into the new flat, to be caretakers and for Mr. Pitcher to be Verger.

Philip Turner's idea of a Nave Altar was to be followed further. There had been problems obtaining the necessary Faculty, but the platform was fixed at the Chancel steps and the portable altar, the gift of the Misses Agutter in memory of their parents, was put into position. When it was not in use it could be placed under the Graham Sutherland painting. The Mothers' Union contributed 200 new hassocks, requesting that they were not used as foot-rests! The first use of the new altar was at the Sung Eucharist on 4th May. Inevitably some of the congregation found the change too revolutionary but many enjoyed the more intimate nature of the service and the fact that the choir was not shut away. The new service times were to begin in October and were scheduled as a year's trial.

Charles and Phyllis Moxon went to Teheran to visit their daughter, son-in-law and the grandchildren for a month, returning to the final arrangements for the Opening of the Parish Centre. This took place on Wednesday 10th September. Evensong was at 7.30 p.m. when the Bishop of Peterborough was to preach; then everyone processed over to the Centre for the Dedication. It was intended as a real family occasion. The keys were handed to the Bishop by Keith Locke who had done so much to oversee the work; the door was unlocked, the plaque unveiled and the building dedicated. Afterwards everyone squeezed into the Hall and celebrated with cheese and wine, prepared by Gwen Smith and her marvellous team of helpers and served by the Guides and Scouts. The dream had come true!

On Sunday 14th September the B.B.C. was to record 'Sunday Half-Hour' from St. Matthew's, to be broadcast on Radio 2 on St. Matthew's Day. Philip Turner was back to supervise the recording and the congregation was boosted by visitors from the Kingsley Park Methodists and from neighbouring Anglican churches.

The Festival, the beginning of the seventy-sixth year but also the climax of the seventy-fifth, was unusual in *not* having any Bishops, but the preachers were still well-known.

As on other occasions the family took the stage, with the arrival of twin sons, Nicholas and Benjamin, to Michael and Sarah Moxon. Two more grandchildren for the Vicarage!

32

Changes Ahead?

In the first magazine of 1969, Charles Moxon explained the importance of Unity in the Church. Unity is not uniformity, the Anglican Church includes a wide diversity of worship. The Anglican-Methodist proposals for the Union of the two churches were to be discussed locally and the January Diocesan Conference was to vote on it, while later in the year, the Convocations would make decisions. The Week of Prayer for Christian Unity had particular significance for 1969.

The questions to be put to the Diocesan Conference were to see if the Assembly,
1. agreed that Unity should be sought in two stages,
2. approved the proposed Ordinal,
3. approved the proposed Service of Reconciliation,
4. agreed to inaugurate Stage 1.

Though the idea of unity was acceptable to most people, the suggested Service of Reconciliation was not popular; the essence of the Service was the Reception of the Methodist Ministers into the Ministry of the Church of England; many people, including the Bishop of Peterborough, felt that this service would be both divisive and evasive. The Bishop believed that the Methodists should be asked to accept Ordination or Conditional Ordination to the Priesthood.

At the Diocesan Conference, 65 per cent of the clergy and 77 per cent of the laity were agreed that unity should be sought, but the clergy rejected the Reconciliation Service by 134 votes to 103, but approved Stage 1 by 125 votes to 112. The laity were in favour in both cases. Later, the clergy were to be asked if they would actually take part in a Service of Reconciliation; if this resulted in a sizeable vote against, it would be necessary to reject the scheme.

The Methodist District Synods showed 67 per cent for going forward, though at the Quarterly Meetings, from which the representatives to Synod would be chosen, the voting was only 60 per cent in favour. Mr Burd, the Minister of Kingsley Park Methodist Church, said that he was somewhat relieved that no larger percentage had been reached. He did not think there was widespread feeling against Unity but there was against the *method* of Unity! Union involves changes and the votes made it obvious that people were not yet ready to accept such changes.

Subsequent votes continued to approve the idea without approving the methods. Though formal union was rejected, there was nothing to stop informal contacts at local level. It was not a time for despair.

Charles Moxon felt that 1970 looked back over a period of change in the parish. New forms of worship, new times of services had been accepted without too much opposition. The new Parish Centre was being usefully and profitably used. There was now need for a time of consolidation to build up numbers; for regular worship and for public witness. The Church needed to stand firm and resolute and everyone needed to show Christ's standards in their lives.

Change was, however, coming in the wider church. The Church Assembly was to become the General Synod; the Diocesan Conference the Diocesan Synod and the Ruri-Decanal Conference the Deanery Synods. The General Synod was to have 500 members (from 700); the Diocesan Synod 250 (from 700). In the past *all* clergy were on the Diocesan Conferences and *every* parish had *one* lay representative. Under the new scheme, the clergy would elect about a third of their number to the new synod and the lay representatives would be elected from the Deanery Synods, not directly from the parishes. To ensure that there would be a 'new look' it was intended that the laity would elect people who would take an active part and be ready to report back; it was also desirable that *young* men and women should be elected as well as others with longer experience. In the Diocese, the Deaneries were to be reduced from twenty- one to fourteen and the Rural Deans would serve for a maximum of nine years. The new Deanery Synods were expected to be a vital link in the chain. They would consist of all clergy together with lay representatives, the number of these would be related to the Electoral Roll of the parish. Deanery Synods were to elect both Diocesan and General Synod Representatives; they were to meet to discuss and express opinions on matters to go to the Diocesan Synod; thus they would be the means of communication between the parishes and the diocese and could bring the views of the parishes to diocesan notice. It was a somewhat idealistic set-up and, understandably, the reality was never to measure up to the ideal!

At the Parish A.G.M., one representative to Deanery Synod was to be elected for every sixty-five names on the Electoral Roll and then, in September, the Diocesan members would be elected.

In St. Matthew's there were 453 names on the Roll (221 living within the parish and 232 outside) so eight representatives were possible; those elected were: Miss Collins and Miss Lightburne together with Messrs. Ball, Leese, Hartwell, Pickaver, Dalziel and Adams. The twenty P.C.C. members were Mrs. Fraiel, Mrs. Goodfellow, Miss Ogborn, Miss Ward, with Messrs. Abrams, A.V. Allen, R. Allen, Bateman, Dowdy, Garrett, Gates, James, Kohler, March, Marriott, Nicholls, Rawlinson, Taylor, Tilsey and Vickers. In future the Electoral Roll would be revised every six years.

The new General Synod was to be opened on 4th November 1970 in the presence of the Queen and Prince Philip, at Church House, Westminster, following a service of Holy Communion at Westminster Abbey. Earlier, on 17th October the Diocesan Synod was inaugurated at Peterborough Cathedral.

The Deaneries were asked to find £73,500 by the Parish Quotas and to discuss the possibility of introducing a Parish Shares Scheme. This scheme was designed to spread the financial load more fairly among the parishes than the Quota System had done. In the old system, each parish had provided figures of total income over the previous three years, back income. Certain allowances were deducted, money spent on clergy stipends and expenses; money given to charities; major expenditure on fabric, etc. The Deanery Quota wsa calculated from these net figures and then decided what each parish should pay. St. Matthew's had never found it easy to raise the money and had not always managed to do so. The Parish Shares Scheme, already used in the dioceses of Lichfield and Coventry, was based on *expected* income from active Church members, the allocation of the shares being done after direct consultation with parish and Deanery representatives. One wonders if the time needed for such detailed consultation had been considered!

In November 1971, after much discussion, the Parish Shares Scheme was accepted by an overwhelming majority at the Diocesan Synod. It was to come into effect from 1st January 1972, phased in over four years. The key factor in the calculation was to be the size of the potential income. Each parish would complete a questionnaire, bearing on the finances'; submit the latest Balance Sheet and Parish Accounts and there would be an interview with the Incumbent and three P.C.C. members. These interviews would be in the May/June period and the amounts of the Shares would be available June/July. Each parish would have thirty days to lodge an appeal if it so wished.

At St. Matthew's, money was desperately needed to boost the income and at every Stewardship Service on Stewardship Sundays, Charles Moxon would appeal for more to join the scheme and for everyone to be realistic in their giving.

Costs were constantly rising, the money obtained from the sale of the land adjoining the Nursing Home, was to be used for the maintenance of the Parish Centre. The Church Commissioners had paid a proportion of clergy salaries from Historic Resources, but there remained a proportion to be paid by the parish and the parish was also responsible for clergy expenses. Charles Moxon received less than £800 a year from the Commissioners and the rest had to come from the parish and the diocese. St. Matthew's had no endowments or reserves and, by this time, needed £6,500 a year; about £120 a week; £85 for general upkeep; £25 for the Quota and £10 for charitable giving. This did not allow for any emergencies!

Back in May 1970, there was a new venture for the diocese. This was a Children's Pilgrimage to the Saxon Church of Brixworth. It was intended for ten to thirteen-year-olds, who would spend time exploring the church and learning about religious communities, with a service at 3.30 p.m. which would be open to everyone, an act of worship at which the work of the day would be offered to God. The response was over 160 attending and a second Pilgrimage was held at Barnack in September. It was a most successful idea.

In July 1972, Bishop Eastaugh was to retire, following his tenth Anniversary as Bishop of Peterborough. He was to be followed by Bishop Douglas Feaver, who had been Vicar of St. Mary's in Nottingham for fourteen years.

Charles Moxon was Chaplain to the Mayor for the year, which added to his responsibilities. The Mayor and Mayoress, Kenneth and Mrs. Pearson, were to attend the Festival Solemn Eucharist when the Bishop of Lynn was to preach and Bishop Graham-Campbell would preside. In the old days the Solemn Eucharist was always held on the *morning* of St. Matthew's Day and people were expected to take the day off work to attend. For the last eight years it had been changed to an evening time to make a large attendance more practical.

The Mayor celebrated his year by planting a tree in the Vicarage garden. There were worries over the increasing trends of church attendance and the shortage of ordinands. People no longer came regularly to two services on a Sunday. The attendance at the 9.00 a.m. service was increasing but that at the 10.15 a.m. was down. Charles Moxon suggested introducing a short sermon to the 9.00 a.m. service. Numbers attending Evensong were also down, unless there was some special occasion. Was there a danger of 'affluence leading to a selfish, materialistic and greedy society'?

There was certainly no room for complacency!

33

The Eightieth Anniversary and After

Nineteen seventy-three was the year of the eightieth Anniversary of the consecration of the church and was the sixth year of Charles Moxon's incumbency. There were usually around 200 communicants at the Sunday Communions, about double on Festival occasions, and financially the parish was about paying its way. The Parish Share had been paid in full and the money for the Organ Restoration was being raised, but there were loans to repay and the savings had been due to the absence of a curate, not a desirable economy. There was some hope during the year that Alan Deboo, whose father had been a contemporary of the Vicar's, would join the staff, but in the end he went to Brackley.

To celebrate the year, it was hoped that money could be raised to buy new cassocks, surplices and albs for the choir and the servers, and to provide new hymnbooks. Cassocks cost £10, surplices and albs £5 each and the hymnbooks were 60p. It was calculated that £500 would cover what was needed, representing about £2 a head for the congregation. The money was raised before the Festival in September, when there was a real splash of colour, the black cassocks of the past being replaced by red for the choir and purple for the servers.

At the Festival on 21st September, the highlight of St. Matthew's year, the new Bishop of Peterborough, Douglas Feaver, was to preach at the Solemn Mass, being welcomed with the 'Introit' by Bruckner with the organ and three trombones. A newly commissioned work by William Mathias, Professor of Music at Bangor, was performed and, on the Eve of St. Matthew's Day, was given the thirtieth Anniversary performance of Benjamin Britten's 'Rejoice in the Lamb'.

Charles Moxon was somewhat depressed by the world's problems of inflation, violence and vandalism, though he continued to preach his belief that any despair or despondency was not for the Christian. In 1975, he announced that he would be leaving in the autumn to be Precentor and Canon Residentiary at Salisbury Cathedral. His eight and a half years at St. Matthew's had been happy, though challenging and very hard work. He was now looking forward to a new life and found it exciting to be returning to a Cathedral and all the changes that entailed. He was helped in the parish by Father Leslie Bearman, who had retired, and he was glad to be leaving the parish with its finances in reasonably good order. The Parish Share of £1,870 had been paid; all domestic commitments had been met; money had been given to Missions and there was money in the Reserve Funds for the Organ and the Fabric. However, he warned the Annual Meeting that costs were rising, that they were 'saving' by having no curate nor other paid Parish Worker and that, as clergy stipends were to rise, the Parish Share would also increase. We in the Church of England, he said, have always had our religion on the cheap, due to the generosity of past benefactors, but the time was coming when, like the Free Churches, we would have to pay our way.

Charles was to be installed in Salisbury on 1st October so they would move during the Festival, returning for the final service.

St. Matthew's Day was on Sunday in 1975. The anthem on the Eve was to be Gerald Finiz's 'Lo, the full, final sacrifice', words by the seventeenth-century poet Richard Crashaw, commissioned for choir in 1946. At the Solemn Eucharist, the preacher was the Rev'd. Eric Abbott, the former Dean of Westminster. Michael Moxon was to be the celebrant and would also preach at Evensong. A fitting tribute to him and to his father. On the Sunday of the Octave, Charles himself would celebrate at both morning Eucharists and would preach at Evensong.

For eight and a half years, said Charles Moxon, he had had the privilege of serving the parish and digging up roots would be painful to him and to Mrs. Moxon, and the whole family would find it difficult to shed the links with St. Matthew's. Phyllis Moxon had done a great deal in her own right, she had taught at the local Church school and come to know the staff, the children and their parents. She had worked very hard to make the Christian Aid Shop a success and channelled the money off to many useful projects. She had always time for the people of the parish, who found her a real friend and loved her for her gentle and loving personality. She even found time for the clergy of the Seven Parishes, especially those who had come new, and their wives. Friendships made by both Charles and Phyllis were long-lasting and they never lost their love for St. Matthew's.

Charles prayed that the new Vicar would be upheld as he had been; he would need, he said, 'your friendship and affection, for being the Vicar of this parish is no easy task!'

Once more St. Matthew's congregation was plunged into an Interregnum.

34

Music from 1965 – Michael Nicholas

Michael Nicholas, who came to St. Matthew's as Organist in 1965, when John Bertalot had gone to Blackburn Cathedral, had an amazing capacity for work, running the Bach Choir and the St. Matthew's Singers, as well as the Church Choir. He also taught music at Northampton Boys' Grammar School. He had a dry wit, which rarely repeated itself, and could be sarcastic, but he kept his choirs to a very high standard and they worked for him enthusiastically. He was immensely interested in producing new works for the Bach Choir Concerts and the Church Festivals.

From lack of space in his lodgings, he kept his grand piano in the church and a story is told of it being played one evening as dusk approached, and the pianist looking up to find a 'grey lady' listening. The ghost was Deaconess Sankey, who had silently entered the church!

At his first Festival, in 1965, the choir sang Kenneth Leighton's new anthem, a jazzy setting of George Herbert's 'Let All the World in Every Corner Sing' and the Canticles were also set by Dr. Leighton, as written for Magdalen College, Oxford. At the Sung Eucharist, the setting was Byrd's Four-Part, with Dexter's Gloria in D, the basses joining the congregation in the nave for an exciting climax.

Around the same time, four choirboys had passed Grade V and two had gone to the Louth Festival and to sing in Lincoln Cathedral. In October, the choir had gone to sing Evensong in Peterborough Cathedral and, in early November, to Christ's College, Cambridge, with a later visit to St. Alban's. The same month had the Bach Choir presenting a mix of Bach and Vaughan Williams, and two weeks later the new Cantata Orchestra of London performed in the church.

Michael Nicholas' monthly 'Music Notes', in the parish magazine, were short but stimulating and must have helped to encourage audiences to the concerts he was initiating. He also listed full details of the music used in Sunday services and the organ voluntaries, carefully mixing new and less usual music with old favourites.

It was Michael Nicholas who really got the organ restored, though the need had been obvious for some time. He finally brought attention to its problems, an unusable manual; noisy pedal stops; other stops and couplers which sometimes refused to work at all and the need to replace many of the hundreds of leather purses on the swell. It was also desirable to complete the electrification. Too much had been spent in temporary repairs.

He was a supporter of the new Training Scheme for choirboys inaugurated in December 1965 by the Royal School of Church Music; the St. Matthew's Choir was represented at the inaugural service, and he took the choir to Blackburn Cathedral in June 1966 and to Coventry in July.

There was an exciting concert season ahead, some in aid of the Organ Fund. The church was building a reputation for concerts, as well as for exciting music at services. On 29th June 1966 there was a special recital by the church choir of seven of the anthems specially commissioned for St. Matthew's.

Naturally 'Rejoice in the Lamb', Britten's 1943 contribution, was one, with others by Leighton, Rubbra, Finzi, Berkeley, Judge and Arnold; as well as the organ-work first played in 1946, Britten's 'Prelude and Fugue on a Theme of Vittoria'; a most ambitious programme. In July there was a recital by a choir from New Jersey, U.S.A., and another from Denmark, both much enjoyed, though there was natural disappointment that Alec Wyton's visit had to be cancelled.

The Festival of 1966 took place during the interregnum and the special commission, as already recorded, was John McCabe's 'A Hymne to God the Father' from a poem by John Donne; the poem, Michael explained, though it might seem an odd choice, was the one chosen by the young composer. The music, he described as strange and new but lovely, the words being searching but introspective. As the church was facing the need to raise money for the organ, Michael Nicholas and the choirmen had decided to pay for the new work themselves. During the Festival week, there was a special concert by the Midland Sinfonia Orchestra under its conductor, Neville Dilkes, playing two of Bach's Brandenburg Concertos. The church choir sang Purcell's 'My Beloved spoke', to the orchestral accompaniment.

An important innovation around this time was the sending of more of the choirboys on summer R.S.C.M. courses, half of the cost being met from the Choir Fund.

On 5th November, after the Festival, Choral Evensong was for the A.G.M. of the Northampton Organists' Association, Ron Gates was to be installed as the next year's President. On the 9th there was a programme of Bach by the St. Matthew's Singers and on the 19th a Bach Choir Concert!

Philip Turner, as Vicar, greatly encouraged the music and was interested in using music in the religious plays he wrote. With the arrival of Charles Moxon, they had someone with experience of Cathedral Choirs, who sang the Office beautifully and was deeply concerned with the dignity and beauty of all services. Music at St. Matthew's was set fair! Many programmes were arranged to raise money and many visiting musicians were persuaded to help.

In May 1967, the choir of the University of Bristol visited St. Matthew's and on the 28th there was a recital of clarinet and piano by Peter David and Donetta Wallace, a combination particularly suited to the acoustics of the church.

The 1967 Festival produced the work 'Five Christmas Carols' by Richard Rodney Bennett, an unexpected opportunity as his works were mostly instrumental; these now appear in 'Carols for Choirs', dedicated to Michael Nicholas and the St. Matthew's Choir; at the same concert, the organ recital was by Harry Gabb. Other concerts included the Ely Cathedral Choir and the Bloomsbury Singers' performance of Britten's 'A Boy was born'. This is rarely performed as it is a difficult work, so it was another unusual opportunity. The choirboys had a part to sing!

In February 1968, there was to be a performance of Schubert's song-cycle 'Die Schone Mullerin' with Vaughan Meakins, baritone, and Terence Allbright, piano; it was in German but translation was to be provided. In March there was to be music for voices and wind-instruments played by members of the London Brass Consort and others, including Purcell's Music for the funeral of Queen Mary; Stravinsky's 'Mass'; and Matthew Locke's 'Music for His Majesty's Cornetts and Sackbuts' of 1661. The choir was the Church Choir together with the St. Matthew's Singers.

In May two important vocal works by Benjamin Britten, 'A Charm of Lullabies' and Canticle II 'Abram and Isaac', were sung by Diana Gillingham and Stephen Meakins, both well known in Northampton and also more widely. June brought back John Bertalot with the Blackburn Bach Choir and, in July, the Northampton Bach Choir was to sing Handel's 'Messiah' – 'as Handel intended it to be heard'.

Nineteen sixty-nine was also closely packed with musical occasions, three choral concerts in May and the Lawrence Lloyd Singers gave a concert in April for the Organ Appeal. Under their conductor Stephen Meakins, they performed Herbert Howells 'Motet on the Death of President Kennedy', for the unaccompanied choir with its text from Latin lyrics translated by Helen Waddell and Gerald Finzi's anthem from the 1946 Festival, as well as organ solos by Terence Allbright. Later there was a concert by the Alan Civil Horn Trio with Alan Civil on the French horn; Hugh Bean on the violin and David Parkhouse at the piano.

Variety is important and the musical occasions in June concluded with a recital by Desmond Dupre of lute and guitar; while the Choir was off to Coventry Cathedral and later to the Wollaston Festival.

The 1969 Festival had the London Mozart Players with a concert of symphonies by Haydn and Mozart; a 'Concerto Grosso' by Handel and two modern works, Malcolm Arnold's 'Oboe Concerto' and Michael Tippett's 'Little Music for Strings'. The Eucharist on St. Matthew's Day was to be to a setting by Edmund Rubbra, for double choir, in the composer's characteristic and contrapuntal style, it was originally written for Canterbury Cathedral in 1945.

Michael Nicholas had many of the Choir's performances recorded, and usually the person in charge was hidden in the Minstrel's Gallery, the microphone being slung on a wire fixed across the screen. There was at least one occasion when the large banner carried in the final procession got caught up and only untangled when the bearer backed away and then processed for several yards with bent knees!

In complete contrast, in October 1969, there was a concert by the Michael Garrick Sextet, a top jazz group!

In November, the Laurence Lloyd Singers celebrated their tenth birthday by a concert conducted by Stephen Meakins; this included two choral contributions written by former members of the Singers and ended with Mozart's 'Coronation Mass'. In the same month, Michael Nicholas conducted Bach's 'Joyous Magnificat' and Vaughan William's Christmas Cantata 'Hodie', repeated by popular request, and the audience was asked to join in the 1953 Coronation setting of the 'Old Hundredth'. In December there was the ever popular carol concert!

Nineteen seventy was another music-packed year. Michael Nicholas was to give four recitals of Bach's Organ Music. In May, Christopher Robinson, the organist from Worcester Cathedral, gave a recital; the programme included Elgar's 'Sonata in G'; the Mozart 'Fantasia in F minor' and the First Movement of Vidor's 'Fifth Organ Sonata'. In July, the John Alldis Octet presented a varied programme. At all times the choir was kept busy in addition to the normal services; their visits varied from village church to Cathedral; Hardingstone Patronal Festival; Salisbury Cathedral; Great Horwood, in Buckinghamshire; Earls Barton – a recital with David Kossof and Bob Cort; Westbury-on-Trym near Bristol; and back to St. Matthew's for the Northampton and District Organists' Association, an occasion which included Kelly's Latin-American style canticles and Brahms' 'How Lovely are Thy Dwellings'.

In 1971, the organ was finally dismantled but concerts still went on! The Northamptonshire Festival of the Arts held the Opening Service at St. Matthew's on 28th February, the Church Choir with String Orchestra, playing Purcell and Elgar. The Festival stretched from March to May and the church took an active part.

It was a considerable shock to everyone when Michael Nicholas announced his appointment to Norwich, though no one had really expected him to stay for ever and his talents deserved wider experience and recognition. He had brought great talents and great enthusiasm to his work in the six years he had been at St. Matthew's, and Norwich Cathedral would reap the benefit.

Though Michael left Northampton just after Easter, the impetus continued. The invaluable and talented Charles Barker once more filled the gap.

St. Matthew's musical reputation was not dimmed!

35

Music with Stephen Cleobury

Stephen Cleobury's arrival heralded some changes but no diminution of enthusiasm nor of musical occasions. He was an excellent musician with a brain which could remember every detail; somewhat less witty than his predecessor but mature in his approach despite being only twenty-two; he maintained an excellent standard and the same momentum of hard work. Charles Barker finally decided to resign as assistant organist, so Ron Gates was appointed in his place, starting new with Stephen Cleobury, the two making an excellent team.

On New Year's Day 1972, the choir sang Choral Evensong at St. Paul's Cathedral in London. The Vicar, Charles Moxon, sang the service (back in his old haunts!) and it was a glorious occasion as testified by the people who travelled with him. A new idea which followed was that of singing madrigals by candlelight, initiated by the St. Matthew's Singers and repeated in successive years.

In March, there was a recital by the internationally known guitarist Turibio Santos, Brazilian by birth but then Professor at the Paris Conservatoire. In April, the Birmingham Cathedral Choir gave a programme of Early Church Music and some from the Victorian Period, starting with Handel's 'Zadok the Priest'. An exciting idea was to have special organ recitals on the restored organ by 'St. Matthew's Men': Stephen Cleobury, organist in residence; Alec Wyton, on a whistle-stop tour from the U.S.A. and John Bertalot from Blackburn (the last piece in his programme was described as 'A Concert on a Lake, interrupted by a thunderstorm')! The recitals were followed by refreshments in the Parish Centre and the occasions were popular and well attended from the joy of meeting old friends, as well as for the musical feasts! The Bach Choir continued to give regular concerts, in fact so

Music with Stephen Cleobury

Stephen Cleobury at the organ console.

much took place that even reading the programmes leaves one breathless!

The Northampton Arts Festival again involved St. Matthew's. The Bach Choir presented music by the Bach Family, not only that of Johann Sebastian but also by his sons Carl Philip Emmanuel and Johann Christian, with pieces for harpsichord and an instrumental ensemble. In November the Bach Choir and Orchestra and the St. Matthew's Singers presented an exciting concert, with Stephen Cleobury's brother as a soloist in a Handel's organ concerto. This was followed two weeks later by the Laurence Lloyd Singers with two of St. Matthew's commissioned works; Britten's 'Rejoice in the Lamb' and Judge's 'Ambrosian Prayer'.

It was also in 1972 that Vaughan Meakins, who had joined the church choir when he was eight, and worked under both Robert Joyce and John Bertalot, had received three awards at the end of his fourth year at the Royal College of Music, one for being the most distinguished male student of the year. He also won a prize for conducting and he conducted the College Choir and Orchestra in the presence of the Queen Mother, to whom he was presented. A great honour for Vaughan and with some reflections on St. Matthew's!

Nineteen seventy-three welcomed the choir of Worcester Cathedral where Stephen Cleobury had sung in his schooldays. In March, the Bach Choir gave a complete performance of Bach's 'St. Matthew's Passion', given in two parts from 6.00 to 7.30 and 8.00 to 10.00 p.m. Stephen wrote suitable programme notes on the history of the music, showing how Bach's Passion settings developed from the early Liturgical Drama and explained some of the symbolism employed.

During Lent it was decided not to use the organ at Evensong except for the final hymn and the voluntary, thus partly following historic custom. The choir was to sing mostly Plainsong, but also, as an anthem, Tompkin's setting of 'David's Lament for his son Absalom'. On Passion Sunday, Stainer's 'Crucifixion' was to be sung, with the congregation joining in the hymns which are an important part of the work. On Palm Sunday and Good Friday, Vittoria's settings for the St. Matthew and St. John accounts of the last few days of the life of Christ were used, the words of the crowd were sung by the choir, the other passages, in Plainsong, dating from the fifth century. Also on the Good Friday, the St. Matthew's Singers performed Liszt's 'Via Crucis'. In the original the worshippers moved in procession between the Stations of the Cross but, on this occasion, they remained still and the action of the fourteen Stations were mimed. Catherine Richardson (Clarke) was responsible for the production which became a most moving religious experience for everyone, not least for those participating in the mime, who found themselves 'being there' rather than acting.

May brought a complete change with a recital by the Philip Jones Brass Ensemble. The summer concerts cleared the last debt on the organ. These included an organ recital by Michael Nicholas and the Halcyon Wind Quintet and the Bach Choir, with Graham Mayo playing the organ and the St. Matthew's Singers with a String Orchestra. While the Church Choir was off to Ely Cathedral in July.

Nineteen seventy-three brought the eightieth Anniversary with all the celebrations, which have already been described. At the Arts Festival in October the London Gabrieli Brass Ensemble played in the church.

In December 'from a tinkle to a clamour; a tap to a boom; humour, exuberance, solemnity – the whole descriptive range that makes up the World of Percussion' – this was the introduction to an illustrated talk, with piano accompaniment by Joan Turner, by the timpanist and percussionist James Blades, at the Parish Centre. A most unusual opportunity, to bear witness to the versatility of St. Matthew's and its people.

One begins to wonder how anyone had time to draw breath. The New Year of 1974 brought the choir of St. John's College, Cambridge, another choir with an international reputation. Unfortunately, in the dire state of the heating system, the concert had to be held at St. Giles' Church and the return visit of the Alan Civil Horn Trio had to be held in the Carnegie Hall, but the celebration of St. Valentine's Day took place in the reasonable warmth of the Parish Centre. 'More Heat for St. Matthew's' needed £8,000, some of which was raised by a sponsored walk. June was enlivened by a Bach Choir Concert with Dvořák's 'Mass in D' and Britten's 'Hymn to St. Cecilia'. There was also a recital by the Laurence Lloyd Singers with Nicolas Kynaston at the organ. The organ fund having been closed, there was now the Heating Fund to be worked for!

Stephen Cleobury's departure to Westminster Abbey was preceded by his Organ Recital in aid of the Heating Fund. The recital was very well attended as the audience was also saying its farewell to Stephen, Penny and baby Helen. They would be much missed but were wished a happy and successful future.

The musical life of St. Matthew's was left in very good heart.

36

And Afterwards

Timothy Day was the organist from 1974 and gave an organ recital to raise money in March 1976, though he was to leave that summer; it was the same year as the marvellous, co-operative effort that produced 'St Joan' in the round! The costumes were particularly effective and the five performances were seen by almost 600 people, raising money for the Heating Fund.

Ray Allen retired from the choir that year, after fifty years, having joined as a boy chorister in 1925. One of the great characteristics of the St. Matthew's choir, still true today, is that, when a boy's voice breaks he is not lost to the choir, resting for a while if necessary, then singing alto until his voice has 'settled down' as a tenor or a bass.

In September, the Piacevole Orchestra, conducted by Richard Roddis, gave a concert including Sibelius' tone poem 'Finlandia'; Dvořák's Seventh Symphony and the 'Clarinet Concerto' by Mozart, the clarinettist being Mark van de Wiel. This also added to the Heating Fund. In November, the Bach Choir and the Bach Orchestra performed Mendelssohn's 'Elijah', under the auspices of the St. Matthew's Concert Society. Early in 1977, they gave Schubert's Mass in E flat and later, Handel's Chandos Anthem 'The King shall Rejoice' and Haydn's 'Clock Symphony'. In February, one Saturday evening was devoted to a programme of words, song and scripture readings, with rock and soul music.

David Ponsford, arriving as the new organist, found himself involved in a busy programme of music. Malcolm Tyler conducted the Northamptonshire Choir and Orchestra in Haydn's 'Creation' in April, and one week later, the Concert Society sponsored the Fitzwilliam String Quartet at the Parish Centre, playing items from Mozart, Beethoven and Shostokovitch. A concert was arranged for each Saturday in June; an Organ Recital by

Andrew Newberry, the sub-organist at Peterborough Cathedral; the Music Society presented the Schola Cantorum of Oxford; then there was the Bach Choir Summer Concert and an evening of Gilbert and Sullivan – plenty of variety!

In September, David and Liz Ponsford (Elizabeth O'Dell – soprano) gave a recital with David playing the harpsichord, featuring works by Purcell, Bach, Rameau and Charissimi and in November, the Concert Society, chaired by David and with Liz as Secretary, sponsored six ex-choral scholars of St. John's, Cambridge, who had been singing together for five years, in a concert which demonstrated a variety of styles of choral music: English Tudor; European Renaissance; Elizabethan Secular and Sacred; Victorian Part-Songs and Negro Spirituals.

Nineteen seventy-eight produced another busy year, starting with the Medici String Quartet. In July on U.S.P.G. Sunday, there was a Festal Evensong at Ecton, when the Bishop of Zululand preached, and later that month, a large choir from Poitiers (Northampton's twin town) was invited to Northampton. The Children's Concerts were becoming very popular and were often arranged to precede an evening concert as, in October, James Blades gave a talk/demonstration at Nene College in the afternoon on 'The World of Percussion' and in the evening gave 'Then and Now' at the Parish Centre.

In November, the London Early Music Group gave a concert of Renaissance and Early Baroque Music with viols, crumhorn, lute, etc., and in the same month the Bach Choir sang Bach's 'Christmas Oratorio', followed by their much appreciated Christmas Concert in December, conducted by their new conductor, Malcolm Tyler, and with Marisa Robles playing the harp. The Bach Choir was no longer being conducted by the Organist of St. Matthew's Church, but was still using the Parish Centre for rehearsals, so there was still a connection with the church, though not such a close one as before.

In the summer of 1979, Derek Gillard took over as organist, and the great number and variety of concerts continued. The January 1980 Children's Concert at Nene College involved talks on early instruments; the serpent, sackbut, euphonium and ophicleide. The concert was, as usual, followed by an evening version in the Parish Centre. When the Coull String Quartet from Warwick University performed, they included a piece to celebrate Sir Michael Tippett's seventy-fifth birthday. In June, the Bach Choir performed Durafle's 'Requiem' and Stravinsky's 'Mass', with Andrew Newberry as organist. The Concert Society sponsored the King's Singers in September but at the new Spinney Hill Hall attached to

Northampton School for Girls. In October, the Early Music Group gave a fascinating concert of songs and music of the medieval troubadours (1150 to 1300) using lute, psaltery, recorder, regal, dulcimer and rebec.

In May 1981 came the welcome news that the Bernard Sunley Charitable Foundation had voted £3,000 towards the replacement organ blower motor and there was also a gift from the Page Trustees.

The St. Matthew's Concert Society arranged the 1982/1983 season with four evening concerts and two afternoon concerts for children, as well as a family concert for the County Youth Orchestra. The programmes to be by the Georgian Drawing Room; the Delmo String Quartet; the Deakin Horn Trio and the pianist Miss Mitsuko Achida, playing Mozart. To aid finances, people were encouraged to buy tickets in advance for the complete series: £10 for five concerts or £18 for a double ticket, with £7.50 for a junior to attend all seven. The Georgian Drawing Room, whose concert was in September, dressed in eighteenth-century costumes and gave music and readings from Handel, Bach, Purcell, Telemann, Arne, Croft and Hook, using harpsichord and baroque flute.

In the 1983/1984 season there was to be a concert by the choir of King's College, Cambridge, under Stephen Cleobury and Davis Briggs. The programme included the fortieth performance of Britten's 'Rejoice in the Lamb' at which it was hoped that Dean Hussey would be present.

The Bach Choir, in 1982, performed Mozart's 'Requiem' and Purcell's 'Ode for St. Cecilia's Day' with the Milton Keynes Orchestra, and their December Carol Concert included the 'St. Nicholas Cantata' by Benjamin Britten with Ian Clarke at the organ. They gave a Brahms' evening in March 1983 and music by the Bach Family in November; their Christmas Concert in 1983 included 'Daystar in Winter' by Geoffrey Bush.

From 1984, concerts were increasingly held in other venues, at Nene College, Northampton High School and the Spinney Hill Hall, though some were still at St. Matthew's Church, like the choir of the Martin Luther Gymnasium from Marburg in Germany and the Bach Choir Carol Concert with the Eleanor Wind Quintet.

In the summer of 1985, Derek Gillard left for his new post as a Headmaster in Ealing and it was decided to replace him with another professional musician. The post was widely advertised and, after interviews, the youngest applicant, Andrew Shenton, was appointed. Andrew had been educated in Canterbury and at the Royal College of Music in London; he had been Organ Scholar at St. Paul's Cathedral; had been organist for the Young Musicians Symphony Orchestra and, while doing postgraduate work, had taught at Harrow School. He was very well qualified for his new post.

37

St. Matthew's Voluntary Aided Junior Mixed School

The Church School was always a most important part of the parish, Charles MacKenzie called it the most important single asset, it was regularly visited by the clergy and the pupils attended regular services in the church. Under the Headship of Mr. Ernest Ashby it had progressed as a good and happy school.

The Education Act of 1944 was an attempt to advance educational standards in the country after all the immense problems brought by the exigencies of war. It established a Ministry of Education with Advisory Councils to replace the Board, and the Local Education Authorities were required to secure adequate provision of both primary and secondary schools, and to submit a plan to cover the whole of the educational field in their area, including provision of Nursery Education for children under five.

Agreements had begun before the war for some Voluntary Schools to become Grant-Aided, receiving a fifty per cent grant towards repairs and alterations, other repairs and the salaries of teachers being paid by the Local Authority. The Act made it possible for these plans to be revived and laid down that Voluntary Primary Schools were now to have not less than six Managers, including L.E.A. representatives. The School Leaving Age was to be raised to fifteen and, later, to sixteen. The concept of Elementary Education was to be swept away.

One great difficulty, which complicated the enforcement of the provisions of the Act was the financial difficulty of up-dating out-of-date and unsatisfactory buildings, particularly as building materials and builders were in short supply. Many towns had had school buildings badly damaged or destroyed and their replacement was a priority, as was the rebuilding of other essentials.

On 21st November 1949, the Church School was finally established as an Aided school under the 1944 Act. The school building was in great need of improvement, some needs were very basic, the coke stoves needed replacing; the lighting was poor; floors were uneven and worn; there was no hot water; no telephone (one was installed in July 1950); roof and gutters needed repair; the playground surface and surrounding walls were dangerous and the lavatories were a complete disgrace. The Managers' Meetings in 1950, at which the Headmaster was finally permitted to attend, discussed all these but the constant problem was money – who paid? – were these changes or repairs? In 1951, the Managers finally decided to have the school decorated!

In May 1950, the H.M.I.'s Inspection took place and the report, published in July, pointed out that numbers had declined sharply so that 161 pupils (100 boys and 61 girls) were half those of five years earlier. Of course, the decline in numbers had made the building situation easier. The classrooms led out of each other, without corridors, and the reduction made it possible to use certain rooms as specialist rooms for Art, Handwork, Music and History. There were five classes, one for each of the first three years, and two for the fifty-two children of the final year, the slower ones being in a small group. This was the vestige of the two-stream system, though, interestingly, it was built up again in the years that followed. The five Assistant Teachers were experienced and made a loyal and united team.

The Inspectors found the work done to be reasonably good, except for written English which needed more stimulation and remedial work, together with more interesting books to encourage reading. Singing and Percussion Band were commended, as were all P.E. activities.

The school, the Inspectors said, had high aims and a strong purpose and was particularly commended for the Morning Assembly, which was carefully prepared and devoutly conducted, and they approved of the close links between the Church and the School; and between the School and Parents, for whom concerts, plays, Open Days and Special Parents' Meetings were regularly arranged and well attended.

By September 1950 the school roll had risen to 181; the following year to 227; reaching 290 in 1952; 336 in 1953 and 363 in 1954, by which time the two streams had been re-introduced in each year and over-crowding was causing problems!

However, the radio played its part in education and the news of the death of King George VI was heard by the children, as was the proclamation of Queen Elizabeth II in February 1952. On the day of the King's Funeral, a service was held in the school. The school was decorated for the Coronation in May 1953 and there was a special service on 22nd May for Empire Day at which Canon Hussey presented the Coronation mugs, after which the school closed for the Whitsun and Coronation holidays, re-opening on 4th June.

In 1955 the school said its farewell to Walter Hussey and welcomed Charles MacKenzie, and it was that year that the Managers finally opened a Managers' Bank Account with a deposit of £50. A Banda duplicator was acquired and buzzers for the classrooms were installed. The school was creeping into the twentieth century!

The New Development Plan of the Local Authority was feared to have the school scheduled for eventual closure, despite the objections of the Bishop, the Diocese and the Parish, all of whom wanted a new building on a new site within the parish. The need for flushing toilets was again considered and this time plans were drawn up and estimates obtained. The Managers said it was a 'repair', the L.E.A. said it was an 'alteration' and so the Managers should pay. Appeals to the Ministry supported the L.E.A.; the Managers had only £180 in their account, so they asked the L.E.A. to *repair* the disused lavatories which had been out of action for twenty years!

By the end of 1956 new floors and a hot water system had been installed and, wonder of wonders, there were now flushing toilets, proper pedestals with separate cisterns, the cost being borne by the Managers with the help of donations, though half would be refunded by the Ministry of Education. Peterborough Diocesan Education Committee was developing a new scheme for the upkeep of their school buildings, though, to start with, the Managers had to pay £95 a year, but might benefit later. The Summer Session of the Church Assembly discussed Church Schools; there were 2,500 Aided Schools which would involve the expenditure of at least £3 million; £2 million to come from the dioceses and parishes, with £1 million from the Church Assembly.

On Ascension Day 1957, a Sung Eucharist involving the School and the Church Choir, was broadcast on the Home Service. It went well and many letters of appreciation were received. In July that year, there was a much enjoyed school outing to Dovedale and Matlock Bath. In the summer holidays more improvements were made and an Inspectors' Report afterwards praised all the improvements and showed reasonable satisfaction, though the report still regretted the lack of a proper hall. The numbers were about 300, about equal boys and girls. In February 1959, the

Bishop inspected the school and took tea with the staff, he was able to see the new 'contemporary' decorations which had transformed the old drabness!

The year 1959 ended with the great shock of the sudden death of the Headmaster, Ernest Ashby. He died at his home on 31st December aged only fifty-nine. He had been at the school since May 1934 and had done a tremendous lot for both the school and the church.

John Bedford, the Deputy Head, took over during the interregnum. When the post was advertised there were 101 applicants, eight were short-listed and interviewed by the Managers, together with Mr. Skerrett, the Chief Education Officer and the Rev'd. E. Wild who was the Diocesan Director of Education. The post was offered to Mr. J. L. Fallows, who was Head of a school near Carlisle.

Two Parents' Meetings were held soon after the beginning of term, at which Laurie Fallows outlined the plans for these structural and academic changes. As a new school building still seemed a distant dream, it had been decided to refurbish the existing one over the next five years. The next priority was to replace the stoves with oil-fired central heating. Schemes of work were also being considered. The broad aim was to make the school a vital part of a continuously expanding process and to establish firm foundations for secondary education: to develop personality, individuality and self-confidence; to develop in the children self-esteem together with acceptable social behaviour. There was no room for complacency; the school uniform would bring a pride in the school with an improvement in behaviour and it was an aim which required the co-operation of all; of parents, teachers and children.

By September 1961, the school had 250 pupils to enjoy the new heating system but in October, with the rest of the parish, they suffered the great shock of Charles MacKenzie's sudden death. It had been 'his school' and he was to be missed in so many ways. The children contributed to buy flowers and for the Testimonial Fund. They had lost a real friend and someone who had believed in the school and fought hard for its very survival. He had been the driving force in the changes which had been effected over the last six years. Every Tuesday he had taught the top class and he had persuaded the Bishop to allow Methodist clergy to teach in the school as well. Uniform was now worn by over seventy-five per cent of the children and the passes of the last eleven plus examinations had been among the best in the town.

In 1962, Philip Turner was inducted and soon showed his interest in the school. He showed his confidence by enrolling his son.

St. Matthew's Voluntary Aided Junior Mixed School

At the end of the school year much had been achieved; the rooms were warmer and brighter; old desks were being replaced with modern tables and chairs. Educational journeys were enjoyed, as always, with local trips augmented by longer summer outings. That year they had been to Coventry Cathedral, the Malvern Hills, Tewkesbury; with tea at Stow-on-the-Wold and a visit to the Model Village at Bourton-on-the-Water, and there had been notable achievements in sports, art, dancing and handwriting competitions. School examinations were followed by an Open Day, for parents; with a second one for the P.C.C. and the Mothers' Union, these inevitably produced reminiscences about the school from 'old pupils'!

By September, when the new school year started, the rooms were even brighter as fluorescent strip lighting had been put in; the staff room had been enlarged and a new office constructed for the School Secretary. Mr. Fallows' room was thus enlarged. Finance had come from the diocese, the people of the parish and the Bluecoat Foundation.

The St. Matthew's clergy had always taught in the school and were also in the habit of 'popping in' particularly at Break when coffee was being made! There were also others who came to teach, from the Methodist Church and the Rev'd. N. Abbott, the curate from St. Michael's. Other curates also came, Laurie Fallows recorded fifteen during his years at the school. All the curates were treated as student teachers, their lessons being observed and criticised. The school came to have quite a reputation for training curates from various parishes in the town!

In December 1963, a report on the school was printed in the St. Alban's Parish Magazine. It quoted the school as having 265 pupils aged 7 to 11, taught by the Headmaster and 8 Assistant Teachers. It explained that children of all religious persuasions, or none at all, were accepted at the school, though preference was given to children from Anglican families. There was an automatic intake from the Spinney Hill area and from Kingsley County Infants' School. The Headmaster was quoted as saying that, 'we balance intensive academic work with sport, most children can swim the length of the Barry Road Baths by the time they leave and there is a good tradition of netball, football and athletics. Scottish Dancing is popular.' All staff, said the report, were practising church members. The school met regularly for Holy Communion in the church, the children being involved in every possible way. The Vicar of St. Matthew's had now entered his second son into the school. The uniform consisted of a black blazer, a maroon and gold tie and a maroon badge, showing the winged sword of St. Matthew in gold. The church people of St. Alban's were encouraged to send their children to the school.

The 7th of January 1964 was the school's seventy-fifth birthday; it was still hoped that the building would soon be replaced with a new building elsewhere in the parish, the need had been recognised by the Diocesan and Borough Education Committees. Bishop Otter-Barry gave the address at the Anniversary Service, to which many had been invited. Unfortunately Dean Hussey was unable to be present, but the Mayor was there; the Chief Education Officer; the Diocesan Director of Education; the Rural Dean and many other clergy, including Mr. Bailey, the Minister of Kingsley Park Methodist Church and many former staff, including Mr. Tucker, who had been Headmaster from 1924 to 1934; as well as many former pupils. After the Service, prizes were presented and the Exhibition was enjoyed by everyone. There were old school photographs to be exclaimed over, boys in knicker-bockers and jackets, with starched collars and girls in starched and frilled pinafores! It was a great occasion.

The end of 1965 saw the departure of John Bedford to be Headmaster of Far Cotton School, after nine years at St. Matthew's. He was renowned for his success in getting Grammar School places and also as a Sports Coach, particularly for football, at which he frequently refereed at amateur matches. His leaving would be a great loss to the school.

In 1966 the nine classes included five which were over the maximum of forty; in fact there was only one spare chair in the school! Work continued enthusiastically despite the over-crowding. The Nuffield schemes were encouraging learning by experience and discovery and, at the end of the Summer Term, the first Swimming Gala was held at the Barry Road Baths.

As from September 1967, the Parklands children would have a new school and the Links View children would not be admitted unless they had siblings already in the school, or close church connections, in which cases applications for admission would be given special consideration.

However, in the summer of 1967, the school had to say 'Farewell' to the Headmaster, Laurie Fallows, who was leaving to go to Blackburn as a School Organiser. His duties would be to develop and strengthen the quality of teaching in the primary, secondary and special schools. Philip Turner had left the parish the previous year and Charles Moxon had recently settled in, so it was a period of change. Laurie Fallows had thus worked with three vicars and during two interregnums. His contribution to the school was without parallel.

Mr. A. North of Duston Eldean acted as Headmaster until the arrival in January 1968 of Mr. H. S. Abrams, who came from Swanage.

The School played its part in the seventy-fifth Anniversary Celebration of the parish, remembering how it had grown from the little two-roomed

Infant School. The acquisition of the new Parish Centre was much welcomed by the school as School Dinners could be held there, so the numbers of children staying increased rapidly. Also, the school was able to use the Centre on three afternoons for Physical Education, with the Borough Education Committee providing the necessary apparatus.

Mr. Abrams left after three years to go to Chichester; he had been a Reader and was Secretary of the P.C.C., so was missed by the parish as well as the school. He was replaced by Raymond Foulgar from January 1972, who came to a flourishing school, though there was still a threat of closure looming!

38

A New Year and a New Vicar – John Ivan Morton

John Morton was instituted to the benefice of St. Matthew's on Monday 8th December 1975, by the Bishop of Peterborough, and inducted by the Archdeacon of Northampton. A group of parishioners from West Kirby was there to link his ministries and afterwards, at the Parish Centre, everyone had a chance to make his acquaintance. His arrival was just in time to celebrate Christmas in his new church.

In the parish magazine he wrote that he was in a curious limbo (he had written this before his institution); they would all feel sadness, he for his previous flock; they for a loved pastor; all would feel apprehension for the challenge to come. He assured them that he would hope to enhance the worship as he came to know the church and its people; and he would continue the Daily Eucharist and have a second celebration on all Red Letter Days. He had, he explained, developed certain convictions about Christian communities. First, that a parish congregation must be a Eucharistic community, rooted in prayer. Then, that every Christian community must be a sign of God's care for the neighbourhood and the wider world and also, that every member of the community must be sacrificially committed to its life, worship and work, including sacrificial giving – 'a new year – a new priest – and, God willing, a new vision.'

When Christmas was over, the new Vicar expressed his delight in the dignified ceremonial, the beautiful music and the well-filled church. He hoped that, at the season of new resolutions, everyone might determine to attend communion every Sunday, so that the church might be well filled every week. He hoped also for larger congregations at weekday services; especially the Communion Services on special days.

A New Year and a New Vicar – John Ivan Morton

Canon John I. Morton, vicar of St. Matthew's since 1975.

Sadly, 1975 had ended with the death of Deaconess Mary (Molly) Sankey, with a Requiem Service conducted by Charles Moxon on 29th December and the interment of her ashes on 7th January. Molly Sankey was eighty years old and had led a long and rewarding life. She had started in the church as a Lay-worker in the diocese of Lichfield; in 1950, she had become a Deaconess and soon afterwards had moved to the diocese of Peterborough, first working in Kingsthorpe and then at St. Matthew's, where she had continued to work even in her official retirement.

As Lent approached, John Morton gave his flock as a slogan, 'Keep Lent with the Church for the World'. On Ash Wednesday he introduced again the imposition of the ashes as an 'outward expression of the inner disposition with which we should begin Lent', and on the first Sunday of Lent there was to be the Liturgy of Penance. Later there were to be two Hunger Lunches joining with Kingsley Park Methodist Church. On Palm Sunday, there was a Procession from the Parish Centre to the Church and the services of Holy Week were to be a reminder of the historical events by word, act, symbol and ceremony. On the first three days, there were two Communion services each day and, on Maundy Thursday, the evening celebration was followed by a vigil in the Chapel, made into a garden with flowers and candles. On Good Friday there was an hour's service from 2.00 p.m. to 3.00 p.m. and then the Liturgy of the Day, with an ancient form of prayer, when the Cross was brought in so that people could kneel before it and swear allegiance to their Crucified Lord; this was followed by Communion from the Reserved Sacrament, all leaving the church in silence. On Holy Saturday, came the great Vigil service which provides the liturgical and psychological link between the Cross and the Resurrection. It began in a darkened church, a world without God; the great Paschal candle was lit, the symbol of the Victorious Christ; and then individual candles were lit, followed by the first Eucharist of Easter. A wonderful Easter.

In his report at the Annual General Meeting after Easter, John Morton posed two questions for them all to face – 'Why am I going to St. Matthew's?' 'What am I and that church for?' We must not, he said, be content with facile answers but seek real answers to do with worship, care and mission. Our worship, he said, was dignified and well-attended, but is it sufficiently flexible? Is it real, heart-felt and communal?

Care – Do we know each other and share? Do we meet socially, face to face?

Mission – Outreach – this should be the permanent preoccupation of every church member. There is plenty to challenge!

As the summer holidays of 1976 were coming closer, three problems loomed. The money for the essential new heating system; the Sunday School and the future of the Church School. Sunday Schools should not be considered as optional extras, they provide Christian teaching *and* worship. The children of the Sunday School had sent money to the Diocesan Children's Project; to the Children's Village at Thandigudi in India; to the Save the Children Fund; the Wantage Sisters in India; the Northampton General Hospital's Toy Fund; they had collected used stamps and foil and they had knitted squares for blankets. Many had won awards in the Junior Quest Scheme. It was hoped that new volunteers would come forward to replace those helpers going on to Further Education or to work.

The School Building was obviously old and inadequate; in the three-tier system adopted by the town, the area was to have its own Middle School for children of nine to thirteen years. This was to be at the old Girls' School in St. George's Avenue, and to it would go the majority of the St. Matthew's children in September 1977. There was still the possibility that it could become a Voluntary Aided School but only if the money could be

A memorial ceramic panel for the former St. Matthew's Church School and headmaster, E. G. Ashby.

raised to buy the building. By the end of the holidays it was obvious that this would not be possible, so the Managers pressed the Local Education Authority to grant the new school Controlled Status so that the church would have some representation. Mr. Raymond Foulgar had been Headmaster from January 1972, and he had been working closely with Charles Moxon and now with John Morton, to bring the school and the church closer together. A new Eucharist had been used, a said version for the youngest children, with the children reading prayers, acting as servers and taking up the elements. The children who had been confirmed took communion alongside the staff. It was doubly disappointing that these activities should have to stop. Despite all efforts, in the following January, the Local Authority rejected the idea, so the Church School was to be closed in July 1977, a sad decision. The two available Anglican Middle Schools were All Saints and Emmanuel. Mr. Foulgar and his staff were to be scattered to other schools.

Summers tend to be times of change. The verger, Ray Pitcher, and his wife were off to Norwich Cathedral, they would be greatly missed at St. Matthew's. The new verger was John Ducrow, a Londoner, who with his wife, would arrive in October. Another departure was that of Timothy

Day, the organist, apparently a sudden decision, but he never seemed to have settled altogether happily at St. Matthew's; an excellent musician, he was not really suited to the work in a parish church, though he made a success of posts in other spheres. On a happier note, the church celebrated both the Diamond Wedding of Herbert and Elizabeth Adams and the fortieth anniversary of Father Bearman's priesting. Tim Leese was to give up the leadership of the Youth Club after eleven years and Ray Allen was retiring from the choir after fifty years' service.

Gifts at this time included a crucifix and frontal for the War Memorial, and later candlesticks, cruets and hassocks were also given. The summer fête was a great success and the eighty-third Festival, the first for the new Vicar, brought an interesting group of visiting preachers. These were, Dr. D. Hope. Principal of St. Stephen's House, Oxford; Bishop Rogers, the Assistant Bishop of Peterborough; Bishop Hewlett Thompson, Suffragen Bishop of Willesden and once a curate at St. Matthew's; and Canon F. Sampson, Vicar of St. John's, Tuebrook, Liverpool.

In the autumn, a six month course leading to confirmation was planned, with classes for both children and adults. A 'School of Religion' on the lines of the Lenten meetings was planned, to meet weekly or fortnightly, to offer an exposition of the whole field of Christian Belief. There was also to be a newly formed Parish Missionary Committee.

The Festival of Christmas brought full-circle John Morton's first year at St. Matthew's . He had 'unashamedly' (his word) used the magazines to teach his flock, necessary, he thought, in these days of short sermons, and he went into great detail to explain the occasions of the liturgical year, the relevant Church History and the symbolism involved. He also described something of the lives of various saints, so that their days could be celebrated meaningfully, as well as the cycle of the Feasts of the Virgin Mary and the great Church Festivals.

So began the new year of 1977, a year with many challenges.

39

1977 to 1983

A new year with, according to newspaper reports, disasters on all sides! At St. Matthew's, John Morton was pleased to report increasing numbers for services and also, he felt, more cohesion between choir, servers and the main congregation. The new organist, David Ponsford and his wife, had arrived. Both were in their late twenties, both were accomplished musicians, Liz as a singer and David as an organist and a harpsichord player. A Welshman, David had studied at Manchester College of Music and then at Cambridge and he had been sub-organist at Wells for six years. Stephen Meakin and Ron Gates were to be congratulated on the work they had done to 'bridge the gap' and to keep the choir up to standard.

The closure of the Church School meant also the end of the income from the Local Education Authority for the use of the Parish Centre and it meant the end of easy contact with families in the parish. Together with Miss Wicks, the Minister at Kingsley Methodist Church, there was started a house-to-house visitation hoping that a street stewardship scheme might evolve. Once again one sees shades of Rowden Hussey and the then Street Visitors! In May, before the school finally closed, a social group for the choir boys and those boys who had recently been confirmed was formed, as choir rehearsals prevented the choristers from joining the uniformed associations. One of the last visitors to the Church School, on its very last day, was Sydney Gould who was so popular in the area when he was a curate at St. Matthew's. Sadly, he died very suddenly about two years later. He had battled with ill-health ever since his war experiences.

In the summer of 1977, other changes included Henry Hartwell's resignation as Sacristan and Head Server. He had been a server for forty-seven years and Sacristan for twenty-one. Words could not express the gratitude owed to him.

With less money from the Parish Centre and increases in costs due to inflation, money was again a problem, the new heating system was to be installed in October, luckily helped by a legacy from the estate of the late Mr. Vickers, and great savings were made when Mr. Leese and Mr. Osborne organised a team to carry out much of the preparatory work. But even then, the efficiency of the new system would still depend on the parish's ability to pay its bills! Back to Stewardship! The estimated expenditure for 1978 was £11,660 and the estimated income £8,880, a shortfall of £2,780. In the magazine, John Morton declared: 'We need money for manpower and for mission – not just that Northampton shall have a lovely neo-Gothic concert hall for the future! We are giving so that there shall remain one splendid building in which Christ is worshipped by a large and devoted group of people, who in turn carry Him out into the lives and hearts of others.'

The winter of 1978 brought the comfort of a warmer church but with it the news that the organ was threatened by the changes of temperature and that £770 was needed for a humifier. Parishioners were asked for gifts or loans as it was essential to preserve the organ.

Petertide saw the arrival of a full-time assistant curate. Welcome relief to the clergy, though he would need training and would be an added expense to the parish! Richard Pringle was to be ordained as a deacon. Richard soon made himself at home and developed his personal ministry. He was duly priested a year later and experienced the excitement and joy of celebrating his first communion.

Other changes were around in that lay members of the congregation now took up the elements and the congregation was encouraged to exchange the Peace with those nearby. In 1980 the new Alternative Service Book reached the churches, though the rites were already known. The congregation at St. Matthew's were using Series II and had done so for some ten years. John Morton made it clear that not everything about the 'old' services was perfect and that one could not condemn a service one had never tried. The new services might reflect trends or fads, but the old form grovelled before 'godly princes' who were probably tyrants, and was concerned with predestination; they must be studied seriously but neither 'old' nor 'new' was automatically best!

The winter of 1980/1981 brought further financial problems; a new organ-blower would cost £3,500; a new lawn-mower £150 and there was a wage-rise coming for the clergy. In 1980 the average wage was £81 a week (£4,212 a year), including £54 from the Church Commissioners. In 1981 the clergy were guaranteed £57 a week from the Commissioners and the Peterborough Diocese was likely to recommend £5,100 per annum, though that was still £300 below the maximum recommended. The Quota of £6,000 was likely to rise to £9,000 and the church had no reserves. The advantages of Covenanting one's giving were emphasised yet again; during 1979 the church had recovered £2,253 in taxes but far more people could help in this way if they would only agree to do so.

Summarising the 'state of the parish' in the January 1981 magazine, John felt that the 9.00 a.m. service, which now had two hymns and an address, appealed to the younger parishioners. Attendance at the 10.15 a.m. Solemn Eucharist was fairly static, while Evensong had much less appeal. It was rare for anyone to attend two Sunday services. Derek Gillard was working well with the choir and under his energetic direction it had returned to healthy numbers. Enthusiasm was also evident amongst the members of the Junior Club, some of whom were joining Sunday School and Confirmation Classes. Christian education for adults he found less easy to organise.

In April 1981, Phyllis Oldaker died after many years of loyal service to St. Matthew's. She was sixty-nine. She had been born and educated in Birmingham, serving first with the U.S.P.G. and then, when trained, she lectured at St. Christopher's, Blackheath. Back in Birmingham again she became Assistant Sunday School Organiser and then Adviser in Religious Studies for the Lichfield Diocese, where she met and became friends with Deaconess Molly Sankey. Later they both worked in Northampton. Phyllis was Adviser to the Peterborough Diocese until 1962 when she joined the St. Matthew's staff under Philip Turner. She retired in 1975 after a serious operation, though, like her friend, she worked hard in her retirement. She continued her ministry even when her sight began to fail and, finally, a stroke brought her most useful life to a close. After her funeral, an appeal was launched and £400 raised. It was decided that new Stations of the Cross would be a worthy memorial, though more money would be needed and it would have to be a memorial of wider significance. Discussions with the Diocesan Authorities took place, slowing down the process of decision. By 1983 three contemporary artists were asked to prepare drawings, by that time the fund had been increased by benefactions. Eventually, the commission was given to David Thomas, a sculptor born in 1919, who had studied and later lectured at the Courtauld Institute. These Stations of the Cross were his first religious work. The reliefs were modelled in clay and cast to represent terracotta. Interestingly, David Thomas had first visited St. Matthew's in a group from the Courtauld back in 1953, when the group had been received by Canon Walter Hussey.

Number 5 of 14 Stations of the Cross (1987), the work of David Thomas.

In July 1981, Richard Pringle was leaving to go to the parish of Seaton Delaval and Seaton Sluice, in the diocese of Newcastle, where he would be curate-in-charge of New Hartley. In the three years he had become very popular and particularly effective with the young people of the parish. The timing of his going prevented any new deacon being appointed for at least twelve months and, as John Morton had carried the responsibilities of being Rural Dean for some time, he was going to be dependent again on his Honorary Assistants. Leslie Bearman was still helping, as was Walter Hobday, and, in September, Canon Methuen Clarke came to live in Kingsley Road, having retired from All Hallows, Wellingborough. He had been away for twenty-nine years and found it most exciting to be back.

In 1982, Michael Fountaine was to join the staff. He had been born in Pytchley and had been a student at St. Stephen's House, Oxford, a college originally founded on the tractarian tradition. In March 1982, Walter Hobday was to celebrate the Silver Jubilee of his priesthood. He had been ordained in London, serving in Perivale, and moved to Litchborough in 1972. In June 1983, John Morton celebrated his own Silver Jubilee, having Dean Jowett of Manchester to preach at the service.

The Graham Sutherland painting went to London as part of an exhibition at the Tate Gallery and returned some time later, cleaned and restored.

There had been many changes – now with two full-time staff and three retired assistants, as well as Mr. Riley, who was a Reader, the parish was better staffed than it had been for a very long time.

40

The Last Decade of the Church's Century

Nineteen eighty-four saw Michael Fountaine priested at the Cathedral.

In July, Bishop Douglas Feaver announced that he was to retire in October, twelve years after his consecration; he and his wife were to live in Cambridge. In September, it was announced that the Right Reverend John William Westwood, Suffragan Bishop of Edmonton, would be the next Bishop of Peterborough.

By December 1984, the new Stations of the Cross were definitely ordered and the necessary faculty obtained. Some parishioners had offered £500 covenanted for four years, which would produce the £700 needed for one plaque. By the end of the year the project was fully funded. Each panel took a month to complete before casting, so it was not until April 1987 that they were all finally finished and installed. On 9th April there was to be a Confirmation Service and the Bishop would also dedicate the Stations of the Cross; it was felt that they were powerful and sensitive, and that the warmth of the material transformed the starkness of the nave walls.

Just before the Festival, news came to St. Matthew's of the death of Dean Hussey, who as Walter Hussey had been Vicar of St. Matthew's from 1937, when his father retired, to 1955, when he became Dean of Chichester. His unique place in the modern church had been to recognise genius in music and the arts, and to draw from it for the glory of God. His great friend, Canon Methuen Clarke, said, 'He was a faithful son of the church who loved God and Christ's Church; he loved life; he loved art in all its forms and he loved his fellowmen.' Dean Hussey had retired in 1977 to live in London, from where he could enjoy the Art Galleries,

The Lady Chapel, showing Triptych and Stained Glass Windows. Standing in front of the altar is Michael Fountaine (curate).

Concerts and Auctions; also the company of his many friends. His careful husbandry and economies in personal spending and his skill in buying and selling had resulted in a wonderful collection of art treasures. He left those with local interest to Northampton Art Gallery. He also left generous sums to St. Matthew's Church for the upkeep of the gardens, the fabric of the church, the organ and to commission a new piece of music for the Festival.

His generous gifts to the church were much needed and the Memorial Service held at Chichester Cathedral, on a fine, bright, autumn Saturday in October, was a wonderfully uplifting experience.

The loss of Walter Hussey was followed all too soon by news of the serious illness of Canon Charles Moxon, at the beginning of his retirement, he died soon after. The funeral service at Salisbury Cathedral vibrated with Easter joy. A Solemn Requiem was held at St. Matthew's and great love and prayers went to Phyllis, his widow, and the children and grandchildren.

In January 1986, another great loss came with the death of Charles Barker. Despite an illness ten years before, he had returned to the choir and notched up a total of forty-five years. He was devoted to music and particularly to church music but had kept it as a hobby. He was Deputy Organist and accompanist to the Bach choir and happily remained in the second place by preference, though he often stepped in to cover vacancies.

During 1986, the P.C.C. decided to seek for designs for a figure of the Risen Christ to hang over the Victorian iron cross which hangs over the Chancel Screen. This was something that John Morton had long felt desirable. Initially, Malcolm Pollard, a local sculptor, was to be approached and the Diocesan Advisory Committee would be asked for guidance. The figure, as conceived by Malcolm Pollard, was to be contemporary but in keeping with the building, and made in fibre-glass or wood. In January 1990, he described it as to be 'suspended like a bird'. In principle, the P.C.C. and the D.A.C. approved the design. It was to be a memorial to Dean Walter Hussey and would cost about £11,000. Donations were requested. The project was around for a long time and seemed likely to be abandoned, but in September 1990, the figure suddenly appeared above the heads of the congregation! Of course, there was criticism, but people reminded themselves of the criticisms levelled at the Madonna and the Crucifixion. Taste is, after all, a matter of opinion. It was, said Malcolm Pollard, based on the Byzantine style, simple, with the face 'unfinished' the arms outstretched but uplifted in welcome; the body elongated to dominate the cross which has been overcome. The figure was removed for finishing and for the Rood Cross to be partially gilded to make a visual link. It was to be completed for the Centenary.

Also, during 1987, Bert Pickaver, churchwarden for two decades, died suddenly. He was born within sight of the church and had sung in the choir as a boy.

At the Ordination at the Cathedral at Petertide 1987, there was the great excitement of the ordination of the first women deacons. Seven women were ordained including Geinor Downs, who was to serve at All Saints, Wellingborough. The others were Valerie Barford, licensed to Weston Favell; Pamela Hayward to St. Mary's, Far Cotton; Gillian Orpin to Passenham; Ethel Reed to Corby; Judith Rose to All Saints, Kettering and Helen Woodhead to Daventry. Six men were ordained as deacons at the same service, though only the men were able to be priested in 1988. Three years later, Geinor Downs went off to Chichester to lecture at the Theological College, still a deacon!

In the magazine for January 1988, John Morton outlined the Bishop's new system of support for the clergy, pointing out how difficult it was for them to assess their work. Such a course would be welcomed. Similarly, whole congregations needed to re-assess their aims. The fundamental duty is to provide worship which proclaims the gospel and offers a focus for faith; then to advance the Kingdom of God and serve a wider community. The P.C.C. approved the Bishop's intention to train Lay Pastoral Assistants and for the use of Lay Eucharistic Assistants, who could carry the Communion to the housebound. There had also been the purchase of the New English Hymnal, a conservative revision of the old one, originally published in 1906! There was intention to use the A.S.B. Rite A at the monthly Parade Services. It was felt that one reason it was proving difficult to find a deacon, was that the services were all Rite B, and the church was seen as resistant to modern ways. As the year progressed, it was obvious that this change was a good one and maybe the newness had enabled others to find a new message in the liturgy. The choir, under Andrew Shenton, had been helpful and adaptable.

On January 1989, the first ever Suffragan Bishop for the Peterborough Diocese was consecrated at Westminster Abbey. Paul Barber had been educated at Sherborne School, at St. John's College, Cambridge and at Wells Theological College. He had served his ministry in Surrey and, in 1980, had become the Archdeacon of Surrey.

Bishop Paul soon took over the Chairmanship of the Church Urban Fund Appeal for the diocese; this was a country-wide appeal to raise funds for work in the inner city areas. Targets were set for dioceses, and then subdivided for the Deaneries and their parishes. The target for St. Matthew's was £850. As a start, votive candles were on sale at £1 each to launch the campaign. The money was to be used to bring social projects into action in these areas, so that the quality of life could be thereby improved. 'This,' said John Morton, 'is Christian Evangelism as it should be; the Church of Christ should be at the centre of such activity. The Urban Fund must touch our pockets but it also needs our daily prayers and sustained support.'

Spring 1989 brought the news that Simon Tebbutt was to join the staff as a deacon after he had been ordained at Petertide. Simon was to be non-stipendiary and he was no raw youngster but a man of sixty-one. The creation of the non-stipendiary ministry for men and women was a valuable initiative, partly dictated by the shortage of full-time priests. Such people continued, and earned their living, in their ordinary work and offered ministerial help in a parish as was possible. Living in Boughton, Simon and his wife, Christina, were well known in many capacities. Christina, in particular, had served on various synods and diocesan committees. They would continue to live at Boughton but Simon would have an office in the Parish Centre and would work for the parish for five days a week, including Sundays.

One of Simon Tebbutt's first jobs was to convene a committee to plan the celebrations for the Centenary in 1993. The pinnacles of the spire were repaired in good time before the centenary. Inside one pinnacle a bottle was found containing a shilling dated 1895 and the names of the Vicar and Churchwardens of that year. When the work was finished, another container was sealed inside, enclosing a shilling of 1989, a magazine and the words:

'The spire and the tower parapet of this church were repaired in the autumn of 1989 in preparation for the celebration of the Centenary of St. Matthew's on 21st September 1993.'
John I. Morton. Vicar.
 Bryan Nicholls. Raymond Allen. Churchwardens.

In March, 1990, the new Electoral Roll recorded 240 names, of which 75 were resident in the parish and 165 came from outside. At the A.G.M., John Morton drew attention to three areas of church life which required a lot of thought and prayer: finance, though one must never put maintenance before mission; the forthcoming Decade of Evangelism; concern for Youth.

The Last Decade of the Church's Century

An aerial view of the church and grounds taken in August 1990. The Parish Centre, built in 1968, is on the left.

Earlier in March, an Ecumenical meeting had been held at Spinney Hill Hall, attended by over 500 Christians (St. Matthew's had fourteen places) at which the two Bishops of Liverpool had spoken, the Roman Catholic Archbishop Warlock and the Anglican Bishop Shepherd had been inspiring to listen to as they outlined their own ecumenical activities and stimulated discussions and questions. Ecumenical activities in the Diocese are another cause for concern.

41

Music with Andrew Shenton, in the Last Decade of the Church's Century

Derek Gillard was to leave St. Matthew's after five and three-quarter years, during which time he had rebuilt the choir, showing great dedication. He was to become Headmaster of Christ the Saviour School in Ealing. His methods with the choir had been painstaking and his manner with the boys was excellent, handling them firmly but with good humour; demanding high standards but without losing the sense of fun and enjoyment which is so essential. He had always seen the choir as part of the whole and not just an end in itself. Such abilities as he had shown obviously needed wider recognition, so, while everyone regretted his going, they wished him well in a wider field. The church had always enjoyed a fine musical tradition which needed musical expertise greater than that usually expected in a parish church. At the same time, a parish church cannot pay the sort of salary which might be paid to someone of such ability, so the organist and choirmaster must have some way of getting further remuneration to give him a living wage.

In his Goodbyes, Derek Gillard said that he left a challenging task, as he left a nucleus of young singers to be developed into a competent choir, but that the 'near disaster' situation he had inherited had been saved. He had found the years hectic but very exciting. Derek's enthusiasm for a challenge was now to be exercised in Ealing! In September, the new organist was appointed, the youngest of those interviewed, but full of ideas and with very high standards.

Andrew Shenton started at St. Matthew's with a number of very definite aims. The first was to update the image of the Choir, the musical standards of which had been somewhat overshadowed by the other musical activities in the area. He was anxious to re-start the idea of regular commissioned works, especially for performance at Festivals, and to increase the Choir's repertoire. The Hussey money provided £500 a year for commissions but more was really needed and he felt that if a Trust Fund could be established, that would help. The standard of music at St. Matthew's had always been high, but with television and radio and the modern methods of recording, the musical knowledge of ordinary people was wider than ever and they were used to hearing music of a professionally high standard. It was therefore harder for choirs to reach the heights.

When he first came to Northampton, Andrew had to live some way from the church, but eventually he was able to move into the flat over the parish room so that he really was 'living on the job'. Also he got the general agreement that this flat would be available for his successors.

At the 1986 Festival, a new work was commissioned and performed. This was 'The Spacious Firmament on High' by Herbert Sumsion, a setting of the words of Joseph Addison, and he also revived the tradition of the Festival Organ Recital playing works by Bach, Messiaen and Liszt. The choir was still making annual visits to sing at various Cathedrals, to Hereford, to Tewkesbury Abbey, Norwich, with a later visit to the Albert Hall to sing at the sixtieth Anniversary Celebrations of the Royal School of Church Music.

It was in 1986, too, that Daniel Ludford-Thomas, aged thirteen, entered the Royal School's competition, reaching the finals and being judged the Choirboy of the Year, winning £2,000 for St. Matthew's and £300 for himself. This was a real triumph for Daniel, who was later to make a recording 'On Wings of Song' with the Choir, with Andrew directing and Ron Gates at the organ. It was also a good 'advertisement' for the training the choristers received at St. Matthew's.

It was thus a good time for the launch of 'The Friends of the Choir' with Stephen Cleobury, now Director of Music at King's College, Cambridge, as Patron. The aim of the Friends was 'to support the pursuit of musical activity at St. Matthew's and the financial, material and social welfare of the choir. Also, monies would be raised for choral scholarships and educational courses; for financing the Choir's Cathedral visits and assisting with the expenses necessarily incurred in concert and recital activities' – this, it was felt, would widen interest in the choir and ensure the future security of music at St. Matthew's and so maintain the vision which had always been there but particularly from the time of Walter Hussey. Choir boys have a busy life, they sing at Sunday services and need plenty of rehearsal time, but they also need to prepare for many other special

Commissioned Music III 'The Spacious Firmament' composed by Herbert Sumsion for Andrew Shenton and St. Matthew's Choir (original manuscript).

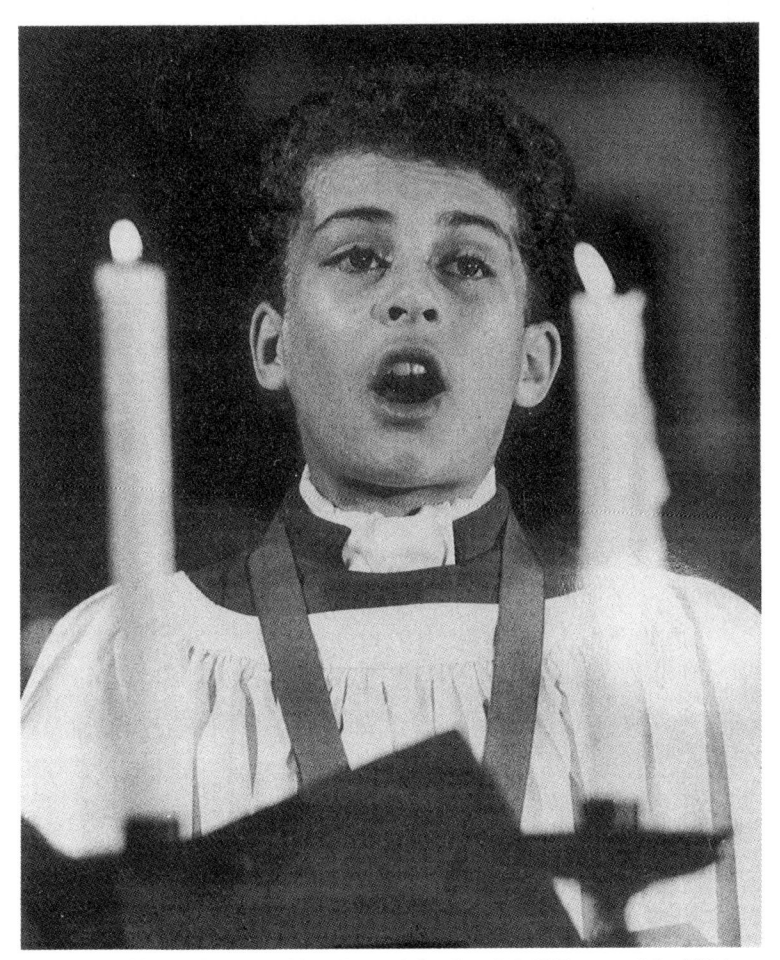

Daniel Ludford-Thomas 'Choirboy of the Year' B.E.T. award in 1986.

services, to be present for services in school holidays, like Easter and Christmas. They learn a wide range of music, including the Canticles at Evensong, they have opportunity to work with bands and orchestras; to sing Masses in Latin; Plainsong and more light-hearted things. The boys are paid small amounts for their services and particularly for weddings; there are regular summer concerts and prizes or small scholarships. They have a Badminton Club, a Boys' Club and have recently combined to beautify a strip of garden near the Parish Centre. Nevertheless, it is a busy life and no boy would survive it if he was not dedicated to it. The boys have, of course, to maintain their School work and other interests. As further encouragement, and indirectly for the general benefit, Organ and Choral Scholarships were founded. The Hussey Organ Scholar gets free organ lessons and endless opportunities to widen his scope. The scholarship is held for one year from September, an allowance of £150 is paid by the Friends, to help buy books and music; if necessary, lodgings are found with someone in the Choir or congregation and opportunities are available for the Scholar to earn some money by working some days a week. The first Scholar was Andrew Barford, who was already a chorister and who went on to get a Scholarship at Liverpool University, singing in the Roman Catholic Cathedral Choir. The second was Robert Costin, who went on to Pembroke College; the third was Andrew Reid, who has gone to St. Catherine's, Cambridge, and the fourth, Michael Phillips, is going to Gonville and Caius, also at Cambridge, in 1991.

In 1987, four boys, Tim Ludford-Thomas, Mark Harris, Ian Clarke and James Halstead, took the Dean's Award for choristers and Andrew Shenton gained a Fellowship of the Royal College of Organists. At the Festival that year, the Anthem was Geoffrey Burgon's 'Song of the Creatures', the premiere of this version of Francis of Assisi's poem, each verse being of a particular musical character. Burgon himself was present and the work was paid for from the Hussey bequest and a grant from the East Midlands Arts Trust. Earlier, on Good Friday that year, the choir sang Pergolesi's 'Stabat Mater' and it was around this time that it was decided that, on Friday evening, the men of the choir would sing Compline to ancient Plainsong.

On Ascension Day 1988, the Northampton String Ensemble performed 'Missa Brevis in D' by Mozart; and in May, the choir paid tribute to Sir Lennox Berkeley's eighty-fifth birthday. At the 1988 Festival, the special work was 'The Call' by John Taverner who had studied under Sir Lennox. This was specially commissioned and was a first performance at Evensong on 25th September. It was an eight-minute work for unaccompanied choir, in four parts, making use of silence. It is based on St. Matthew's Gospel, chapter 9, verse 9 and the words were written by Mother Thekla, Abbess of the Orthodox Monastery of the Assumption in North Yorkshire. The music represents, in three mounting steps, the work of St. Matthew; the ascent of the spirit into silence and the silent prayer and music of the heart. Three, the number of the Trinity, is significant in the compositional form and the phrases 'Let My Voice Be Silent' and 'Lord Have Mercy' each move through three pitches, the last phrase also being in three languages, Church Slavonic, Greek and English.

The Festival Organ Recital was given by Christopher Dearnley of St. Paul's Cathedral, who had played at the wedding of the Prince and Princess of Wales. The Festival started with a recital by the Jubilate Singers with members of the Northampton Chamber Orchestra and the organ was played by Robert Costin. They performed Bernstein's 'Chichester Psalms' which had originally been commissioned by Walter Hussey when he was Dean of Chichester; Vaugham William's 'Serenade to Music' and 'The Angels' by John Taverner.

In the Magazine, it was reported that, 'The organ is the original one, built in 1895 by J. W. Walker & Sons, and given to the church by Mrs. Pickering Phipps, senior. It has four manuals and forty-eight speaking stops, and is housed in a special chamber which allows the 32 feet pedal to stand vertically against the back wall. The original action contained an early example of electric combination pistons.' It was explained that the organ is now in the care of the firm Harrison & Harrison Ltd. and this was the beginning of an Appeal for £150,000 for necessary restoration work.

During 1989, a two-year cycle of the major organ works of J. S. Bach was begun, played by the Organist, Andrew Shenton; the sub-organist, Ron Gates (now an official paid member of the team) and Andrew Reid, the Organ Scholar. Ivan Moody was commissioned to write a piece for Candlemass, the text from the Orthodox Service of Small Vespers, the words by Andrew of Crete.

At the Festival of 1989, there was a celebrity organ recital by David Hill of Winchester Cathedral, including works by Bach, Frank, Guillmant and Vierne. The Festival Mass was by Richard Shepherd, specially commissioned and a first performance – St. Matthew's Mass; as also was Alan Rideout's 'Toccata for Organ'. The Saturday concert included 'Four Motets' and a Requiem by Durufle; the Organ Concerto by Poulenc; sung by the St. Matthew's Choir and the Northampton Festival Chorus and Orchestra conducted by Andrew Shenton. On the Friday of the Octave, there was a previously unperformed motet based on the Day's Lesson from Revelation – 'And There Was War in Heaven', written by Geoffrey Burgon, originally for the Coventry Cathedral Choir. The work included vast crescendoes and great contrasts, this was performed by the Church Choir and that of Grimsby Parish Church. To parallel the music of the Festival, there was an Exhibition of Art and Sculpture in the church, presented by students from the Slade School of Art; including work by Clio Lloyd-Jacob, Mark Handforth, and others. An explanatory folder accompanied everything, as Andrew Shenton tried to get as much into the spirit of Walter Hussey's dream as possible!

In December was performed 'Dieu Parmi Nous' (God Among Us) – which is the last of the nine Meditations on the Birth of Our Lord – called 'La Nativitie du Seigneur', composed in 1935 by Olivier Messiaen, who celebrated his eightieth birthday on 10th December.

Despite the success of the 1989 Festival, there were some disagreements over the cost, and a feeling that it had been too ambitious to repeat, at least until the Centenary which would be in 1993. However, the Choir had built up a reputation again and were broadcast twice.

Nineteen ninety saw a Charity Concert in May, conducted by Andrew Shenton, with the proceeds to the Goodwill Villages in India. The concert was by the Jubilate Singers and the Church Choir, with Alan Leroy as baritone and Ronald Gates and Andrew Reid as organists. The works included Walton, March: 'Crown Imperial'; Howells, Requiem; St. Paul's Service; Finzi, 'Lo, the Full Final Sacrifice' and Vaughan Williams' 'Five Mystical Songs'. In July, the choir sang at Southwell Minister and, after their return, the choristers gave a concert in church, with awards to those who were thought outstanding.

At the 1990 Festival, the Organ Recital was given by Thomas Trotter playing works by Bach, Saint-Saen, Widor and Durufle. The St. Matthew Mass by Richard Shephard and the Alan Rideout 'Toccata', both commissioned in 1989, were repeated and the special commission was an Anthem by Trevor Hold, based on the Beatitudes. This was to be Andrew Shenton's last Festival as he was to go to the United States in summer 1991 to study for a Master of Music degree at the Institute of Sacred Music at Yale University. This is a great opportunity to study to very high standards and to meet fellow students from all over America and from other countries.

In his years at St. Matthew's, the choir, under Andrew's leadership, had regained status and efficiency. As well as being an excellent musician, he was a good disciplinarian and a most successful Choirmaster.

Despite his decision to leave in summer 1991, Andrew was still busy making plans for the future. During 1990 he had had many contacts with the Governors, Staff and boys of the newly founded Northampton Boys' Grammar School at Pitsford. The old Dower House has been converted into a Music School and is to have a three-manual organ installed.

In the past, the Director of Music at St. Matthew's had had a salary, a flat and facilities to give lessons, but no regular job by which to earn enough to live on, though many obtained posts in local schools. In the future, the Director will also be Director of Music at the school, time being suitably divided between the two responsibilities. He will therefore be able to recruit choristers – it is a day-school – and in effect there will be a 'Choir School'.

The School will use the church for special services and concerts, so there will be co-operation based on music. On 10th November 1990 the school Choral Society gave a successful concert in the church.

This is an exciting development with great possibilities!

42

The Centenary Years – 1991–1993

(from Foundation Stone to New Church)

Eighteen ninety-one was the year when the foundation stone of St. Matthew's Church was laid so, in a way, 1991 was the beginning of the Centenary. It was also the year of the 450th Anniversary of the Diocese of Peterborough for which many exciting events had been planned. Events, the Bishop declared, when all in the Diocese could celebrate and have fun together.

So 1991 was to be a year of beginnings and changes. To widen parish interest and communication it was decided to have the magazine issued quarterly and in a new format. It was to be called 'The Spire' – representing the well-known landmark of the area and to inspire and rejuvenate communication within the geographical parish by being fresh and obviously controversial. Copies were to cost 50p. but during the year free copies would be distributed so that, within the year, every house in the parish would have one free copy. For other, more in-church, information there would be a monthly newsletter.

In the first edition of 'The Spire' the Vicar pointed out the financial problems that faced St. Matthew's, warning that the Parish Share was due to rise substantially. In September, just after the Festival, a Stewardship Campaign was launched with the aim of £50,000 annual giving – a target of about five per cent of take-home pay for the givers. It was necessary to ask everyone to look prayerfully and realistically at their giving. Invitations were issued for dinner on Saturday 28th September or lunch on Sunday 29th September when the financial needs of the parish were spelt out. The whole future of St. Matthew's was at stake! Prayers were answered and the campaign was a success – it attained its target –

with particular thanks to Mr. Muir the Campaign Director – and many others.

On Sunday 5th May, the new Director of Music was introduced, though he did not start until 1st September. Coming almost full circle, the new Director was to be once again Mr. King – but this time Andrew King – also to be responsible for the Music at Northamptonshire Grammar School for Boys at Pitsford. Andrew King had been a chorister at St. Paul's Cathedral in London: educated at Chichester and Organ Scholar at Wells Cathedral; at Canterbury Cathedral and at Jesus College, Cambridge, from where he graduated in 1990. He was to live in the Parish Centre flat.

The Hussey Organ Scholar, Michael Philips, had won an Organ Scholarship to Gonville and Caius College, Cambridge, and this year too, Paul Miles-Kingston had a Choral Scholarship to Durham, and Daniel Ludford Thomas had a similar one to Wells Cathedral, while Daniel Farr had reached the Regional Finals of the Choirboy of the Year Competition. Also in 1991, the choir visited Holland, based in The Hague and Voorscholen. The 1992 Organ Scholar was to be Kate Dowdeswell, the first girl to qualify. The choir was well prepared for the coming Centenary.

July 1991 heralded the arrival of the new Archdeacon, the Rev'd. Michael Chapman, who was to take office in July. He had been Vicar of Hale in Surrey since 1984 and Rural Dean of Farnham since 1988. At fifty-one, he had been ordained at Durham in 1963, after training at Mirfield. He had served in a mining parish and had spent sixteen years as chaplain in the Royal Navy, serving in submarines. His wife had been a Naval Nursing Sister and they now had a teenage son and daughter.

On 29th July Leslie Bearman celebrated his eighty-second birthday – St. Michael's Day – by celebrating Mass at St. Matthew's, though he had recently preferred to be in the congregation. He was born in Leytonstone in 1909 and this year too, celebrated the fifty-fifth anniversary of his priesting.

The Festival this year was celebrating the Laying of the Foundation Stone and was the ninety-eighth Feast of the Dedication. The preacher at the High Mass on the Eve of St. Matthew's Day was the Very Rev'd. Peter Berry, the Provost of Birmingham, and the service was followed by a reception in the Parish Centre. The preacher at the Sunday service was the Suffragan Bishop of Bedford. An Organ Recital by Kevin Bowyer from Warwick was held on Saturday the 14th. And the special musical work was 'Prayer for Church Musicians' by Alec Wyton, which will be published in the U.S.A.

So to 1992, the final year before the Centenary year. In the January Newsletter, Canon Morton reminded his congregation that he had been at

St. Matthew's for sixteen years. He felt that a long incumbency had both advantages and disadvantages. The advantages of knowing your flock and being known by them, but the danger of running out of ideas!

The target for 1992 was communication – the need to re-establish contacts; firstly, with young people, and in this in particular he was glad that they would be welcoming Stephen Cope in May. Stephen was coming from Newmarket with his wife Alison and their two small daughters, Hannah aged four and Rebekah aged nearly two.

However, with the coming of Stephen there was the going of Simon. Simon Tebbutt was to leave by Lent and would be licensed on 8th April at St. Luke's, Duston, as a Team Vicar, where he would work with the Rector, the Rev'd. Peter Garlick. He was going to a large and busy parish, with new estates, and would take the love, thanks and good wishes of the church family of St. Matthew's, to this new challenge. Simon would be missed for many reasons; for his good humour and his friendliness and for his work in services and in the parish; for his time spent in preparations for the Centenary celebrations. A presentation was to be made to Simon and his wife Christina at the last party before Lent.

Preceding the presentation, there would be a service to re-introduce some, who had been confirmed, to the Holy Eucharist. Communicants were asked to persuade a friend to join the service, which would be arranged in a simple fashion and would have some teaching to bring home the spiritual centrality of the Communion. This was another way of communicating with those somewhat outside the church.

Another change, resulting from the fellowship of the Stewardship Campaign, was to be the introduction of a quarterly, combined Communion Service, followed by breakfast. These to be on the four occasions when there are five Sundays in the month. Also, resulting from the popularity of the campaign dinners, there were to be occasional Sunday lunches, so that more members of the congregation could get to know each other. There were also to be more opportunities to worship alongside Christians of other churches, to affirm unity and the faith they all shared.

A century is a long time and the church building shows signs of its age! Dust lurks in unseen corners; vestments become threadbare; round the church the paths have become uneven; and, particularly, the great Walker Organ has been dried out by the efficient heating system. Renewal and replacement for the second century require at least £200,000. This leads to the need for a Centenary Appeal, an Appeal directed largely outside the parish, locally and nationally, particularly to the business community and those interested in church music. A Trust was set up, to be independent of

The Centenary Years – 1991–1993

the P.C.C., chaired by Mr Bowers, the trustees having power to receive and disperse the monies subscribed. Subscribers could designate their particular concern and it was hoped that enough would be raised to restore the organ and the vestments; renew the paths and to install new vestries and cloakrooms in the basement.

In addition to the great Appeal, there was the need to arrange all the special Centenary events. These were to be:

1. special services, with guest speakers of distinction;
2. services of re-dedication for those baptised or married at St. Matthew's and for the members of the uniformed organisations;
3. the church to be flood-lit – thanks to the generosity of the Local Council;
4. the sale of a Centenary History of St. Matthew's;
5. the sale of various mementoes;
6. art exhibitions;
7. a drama performed in church;
8. a Victorian Garden Party;
9. concerts and recitals;
10. a great Festival for St. Matthew's Day with a specially commissioned musical work by a young composer, to parallel those of earlier anniversaries. The church to be filled with flowers.

This was to be a year of planning and organising and also of spiritual renewal, both individually and as a congregation. A great celebration and thanksgiving ahead.

There were to be many social events during 1992 to raise money for new robes for the servers and there was a great Centenary Spring-clean with movable scaffolding to reach all the inaccessible places – so that everyone and everything would be gleaming for 1993. It was a busy time!

November saw the great debate at General Synod on the possibility of the priesting of women in the Anglican Church. This followed years of discussion, with more formal debates in Deanery and Diocesan Synods all over the country. It was clear that the result would be close. The Synod was held with much prayer and discussion. Eventually the question was put, the voting being in Houses – Bishops, Clergy and Laity. The motion was passed with the necessary majority in all three houses.

This is another beginning, which coincides with the second century of St. Matthew's. The decision has brought delight and despair – and a real

Malcolm Pollard's 'Risen Christ' was dedicated by the Bishop of Blackburn, the Right Reverend Alan Chesters, on St. Matthew's Day, 1992.

Parish outing on 25.7.92 to Derbyshire Well Dressing. Church members grouped round one of the displays at Stony Middleton. Amongst the parishioners is Ray Allen (churchwarden), second from right.

The church boasts a Carillon of twelve bells played via this keyboard. Bellringer in this instance is Matthew Hobden.

challenge to everyone – a challenge to the unity of the church, asking people not to be swayed by prejudice; a challenge to Christian love and understanding; to working together for God's purposes; so that the work of God will be carried on even when it doesn't seem to be going our way.

In the Vicarage there are three drawings which are passed to successive occupants. These are architect's drawings of the church; two of the exterior which show little significant differences with the church today. One difference is the sculpture of St. Matthew over the porch; another, sadly, the grilles over the stained glass, something the architect of 1893 would never have believed necessary. The third drawing is of fixtures and seating. The church was designed for 800 or more people and was filled with chairs, though even in 1899 only 400 made their Easter Communion. The fittings, however, remain faithful to Matthew Holding's intentions, the founders visualising a cathedral-like style of worship, dignified, ceremonious, distant and mysterious. The congregation at a reverent distance. The iron screen fencing off the chancel.

The Clergy and Choir after the 10.15 service on 28.2.93. Seated centre of second row, from left to right, are – Alan March (ordinand), Canon John Morton (vicar) and Rev. Stephen Cope (curate), flanked by retired priests Leslie Bearman and Methuen Clarke.

The Right Reverend and Rt. Hon. The Lord Bishop of London, Dr. David Hope, in procession with the youth services, Mothering Sunday 1993. The occasion was used for all baptised in St. Matthew's to renew their vows.

The altar set on a platform before the chancel screen, as used nowadays for many services, has changed the arrangement. People learn by doing and modern worship involves the congregation as fully as possible.

The Kingsley for which the building was designed has changed – the world has changed – the culture of the 1890s has vanished, but the church is there for the next century of worship!

We have to live our lives forwards, not backwards. This may be the end of the first century for St. Matthew's and rightly we celebrate the occasion, but it is also the beginning of the second century and the future needs celebrating too!

The future of the church is in God's hands. We are His people.

'And as Jesus passed forth from thence, he saw a man, named Matthew, sitting at the receipt of custom: and he saith unto him, Follow me.

'And he arose and followed him.'

The SW. aspect of the church and vicarage as they appear today.

The Phipps Family

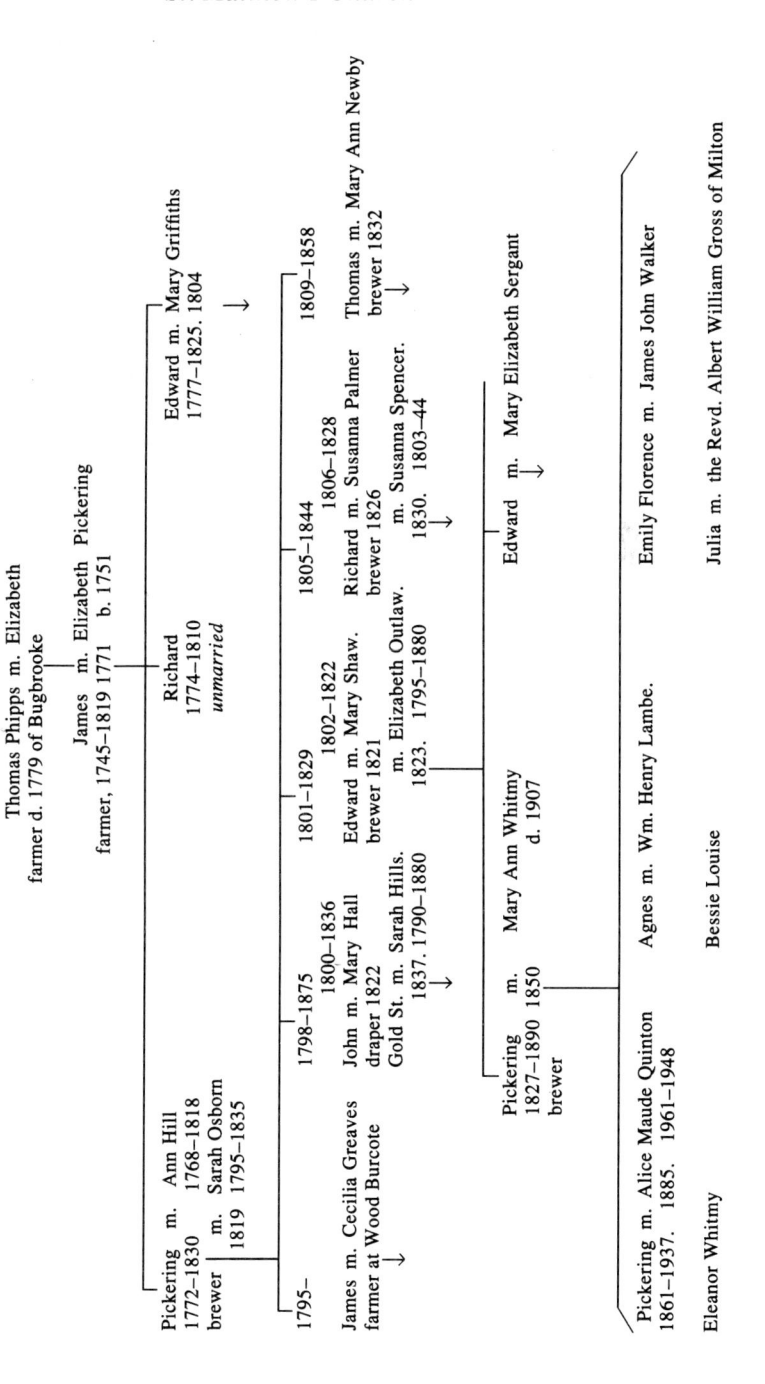

Thomas Phipps m. Elizabeth
farmer d. 1779 of Bugbrooke

James m. Elizabeth Pickering
farmer, 1745–1819 1771 b. 1751

- Richard 1774–1810 *unmarried*
- Edward m. Mary Griffiths 1777–1825. 1804 →
- Pickering 1772–1830 brewer m. Ann Hill 1768–1818
- m. Sarah Osborn 1819 1795–1835

1795–

1798–1875
James m. Cecilia Greaves
farmer at Wood Burcote →

John m. Mary Hall 1800–1836
draper 1822
Gold St. m. Sarah Hills. 1837. 1790–1880

1801–1829
Edward m. Mary Shaw.
brewer 1821
m. Elizabeth Outlaw. 1823. 1795–1880

1802–1822

1805–1844
Richard m. Susanna Palmer
brewer 1826
m. Susanna Spencer. 1830. 1803–44

1806–1828

1809–1858
Thomas m. Mary Ann Newby
brewer 1832

Mary Ann Whitmy m.
d. 1907

Pickering 1827–1890 1850
brewer

Edward m. Mary Elizabeth Sergant →

Agnes m. Wm. Henry Lambe.

Emily Florence m. James John Walker

Pickering m. Alice Maude Quinton 1861–1937. 1885. 1961–1948

Bessie Louise

Julia m. the Revd. Albert William Gross of Milton

Eleanor Whitmy

The Hussey Family

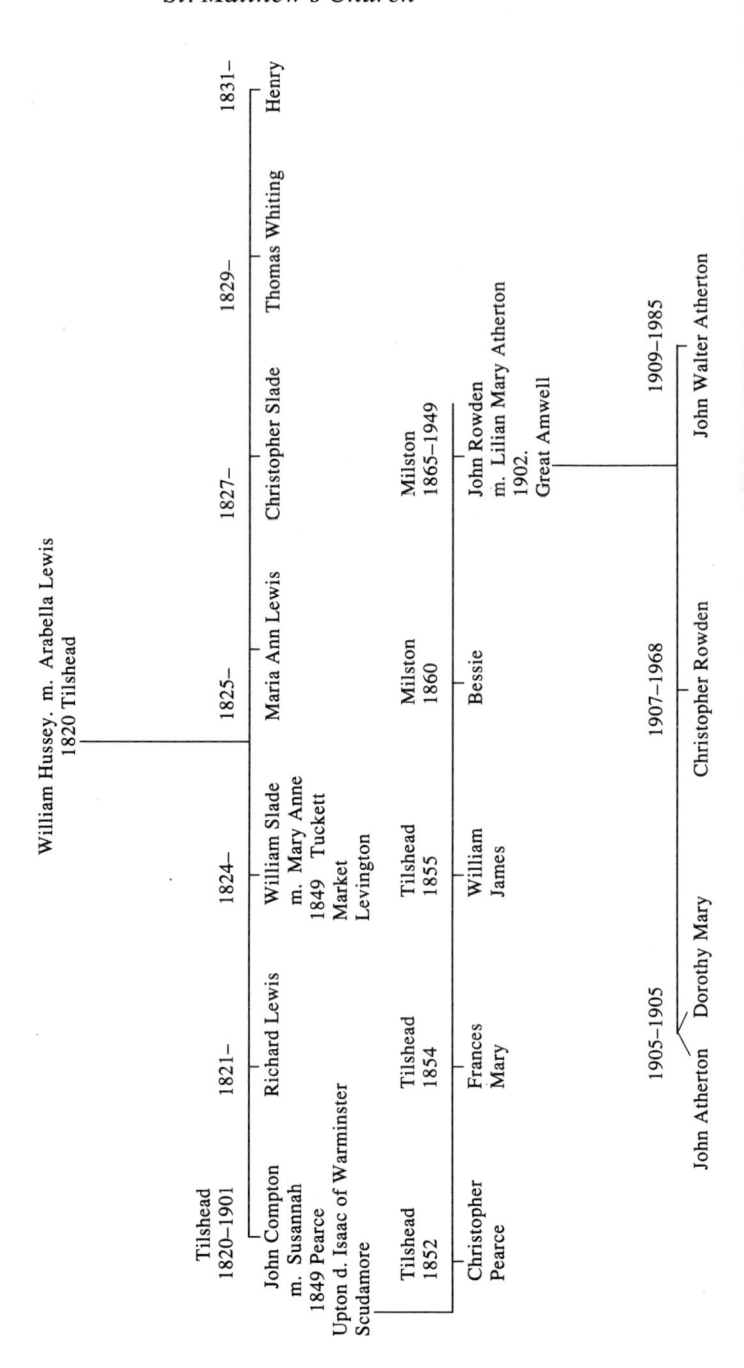

William Hussey. m. Arabella Lewis
1820 Tilshead

1821–	1824–	1825–	1827–	1829–	1831–
Richard Lewis	William Slade m. Mary Anne Tuckett 1849 Market Levington	Maria Ann Lewis	Christopher Slade	Thomas Whiting	Henry

Tilshead
1820–1901

John Compton
m. Susannah
1849 Pearce
Upton d. Isaac of Warminster
Scudamore

Tilshead 1852	Tilshead 1854	Tilshead 1855	Milston 1860	Milston 1865–1949
	Frances Mary	William James	Bessie	John Rowden m. Lilian Mary Atherton 1902. Great Amwell

Christopher
Pearce

1905–1905   Dorothy Mary

1907–1968   Christopher Rowden

1909–1985   John Walter Atherton

John Atherton

The Atherton Family

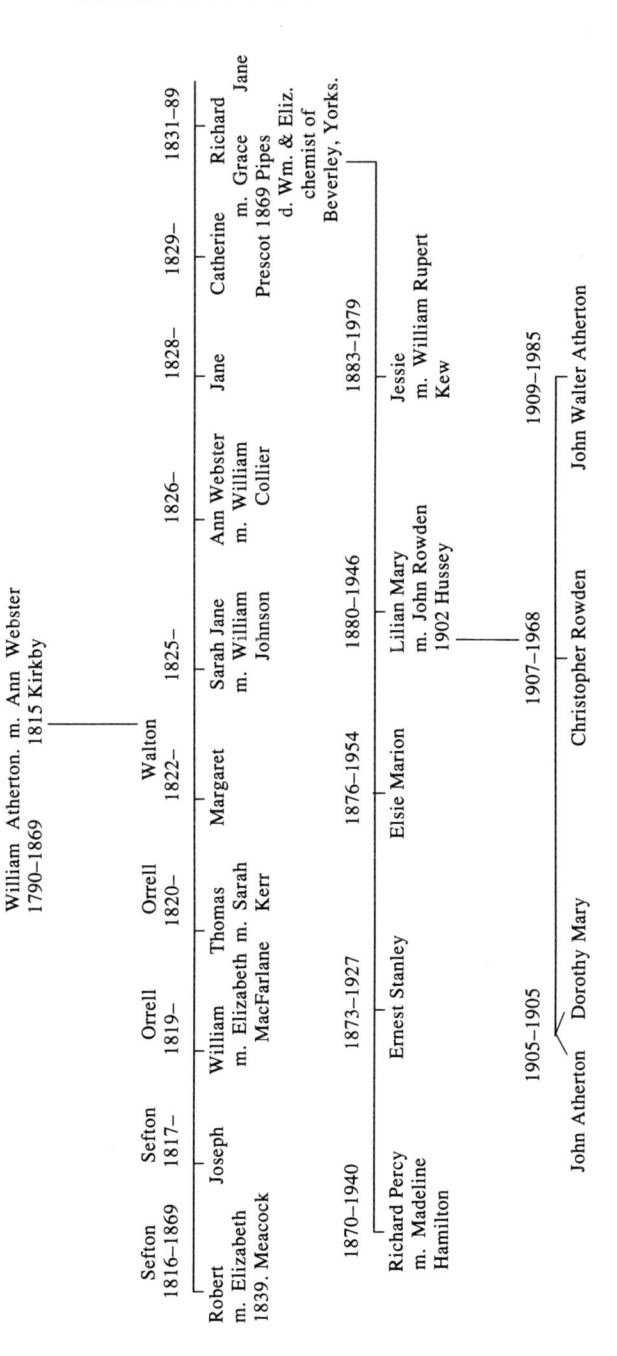

William Atherton. m. Ann Webster
1790–1869   1815 Kirkby

Sefton	Sefton	Orrell	Orrell	Walton		Ann Webster	Jane	Catherine	Richard Jane
1816–1869	1817–	1819–	1820–	1822–	1825–	1826–	1828–	1829–	1831–89
Robert m. Elizabeth 1839. Meacock	Joseph	William m. Elizabeth MacFarlane	Thomas m. Sarah Kerr	Margaret	Sarah Jane m. William Johnson	m. William Collier		Prescot 1869	m. Grace Pipes d. Wm. & Eliz. chemist of Beverley, Yorks.

1870–1940   1873–1927   1876–1954   1880–1946   1883–1979

Richard Percy   Ernest Stanley   Elsie Marion   Lilian Mary   Jessie
m. Madeline   m. John Rowden   m. William Rupert
Hamilton   1902 Hussey   Kew

1905–1905   1907–1968   1909–1985

John Atherton   Dorothy Mary   Christopher Rowden   John Walter Atherton

The Staff of St. Matthew's Church, Northampton

Vicars

John Rowden Hussey	1893–1937
Walter Atherton Hussey	1937–1955
Charles MacKenzie	1956–1961
Philip Turner	1962–1966
Charles Moxon	1966–1974
John Ivan Morton	1975–

Organists

John Eads	1890–1895
Charles King	1895–1934
Denis Pouncey	1934–1936
Philip Pfaff	1936–1940
Alec Wyton	1946–1950
Robert Joyce	1950–1958
John Bertalot	1958–1964
Michael Nicholas	1965–1971
Stephen Cleobury	1971–1974
Timothy Day	1974–1976
David Ponsford	1976–1979
Derek Gillard	1979–1985
Andrew Shenton	1985–1991
Andrew King	1992–

Assistant Organists

Charles Barker	–1971
Charles Ball	
Ron Gates	1971–1993

Lay Staff

Deaconess Molly Sankey   1956–1961
  d.1975
Phyllis Oldaker   1963–1974
  d.1981

Curates

Leonard Pollock	1893–1896
d.1954	
Charles William Peck	1896–1896
d.1931	
Henry Hugh Ingram	1896–1900
	1907–1913
Andrew Carr	1898–1901
d.1929	
Henry John Fry	1900–1904
Reginald Maxwell Woolley	1902–1905
d.1931	
Dr. Noblett Ruddock	1905–1908
Edward Sydenham	1905–1907
Alexander Scrutton	1907–1909
Arthur Orr	1907–1907
Charles Mortimer	1908–1909
Thomas Austin Jones	1910–1914
Robert Churchill	1913–1915
Gerald Thompson	1914–1917
Charles Eastgate	1916–1919
d. 1936	
Cyril Luxmoore	1918–1918
Alfred Seaman	1919–1920
Cyril Arthur Wheeler	1921–1922

Guy Brodie	1922–1937
d.1964	
Edward Ion Carroll	1930–1934
d. 1982	
Frederick Stallard	1934–1940
Methuen Clarke	1938–1949
David Stewart Smith	1941–1943
Fred Whittle	1941–1947
John Wolfe Walker	1947–1949
David Jenkins	1950–1954
Hewlett Thompson	1954–1959
David Griffiths	1958–1961
Alan Wakelin	1960–1963
Humphrey Prideaux	1961–1962
Jeffrey William Bell	1963–1966
Sydney Gould	1964–1967
Haydn Llewellyn Jones	1968–1972
Richard Pringle	1979–1981
Michael Fountaine	1983–1986
Simon Tebbutt	1989–1992
Stephen Cope	1992–

The Choir of St. Matthew's Church, Northampton

A List of Musical Works Commissioned By St. Matthew's Church, Northampton

1943 – Benjamin BRITTEN, Rejoice in the Lamb
　　　　　　　　　　　　　　　　(Boosey & Hawkes)
　　　– Michael TIPPETT, Fanfare No. 1 for 10 Brass Instruments
　　　　　　　　　　　　　　　　(Schott)
1944 – Edmund RUBBRA, Motet : The Revival (Boosey & Hawkes)
1945 – Lennox BERKELEY, Festival Anthem   (Chester)
1946 – Gerald FINZI, Lo, the full final sacrifice (Boosey & Hawkes)
　　　– Benjamin BRITTEN, Prelude & Fugue on a theme of Vittoria
　　　　(for Organ)　　　　　　　　　　(Boosey & Hawkes)
1948 – Christopher HEADINGTON, Festival Anthem : Supreme Bliss
　　　　　　　　　　　　　　　　(MS)
1950 – Malcom ARNOLD, Laudate Dominum   (Lengnick)
1954 – James BUTT, Bless the Lord   (MS)
1956 – David BARLOW, Who shall ascend to the hill of the Lord
　　　　　　　　　　　　　　　　(MS)
1958 – George DYSON, Hail Universal Lord   (Novello)
1959 – Elizabeth POSTON, Festal Te Deum Laudamus (MS)
1960 – Peter DICKINSON, Justus quidem tu es, Domine (MS)
1962 – Brian JUDGE, Ambrosian Prayer   (MS)
1965 – Kenneth LEIGHTON, Let all the world in every corner sing
　　　　　　　　　　　　　　　　(Novello)
1966 – John McCABE, A Hymne to God the Father (Novello)

1967 –Richard Rodney Bennett, Five Christmas Carols (Universal Edition)
    1. There is no rose of such virtue
    2. Out of your sleep arise and wake
    3. That younge child
    4. Sweet was the song the virgin sang
    5. Susanni
1968 –Gordon CROSSE, The Covenant of the Rainbow (Oxford University Press)
    –Herbert HOWELLS, One thing have I desired of the Lord (Novello)
1973 –William MATHIAS, Missa Brevis (Oxford University Press)
1977 –Sebastian FORBES, Quam Dilecta (MS)
1983 –Philip MOORE, At the round earth's imagined corners (MS)
1986 –Herbert SUMSION, The spacious firmament on high (Oecumuse)
1987 –Geoffrey BURGON, The Song of the Creatures (Chester)
1988 –John TAVENER, The Call (Chester)
1989 –Richard SHEPHARD, St. Matthew's Mass (MS - OUP)
    –Alan RIDOUT, Toccata for Organ (Oecumuse)
1990 –Paul EDWARDS, God that madest heaven and earth (ATB) (Oecumuse)
    –Trevor HOLD, Verses from St. Matthew (Oecumuse)
1991 –Alec WYTON, Prayer for Church Musicians (To be published in USA)
1993 –Diana BURAILL, Cantata (UMP)

Also:
1905 –Charles KING, Communion Service in C (Novello)
1949 –John ROSE, Festival Hymn (MS, now lost)
1964 –Christopher LeFLEMING, Communion Service in D (MS)
1988 –Simon LOLE, Carol for Advent (MS)
1989 –Ivan MOODY, Canticle of Simeon (MS)
1989 –Margaret WEGENER, Adoro te devote (MS)

Bibliography

St. Matthew's – Gertrude Hollis	1932
St. Matthew's – Memorial Booklet	1893
Muse at St. Matthew's – Michael Nicholas	1973
Patron of Art – Walter Hussey	1985
Well Remembered – Claude Blagden	1953
Robert Wright Stopford – Robert Holtby	1988
Spencer Leeson – A Memoir –	1958
Founding of Cuddesdon – Owen Chadwick	1954
St. Matthew's Magazines	1888–1992

Articles in *Northampton Independent: Chronicle & Echo; Northampton Mercury* and the files of the Local Studies Centre

Log-books of St. Matthew's Schools, from 1893

Census Records; Parish Registers; Gravestones; Directories

Records of St. Margaret's Convent, East Grinstead

Index of Persons

ABEL	Mr. & Mrs. 133
ABLETT	Mr. – scoutmaster – 72
ABRAMS	H.S. – headmaster – 180, 181
ACHIDA	Mitsuko 174
ADAMS	Herbert 186
ADAMS	R. – scout – 72
AGER	Brian 140
AGUTTER	churchwarden 81
ALCOCK	Dr. – organist 79
ALLBRIGHT	Terence – pianist – 165
ALLEN	Miss – guider – 56
ALLEN	Raymond 72, 172, 185, 196, 210
ARNOLD	Cecily 124
ARNOLD	Malcolm 111, 115
ASHBY	Ernest – headmaster – 71, 175
ATHERTON	Elsie Marion – 32
	Ernest 32
	Grace née Pipes – 31
	Jessie 31, 33, 39
	Lilian Mary (Mrs. Hussey) 32 (see HUSSEY)
	Richard 31, 32
	Richard Percy 31, 32, 33
	William & Ann 31
BADEN-POWELL	Lord & Lady 72
BAILEY	Mr. 180
BAMENT	churchwarden 58
BANKS	Nora – guider 56, 145
BARBER	Paul – Bishop of Brixworth – 195
BARDSLEY	Cyril – Bishop of Peterborough & Leicester – 68, 69
BARFORD	Andrew – organ scholar – 202
BARFORD	Valerie – deacon – 195
BARKER	Charles – organist – 100, 112, 130, 172, 201 obit.
BARLOW	David 120
BAUMER	Rev. L. E. – chaplain – 52

BAXTER	Sidney - scout – 73
BEARMAN	Rev. Leslie – 186, 191, 207, 212
BEDFORD	John – schoolmaster – 178, 180
BELL	Dr. Bishop of Chichester – 94
BELL	Rev. Jeffery – curate – 142
BERKELEY	Lennox 112
BERRY	Rev. Peter 206
BERTALOT	John – organist – 115, 164, 168
BLADES	James 176
BLAGDEN	Claude-Bishop of Peterborough 69, 94, 155
BLANK	Roger 140
BLYTH	Bishop of Jerusalem – 35
BOULT	Sir Adrian 93, 111
BOWERS	Mr. 209
BOWYER	Kevin – organist – 207
BRADLEY	Rev. Andrew 136
BRIGGS	Davis 174
BRITTEN	Benjamin – composer – 92, 94, 100, 111
BRODIE	Rev. Guy – curate – 68, 83, 139 obit.
BROOKES	Rev. Charles – V. of Holy Sepulchre – 29
BROOKS	churchwarden 87
BROWN	William 25
BROWNE	Mrs Montague – Mothers' Union – 43, 69, 79
BUCK	Jean 113
BUDDEN	housekeeper – 68
BULL	Charles 100, 113
BULL	Fr. Paul 59
BYARD	Margaret 143
CARPENTER-GARNER	Bishop of Colombo 100
CARR	Rev. Andrew – curate – 29, 31, 32, 69 obit.
CARROLL	Rev. Edward – curate – 70, 72, 73, 74, 87
CHAPMAN	Ven. Michael – Archdeacon – 207
CHARLESWORTH	George – headmaster – 49
CHESTERS	Alan – Bishop of Blackburn 210
CHOULER	Fred – churchwarden – 4, 6
CHRISTOPHERSON	Noel-Very Rev. Dean of Peterborough – 100
CIVIL	Alan 166, 171
CLARK	Sir Kenneth – Director of National Gallery – 94, 96, 103
CLARKE	Ian – organist – 202
CLARKE	Rev. Methuen – curate – 85, 87, 91, 96, 105, 106, 114, 190, 192, 212
CLAYTON	Mrs. 42
CLEOBURY	Stephen – organist – 168 & onwards, 199
COPE	Rev. Stephen – curate – 208, 212
CORRIN	Mr. 71, 119
COSTIN	Robert – organist – 202, 203
COTTON	Mr. & Mrs. 104, 109, 114
CRAXTON	Harold – pianist – 111, 114, 115
CREIGHTON	Mandell – Bishop of Peterborough – 10, 13
CROUCH	Rev. W. 64
CUTHBERT	Herbert 6
DALZIEL	Gordon 140

Index

DANKWORTH	Johnny 151
DARKE	Dr. Harold – organist – 129
DAVEY	Rev. F. N. 136
DAVID	Peter 165
DAVIES	Dr. Walford – organist – 79
DAY	Timothy – organist – 172, 186
DEARNLEY	Christopher – organist – 203
DODD	Ethel – guider – 56
DOUGLAS-JONES	Rev. L. 120
DOWDESWELL	Kate – organ scholar – 207
DOWNS	Geinor – deacon – 195
DRIBERG	Tom 98
DUCROW	John – verger – 185
DUNN	E. – Bishop of Honduras 58
DUPRE	Desmond 166
DYALL	Valentine – The Man in Black – 112
EADS	John – organist – 29, 112
EASTGATE	Rev. Charles – curate – 50, 56, 82 obit.
EASTAUGH	Cyril – Bishop of Peterborough – 134, 158
EDWARDS	Jimmy – comedian – 107
ELLIOTT-BINNS	Christopher – churchwarden – 140
ENGLAND	Rev. Arthur - V. of Hessle – 60, 62
FALLOWS	Laurie – headmaster – 140, 141, 188, 190
FARR	Daniel 207
FEAVER	Douglas – Bishop of Peterborough – 158, 160, 202
FLAGSTED	Kirsten – singer – 113, 114
FOULGAR	Raymond – headmaster – 181, 185
FOUNTAINE	Rev. Michael – curate – 191, 192, 193
FOX	Joyce – (Mrs. McKenzie) – 117
FRAZER	Celia 143, 147
FRODSHAM	Bishop of Queensland 51
FRY	Rev. Henry – curate – 37
FURNISS	Raymond – scout – 73
FYFFE	Bishop of Rangoon – 66
GABB	Harry 165
GAKWARE	Rev. Festo – of Rwanda Urundi – 144
GARLICK	Rev. Peter – R. of Duston 207
GATES	Ron – organist – 165, 187, 199, 203, 204
GILLARD	Derek – organist – 173, 179, 198
GLOUCESTER	Duchess of – 150
GOODCHILD	Archdeacon – 134
GORE-BROWN	Rev. Wilfred. Bishop of Kimberley – 58
GOUDGE	Canon of Christchurch, Oxford – 66
GOULD	Rev. Sydney – curate – 141, 146, 147, 187 obit.
GRAHAM	Fr. of Mirfield – 123
GRAHAM-CAMPBELL	Bishop – 158
GRAY	Rev. Charles 1
GREAVES	Rev. Arthur – V. of St. Mary's – 38
GREEN	Brenda – cub-mistress – 75
GREEN	Edward – builder – 31

GRIFFITHS	Rev. David – curate – 125, 129, 132
GRIMES	John – Archdeacon – 105, 117
GRIMSBY	Bishop of – 93
GUILBERT	Marjorie 101
HALL	Julian 138
HALSTEAD	James 202
HANDS	Rev. Thomas – V. of St. Laurence – 26, 58
HARRIS	Mark 202
HARRIS	Sir William – organist – 120
HARTWELL	Henry 187
HAVILAND	John – churchwarden – 12, 44
HAYWARD	Pamela 199
HENNINGS	Misses 56, 119
HESLOP	Rev. Alan 144
HOBDAY	Rev. Walter 191
HOBDEN	Matthew 211
HOLDING	Edward – architect – 43, 50
	Matthew – architect – 10, 12, 31, 43
HOLLIS	Gertrude writer – 48, 50, 70, 81
HOLLOWAY	Edgar 25
HOLST	Gustav 100
HOPE	Dr. David – Bishop of London – 186, 213
HOPKINS	Rev. Stephan 136
HORSLEY	Colin 115
HOWELLS	Herbert 155
HUGHES	Marian 144
HULL	Canon – 5, 26
HUNTER	Dr. – organist – 79
HUSSEY	Christopher Rowden – 39, 59, 67, 106
	John Compton – 1
	John Rowden – Vicar – 1 to 100, 106 obit., 117
	John Walter - Vicar – 42, 50, 67, 83-109, 118, 129, 177, 192 obit.
	Lilian Mary – 32, 43, 69, 105 obit.
	Susannah – née Pearce – 1
JENKINS	Rev. David – curate – 108, 124, 129
JOHNSON	David – artist – 131
JOHNSON	Marshall 125
JONES	Canon – of All Saints – 44, 51
JONES	T. – scout – 72
JOYCE	Robert – organist – 108, 115, 120, 124, 169
KEAN	J. 5
KEETON	Haydon – organist – 79
KENWAY	Clifton 66
KEW	William – 33, 38
KING	Andrew – organist – 206
KING	Charles – organist – 27, 29, 57, 69, 70, obit., 79, 83, 110
KING	Bishop of Madagascar – 41
KYNASTON	Nicolas 171

Index

LAINE	Cleo – singer – 151
LANG	Bishop of Leicester – 44, 54, 97, 102
LAW	Rev. William – curate of Belgrave – 6
LEE	Osborne 50
LEESE	Tim 186, 188
LEESON	Spencer – Bishop of Peterborough – 106, 117, 120 obit.
LEROY	Alan 204
LEY	Henry – organist – 79
LINTHWAITE	Mrs. Elsie 126
LLOYD	Miss 87
LOCKE	Keith 153
LONG	Elizabeth 25
LOWE	sidesman – 5
LUDFORD-THOMAS	Daniel – choirboy – 199, 207
	Tim – choirboy – 202
MACLAGAN	Sir Eric – 98
MAGEE	Rev. J.A.V. 58
	William Conner. Bishop of Peterborough – 1, 10, obit., 45
MARCH	Alan 212
MARSH	Bazil – Archdeacon – 133, 141
MARTIN	Dr. George – organist – 13, 27, 79
MARTIN	Henry – builder – 12
MAYO	Graham 170
McKENZIE	Rev. Charles – Vicar – 117-133, obit. 135, 141, 175, 177
MEAKINS	Stephen – 115, 187
	Vaughan – 141, 165, 169
MILLER	Augustus of Wootton – 6
MOORE	Sir Henry – sculptor – 94, 96, 98, 102
MORRIS	Rev. Marcus – 118
MORTON	Rev. John – Vicar – 181 to end
MOXON	Rev. Charles – Vicar – 146-60, 165, 168, 180, 185, 194, obit.
	Rev. Michael – 154
MUIR	Mr. – Campaign Director – 207
NEALE	Rev. John of Harpole – 35
NEWBERRY	Andrew – organist – 173
NEWTON	Eric – writer – 94, 104
NICHOLAS	Michael – organist – 110, 115, 116, 153, 163-7, 170
NICHOLLS	Bryan – churchwarden – 196
NORTH	A. 180
O'DELL	Elizabeth – 173
OLDAKER	Phyllis – Lay Worker – 119, 136, 145, 189, obit.
OLDROYD	Rev. Albert of Raunds – 7
OLNEY	Miss – guider – 56
	churchwarden – 58
ORPIN	Gillian – deacon – 195
OSBORNE	Caroline 25
OTTER-BARRY	Bishop – 180
PEARS	Peter – composer – 94, 100, 111
PEARSON	Kenneth – Mayor – 158

PECK	Rev. Charles – curate – 29
PERCIVAL	caretaker – 5
PERRIN	Dr. – organist – 79
PFAFF	Philip – organist – 83, 103, 111, 112
PHILP	Churchwarden – 12
PHIPPS	Alice 106 obit.
	James 8
	Pickering 47-65, 71, 84 obit.
	Mrs Pickering senior – 27, 39, 43
PICKAVER	A. – scout – 72
	Bert – 194 obit.
PICKERING	8
PIPER	Sir John – artist – 115
PITCHER	verger – 154, 185
POLLARD	Malcolm – sculptor – 194, 210
POLLOCK	Rev. Leonard – curate – 25, 26, 29, 44, 83, 108 obit.
PONSFORD	David – organist – 173, 187
POUNCEY	Denys – organist – 83, 110
PRIDEAUX	Rev. Humfrey – curate – 132, 135
PRINGLE	Rev. Richard – curate – 188, 191
RAYBOULD	Clarence – conductor – 115
REASON	Bill – scout – 74
REED	Ethel 195
REID	Andrew 202, 203, 204
RICHARDSON	Bishop – 35
RILEY	Mr. – reader – 191
RIVETT	Ian – scouts – 75
ROBERTS	E. – scouts – 73, 74
ROBINS	sidesman – 4
ROBINSON	Christopher – 166
ROBINSON	Major John – 131
ROBLES	Marisa – 173
ROGERS	Bishop – 186
ROSE	Judith – deacon – 195
ROSEVEARE	Dr. Ruth – 144
RUBBRA	Edmund – musician – 100, 111
RUDDOCK	Dr. – 'curate' – 38, 42
SABLE	R. – scouts – 73
SAMPSON	Canon F. – 186
SANKEY	Deaconess Mollie – 119, 123, 132, 143, 183 obit.
SANTOS	Turible – 168
SCORER	Mr. – architect – 126
SEAMAN	Rev. Alfred – curate – 56
SEMINO	Norina – cellist – 100
SHAW	Tom – verger – 126
SHELTON	Bishop of Lincoln – 100
SHENTON	Andrew – organist – 174, 198-204
SHERARD	Rev. Charles of Grahamstown – 41
SKERRET	Chief Education Officer – 178
SKINNER	Rev. David – 136
SMITH	Miss – organist – 5

SMITH	Gwen – 152
SNOWDEN	Rev. Arthur – V. of St. Michaels – 4
SPENCER	J. W. – cub-master – 75
STALLARD	Rev. Fred – curate – 70, 73, 75, 83, 85, 87, 88, 153
STANTON	of Holborn – 41
STEPNEY	Bishop of – 39
STEWART-SMITH	Rev. David – curate – 88, 89
STOPFORD	Robert – Bishop of Peterborough – 120, 132
STRINGER	Richard – cubs – 76
STUBBS	Fr. V. of St. Albans – 140
SUTHERLAND	Graham – artist – 96, 102
SYDENHAM	Rev. Edward – curate – 37
TATE	John 25
TAYLOR	Joy (Mrs. Thompson) 108
TAYLOR	Michael 116
TEASDALE	Joy 102
TEBBUTT	Rev. Simon – curate – (& Christina) 195, 208
TERRY	Rev. William Edward of All Saints, Wellingborough – 38
THALBEN-BALL	organist – 93, 111
THICKNESSE	Bishop of Leicester – 13
THOMAS	David – sculptor – 189
THOMPSON	Rev. Gerald – curate – 52
THOMPSON	Rev. Hewlett – curate – (now Bishop of Exeter) – 108, 119, 121, 126, 146, 186
TIPPETT	Michael – 93
TROTTER	Thomas – 204
TROWER	Gerard – Bishop of Likoma – 41
TUCKER	E. W. – headmaster – 69, 71, 180
TUDOR	Kenneth – singer – 113
TURNER	Joan – pianist – 170
TURNER	Rev. Philip – Vicar – 135-45, 154, 165, 178, 180
TUSON	Rev. Edward of Kingsthorpe – 3, 51
TYLER	Malcolm – conductor – 172, 173
VICKERS	Mr. – 188
WAKELIN	Rev. Alan – curate – 132, 136
WALKER	Rev. John – curate – 105
WALLACE	Donetta 165
WALLIS	Fr. – 65
WALTON	William – composer – 93
WARD	Peggy – guider – 56
WARREN	Ethel – teacher – 46
WEED	George – churchwarden – 5, 7
WESTCOTT	Rev. Canon of Cawnpore – 41
WESTMORLAND	Headmaster – 46, 68
WESTWOOD	William – Bishop of Peterborough – 192
WHEELER	Rev. Richard – curate – 68
WHITTLE	Rev. Fred – curate – 88, 105
WICKS	Miss – minister – 187
WILD	Rev. E. – 78
WILLIAMS	A. – scouts – 72

WILLIAMSON	Harold 94
WILLMOTT	Rev. Philip – 136
WILSON	Arthur (Tug) – scoutmaster – 73
WINDLEY	Rev. Francis of Dormanstown – 60
WOODHEAD	Helen – deacon – 195
WOODS	Dr. E. S. Bishop of Lichfield – 93
WOODS	Theodore – Bishop of Peterborough – 51, 61, 68
WOOLLEY	Rev. Reginald – curate – 32, 33, 37, 70, obit.
WORDSWORTH	Dr. Bishop of Salisbury – 1
WYTON	Alec – organist – 101, 105, 106, 112, 113, 115, 129, 168, 207
YOUNG	Polly 25
ZANZIBAR	Bishop of, 35
ZULULAND	Bishop of, 173